To my beloved family and friends

for your encouragement in the Lord

I've known Rhona for over twenty years now – she really is an authentic follower of Jesus.

I love her heart for the poor and I know that her gripping story will encourage any 'ordinary' people who are determined to do extraordinary things for him.

Andy Hawthorne OBE, CEO of The Message Trust.

"I have known Rhona for many years and have admired her Christian commitment and contribution to her own communities in Macclesfield. However her commitment extends beyond the borders of the UK and her pioneering work in Africa has amazed us all. I highly commend her story to you"

Debra Green OBE, National Director, Redeeming our Communities

"There's nothing boring about this book. It reveals a refreshing and exciting lifestyle of Rhona Marshall. With great humility and simplicity she shares her remarkable faith walk.

She shows that God is not absent, neither is He silent. She shows how His Call can be heard and the places He can lead us to. Don't read this if you are afraid of being disturbed. Rhona shows how anyone can be liberated and empowered when they meet Jesus."

Dennis Wrigley, Leader and Co-Founder of the Maranatha Community of which Rhona is an active leading member.

Contents

CHOICES?

I am not the boy who hid under the bed in fear and trembling as my parents were being killed.

I am not the two day old baby girl who was thrown down the pit latrine because my mother couldn't look after me.

I am not the little seven year old boy who was told by my parents to go in the Orphanage and say I have no parents.

I am not the little boy who sat under a Mango Tree watching other children going to school.

I am not the one who was once a Muslim but now a Christian.

I am not the one physically impaired, without a mother, having to live with twenty three children from the extended family.

I am not the girl who at twelve years of age was taken into the orphanage because I was being used as a night dancer and abused by men.

I am not the young man who cooked every weekend at the orphanage to pay for my school fees.

I am not the boy whose parents died leaving me to fend for myself.

I am not, I am not, and I am not………………………………..

But I know about all of these cases and many, many more. Some of their stories are in this book.

Come with me on a journey and I will tell you how God has intertwined my life with some of those mentioned above and given me the great privilege to be used by Him to bring HOPE into their lives. Each one of them now has a future with the wonderful gift we so often take for granted - choices.

UGANDA

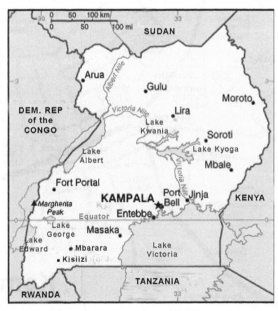

Kamuli

River Nile

Ripon Falls

Busowa Falls

Jinja

Kampala

Entebbe

Lake Victoria

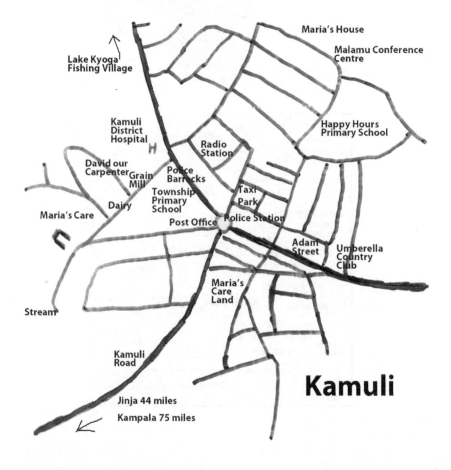

Maria's House

Malamu Conference Centre

Lake Kyoga Fishing Village

Kamuli District Hospital

Happy Hours Primary School

David our Carpenter

Radio Station

Police Barracks

Grain Mill

Township Primary School

Taxi Park

Dairy

Maria's Care

Post Office

Police Station

Adam Street

Umberella Country Club

Maria's Care Land

Stream

Kamuli Road

Jinja 44 miles

Kampala 75 miles

Kamuli

Glossary

bazungu The plural of muzungu

boda-boda The boda-boda taxis are part of the African bicycle culture; they started in the 1960s and 1970s and have their origin on the Kenyan - Ugandan border. The name originated from a need to transport people across the "no-mans-land" between the border posts. This started in southern border crossing town of Busia (Kenya/Uganda), where there is over half a mile between the gates, and quickly spread to the northern border town of Malaba (Kenya). The bicycle owners would shout out boda-boda (border-to-border) to potential customers. These are small mopeds, motorcycles, bicycles or scooters with cushions on the back and are cheap transport as used by locals.

BUU Baptist Union of Uganda

dodo various leafy greens grown in Uganda. Amaranth (dodo), nakati and borr are examples of regional greens

ekwango (singular), ***ebwango*** (plural)   Loofah.

gomez national Ugandad dress; brightly coloured material

jambo hello

mandazas type of food similar to samosa

marum red mud roads

matatu matatu are privately owned minibuses. The Uganda National Road Authority has implemented a 14 passenger maximum rule for Matatu taxis. However this rule is rarely followed, especially in rural areas.

matooke Matoke, also known as Matooke is a meal consisting of steamed green banana (or plantain) and is one of the national dishes of Uganda.

muzungu Mzungu (pronounced [m'zuŋgu]) is the southern, central and eastern African term for a person of foreign descent. Literally translated it means "someone who roams around aimlessly" or "aimless wanderer"

NGO Non Governmental Organisation

nsenene   a seasonal delicacy of a type of grasshopper

panga   like a machete, for cutting grass

piki-piki   Swahili (African dialect) for motorbike / bike

posho   Posho is an East African dish of maize flour cooked with water to a porridge or dough-like consistency. It is the most common staple starch of much of Eastern and Southern Africa. mushroom hut

rondavel   A rondavel (from the Afrikaans word 'rondawel') is a westernised version of the African-style hut.

The rondavel is usually round or oval in shape and is traditionally made with materials that can be locally found. Its walls are often constructed from stones. The mortar may consist of sand, soil, or combinations of these, mixed with cow dung. The floor of a "traditional" rondavel is finished with a dung mixture to make it hard and smooth. The main roofing elements of a rondavel are spars or poles taken from tree limbs which have been harvested and cut to length. The roof covering is of thatch that is sewn to the poles with grass rope.

TSOLS   Training School Of Life Skills

Weebale   Thank you in Luganda

Chapter One

First Steps

How does an insecure young girl from a non Christian family in Liverpool find herself years later in Uganda doing extraordinary things for God? As a child I could never have dreamt of the wonderful plans God had for me. As I look back over the first thirty-eight years of my life before I became a Christian, I realise with wonder how he was preparing me for his good purposes. God gives each one of us different gifts to fulfil his calling on our lives, but each one of us has the choice whether we use those talents and our experiences to God's glory or to fulfil our own ambitions.

I started my career in organising others at Brownies and later Guides where my practical abilities and outgoing character began to develop. I excelled at hands-on tasks in the classroom and at home where I was expected, as the eldest child, to help with different jobs and entertainment. After the humiliation of failing my eleven plus In 1961 I started at Olive Mount Secondary Modern School in Liverpool. In the same year my parents decided to emigrate to Australia. We left Southampton Docks to the cheers of friends and relatives. This was a very special occasion as it was also the maiden voyage of the "Canberra," a P&O Line ship, and my family and I had an exciting adventure sailing in her to Melbourne, Australia. When we arrived mum took the opportunity to visit her pen pal in Werribee, north of Melbourne, with whom she had corresponded throughout the war years.

After I had been at school for less than a year, the family moved again, travelling across the Nullarbor Plain by train to Perth where my youngest brother, Ian, was born.

I loved Australia with all the outdoor activities; everything was so exciting. We had a house on a new estate and I went to Applecross High School. Some of the roads I cycled down to get there were nothing but sand. I can remember everyone had to take a small coin to school to help funds for building the swimming pool which was a real delight once completed. Life was a lot of fun even though I found the academic side of school very hard. I recall being quite rebellious in the sewing class when the teacher asked us to design our own dresses; I drew a dress with a low back which the teacher absolutely disapproved of. I was told that dresses should be up to the neck, front and back. I couldn't understand why since we lived in a beautiful, hot, sunny climate.

I loved Australia, but, sadly, at the end of 1964, the family moved back to England. We sold everything to pay for the fare to return, picking up our passports as we walked up the gangplank. We didn't have a penny. Back home in England my father travelled around looking for work. After two different schools in Australia I said I didn't ever want to go back to school and found retail jobs in London, Taunton and Liverpool. I did go to college however, and studied Child Care and Child Welfare and during the holidays I worked in the restaurant at Bristol Airport. My family moved to Southport and I worked the following year in the 'Tavern in the Town'. In retrospect, I can see that I was given responsibilities early in life and developed social and managerial skills as young as seventeen. Little did I know then how all this experience was going to help me in future years.

Gill was a good friend from those days at college; she later married Larry Benjamin and I stayed in their home recently for a few weeks whilst writing part of this book. After working in Badminton Girls' Boarding School as assistant matron, I eventually moved to Southport where my family lived.

It was there I met and married my husband John. I worked in Marks & Spencer's and was about to go on a supervisor's course when I discovered I was pregnant with our first daughter, Sarah. After her birth I went on a part time youth worker's course and worked at the local youth club. We moved to Macclesfield just after our second daughter, Emma, was born in 1974.

I was very involved in setting up and running the first holiday club ever in Tytherington. Being the eldest in my family, I felt I had missed out on my own childhood so running the club gave me the chance to catch up and splash in puddles, make crafts with plaster of paris moulds and enamelling. We all had so much fun and brought the local community together. I was involved with the PTA (Parent-Teacher Association) at my daughters' primary school where we organised many school events and I enjoyed my involvement with Tytherington Residents' Association, not realising at the time what a significant role this was going to play later in life.

When John was made redundant from his job as a supermarket manager in 1976, Macclesfield Rugby Club asked us if we would run the pub they had taken on, the 'Royal Oak' in King Edward St, and so I became the youngest pub landlady in Macclesfield! It was there that I continued to develop managerial and social skills and learnt how to interact with staff and customers. It was hard work but enjoyable. After four and a half years, we moved to the 'Bull's Head' in Smallwood near Sandbach.

Sadly, the long hours and lack of family life took its toll and in 1985, after 15 years of marriage, John and I were divorced. Needless to say this was a very difficult time; I felt a failure, not in control of my life, empty and without hope. I lost confidence and thought no-one would employ me. I was back in the family home in Macclesfield with the girls and initially found it difficult to cope with all the paperwork, the bills, the divorce papers and so on.

My life did get back on track and, after a couple of years, my friend Rosemary and I set up an outside catering business called 'Wizz Beez", so called because we would wizz in, place the prepared food on a table and buzz off! Some functions required us to serve the food, clear away and wash up; the host would put two glasses and a bottle of wine in the kitchen and Rosemary and I were set up for the night! In most cases the party usually ended up in the kitchen!

My daughters were back at school and I was asked to run a café for a friend. This gave me back some of the confidence that I had lost. I ran Hallé Models Canteen and employed 3 staff; another step of confidence gained. I had a good social life and easily got back in the groove with my many friends. It was during this time that a lady I met whilst serving on the Tytherington Residents Association Committee handed me an invitation for myself and my girls to go to a mission being held at the local church. I looked at the invitation and then showed it to my daughters who instantly responded: "I don't think so, Mum!" That was that, decision made. I had a choice to make and I handed back the invitation.

"Thank you very much but my daughters don't want to go," I said as the lady received it back graciously. The mission came and went and I gave it no further thought. I got on with life, I was busy with the catering business, going to dances at the Rugby Club in Tytherington and enjoying the new-found freedom and confidence I felt I had.

On Sunday, May 10th, 1987, I woke up with the thought going through my head: *I know nothing about God, nothing about the Bible except Matthew, Mark, Luke and John.* As a little girl, I used to bounce two balls against the wall and sing "Matthew, Mark, Luke and John next door neighbour pass it on." I didn't even know that the Old Testament was at the front of the Bible, and the New Testament at the back, and I certainly didn't understand the 'Three in One' concept of Father, Son, and Holy Spirit that I had heard about on the few occasions I had attended a church service. But this morning I suddenly had this overwhelming desire to go to church! I remembered seeing a church in Hurdsfield, about a mile away from my house. As I was thinking, a little voice in my head said: *Why not go to the local church?* Thinking this made sense I rang someone I knew who went to Tytherington Family Worship Church. They told me the service started at 10.30am but advised me to arrive early to get a seat. I remember thinking that this church must get full quickly.

I left a note for my daughters and went along to the primary school where the church service was held. As I walked down the drive, I suddenly panicked and thought: Whatever am I doing? I had my hand on the handle of the front door when someone opened it and I found myself walking in. The first person to greet me was a gentleman called Bob; I had known him and his wife years before, he reached out to me and shook my hand.

"Hello Rhona, I haven't seen you for years! How are you?" I took his hand and promptly burst into tears!

"I don't know why I am here," I said. "Someone will have to talk to me."

Bob told me he wouldn't be a minute and disappeared, reappearing shortly again with his wife Maureen. Despite being a busy elder in the church and leading the service that morning, he still gave the time to talk with me. We sat together as I poured out what my life had been like over the last few years. I was laughing, crying, snivelling, all at the same time it seemed, and we didn't even have a tissue between us!

We walked into the main school hall and sat down ready for the service to start. I tried to stifle my tears, not understanding why I was so emotional. As I looked around I recognised different families in the congregation who had used 'Wizz Beez' in their homes. I was amazed they were here as I didn't know that any of them went to church. I was still upset at the end of the service and, as I handed the church Bible back to a man called Doug, I said: "I want to know more about Jesus."

He explained that a 'beginners' class' had just started on Wednesday evenings. I walked home and found that my daughters had been up, read my note, and gone back to bed.

That Wednesday evening I had a choice. I walked to the house where the Bible study was taking place. I sat down and immediately felt comfortable as I knew nearly everyone there. I realised after a short time that even with this being a 'beginners' class' I still seemed to know less than anyone else. At the end of the meeting I began to cry again. I am sure they didn't quite know what to do with me so they very kindly gave me two booklets and said: "Read these, everything will be alright."

I took the books home and in bed that night read the first one called 'Journey into Life.' Initially I thought it was just a made-up story about sin, God, and Jesus dying on a cross. It spoke of asking Jesus into our lives and spending eternity with him. I had often wondered what the point of life was; we come into the world, we grow up, we work, and then we die. What was that all about? I slept very well that night.

The next day was May 14th, 1987; work had been good, the girls were happy and growing up fast. As I climbed into bed that night I decided to read the second booklet given me called 'Every Day With Jesus.'

I can't remember now what I read but I do remember saying the prayer at the end of the page: "Father forgive me that I go through life on the broken springs of pleasure when I should be cruising in joy. Help me to limp in for spiritual repair and leap out in Jesus name. Amen."

I couldn't believe it! I was having a conversation with God faster than I could speak to someone on the phone (and I can talk fast!)

How did I know it was God?

Because he referred to me by name.

"Rhona!" he said. "You think you have had an exciting life so far, just wait till you see what I have in store for you!" Then, to my surprise, he added: "Throw your cigarettes and lighter in the cupboard and never smoke again as I am not ready for you yet." I had tried previously to quit but found it nigh impossible.

I started asking lots of questions about my family and other situations, and God was answering me.

Suddenly He said: "Go and phone your father and tell him what you have done."

"No!"I replied, "I have got you now and I am not leaving this room."

"Ring your father and tell him what you've done, and throw your cigarettes and lighter in the cupboard and never smoke again."

Wow! This was a command. I jumped up, threw my cigarettes and lighter in the cupboard, ran down stairs and phoned my dad.

"Dad, you'll never believe what's just happened!" I told him everything.

We both cried and dad said: "You are in the Christian family now, I am sure God has great plans for you."

He told me he had been baptised in his sixties; I had been working in Bristol at the time and had no idea, none of the family had mentioned it. I realise now he must have been praying for us all. Dad is now in heaven with his Lord and one day we will meet again, along with other members of my family who believed. I understand now what heaven is about; it is eternal life with God, and hell is eternal life without God. *"For He has rescued us from the dominion of darkness and brought us into the kingdom of the Son he loves."* Colossians 1:13.

Two months later I found myself helping at Benllech summer camp, a Christian-run youth camp in Anglesey. My daughters, Sarah and Emma, and their friend, Darren, reluctantly came to join me. Within four days they heard the gospel message and each became a committed Christian.

I continued working in the centre of Macclesfield. Some of my friends thought I had gone mad and that the change in my life was due to the divorce! Time moved on and I went to as many Bible studies as I could. Tytherington Family Worship Church, the church I now attended, ran a weekly nurture group and I wanted to know so much about the scriptures that I was always asking questions:

"Why do we pray when God knows the answer before we even start to talk to him?"

"If God wanted me across the road to receive a phone call how would he get me there?"

"Why has it taken me thirty-eight years to hear and respond to the truth?"

The leaders answered my questions the best they could or found out the answer for the following week. I wished I had made this commitment to God years ago instead of going my own way for so long. I read in Psalm 25:7, *"Do not remember the sins of my youth or my rebellious ways. Remember me, O Lord, in keeping with your mercy and your goodness."*

People at church encouraged me to get involved with activities which helped to boost my low self esteem. I didn't realise how much baggage I had been carrying, I thought I had been getting on with life remarkably well, considering. It was quite incredible to think that since childhood I had had an ever-increasing number of chips on my shoulder that weighed me down and needed healing. People who know me now would never believe the emotional state I had been in.

I am reminded of Colossians 1:4-6, *"For we have heard that you trust in Christ Jesus and that you love all of God's people. You do this because you are looking forward to the joy of heaven - as you have been ever since you first heard the truth of the good news. The same good news that came to you is going out all over the world. It is changing lives everywhere, just as it changed yours that very first day you heard and understood the truth about God's great kindness to sinners."*

I got involved with Macclesfield Christian Mission that same year and volunteered to help on the 'Choose Life Bus' which parked each Saturday night in different areas of the town. The team met during the week for Bible study, prayer and praise, and I learnt so much during the four years I was involved with them, and would be very sad if ever I had to miss a Saturday night. We asked God where we should park the bus each week and the following Saturday we would pray over the land we visited. We trusted God to watch over and protect us, and I soon learnt about spiritual warfare as incidents arose in different locations around Macclesfield. I learnt so much from Stewart, the director who ran the Mission.

People were often suspicious when they saw the bus and would ask:

"What are you doing? What's this bus about?"

At that stage I didn't have many answers because I had only just become a Christian myself, so I would reply: "My friends can answer your questions, I'm just making the drinks! Do you want tea or coffee?"

Many questions were asked that I couldn't answer but friends on the bus team always came to my rescue. God used these times to teach me so much about the scriptures. When I think back to those days some of us hardly knew one scripture from the other but God was teaching us for the future.

I was baptised in November, 1988; another significant date in my diary. Until then I had never heard of baptism by full immersion. Josh Bowmaker, the leader of our nurture group, read from Isaiah 25:1, *"O LORD, I will honour and praise your name, for you are my God. You do such wonderful things! You planned them long ago, and now you have accomplished them."* Friends and family came to see me being baptised. I felt overwhelmed; I was a new person in Jesus Christ and I had a new life.

During this time I met and fell in love with a man who lived in Wales. He was employed as a transport manager and sent to Ghana and in October, 1988, he invited me there to become engaged. This was such an exciting time in my life. Ghana was wonderful; I was surrounded by African people and, as I walked to the market each day, I drank in the atmosphere. God gave me such a love for this country and the people; even then he was preparing my heart for my future ministry. I loved being with them: their vitality, charismatic personalities, vibrant coloured clothes, love and freedom of expression. We had a wonderful time and my heart leapt as the day unfolded with new adventures, people and places to visit.

I returned to England but, after many letters I wrote to Ghana were not answered, I realised my fiancé had changed his mind. We never did marry; God had different plans.

In 1989, God called me and two friends from church, Peter and Alison, to visit Israel. This was the beginning of another huge learning curve that God had to work in each of us before he sent us onto the mission field. We had so many amazing experiences in Israel as God taught us how to step out in faith and trust him completely. A few years later Peter met and married Lynnette and God sent them to work in China. They now have three children and are currently serving God in Oxford supporting international students. Alison has been a Missionary in Brazil since 1998 and is accomplishing incredible work there. We recognised God's hand on our lives; he taught us to work together using our different gifts and talents, and to work as individuals trusting him. We experienced tiredness and fatigue and saw God move in power. Above all we learnt not to start the day without committing it to God and putting on his full armour:

"A final word: be strong with the Lord's mighty power. Put on all of God's armour so that you will be able to stand firm against all strategies and tricks of the devil. For we are not fighting against people made of flesh and blood, but against the rulers and authorities of the unseen world, against those mighty powers of darkness who rule this world, and against wicked spirits in the heavenly realms. Use every piece of God's armour to resist the enemy in the time of evil, so after the battle you will be standing firm. Stand your ground, putting on the sturdy belt of truth and the body armour of God's righteousness. For shoes, put on the peace that comes from the good news, so that you will be fully prepared. In every battle you will need faith as your shield to stop the fiery arrows aimed at you by Satan. Put on salvation as your helmet, and take the sword of the spirit, which is the word of God. Pray at all times and on every occasion in the power of the Holy Spirit. Stay alert and persistent in your prayers for all Christians everywhere." Ephesians 6:10-18

I recalled one of the elders at church telling me to put on this spiritual protection every day. He said we had no idea of the schemes of the devil and we needed to be protected with the blood of Jesus and the full armour of God.

I was still involved with Macclesfield Christian Mission and in 1990 God called the team to organise 'Cross Beat 1991'; a weekend of concerts in St Michael's Church and the Heritage Centre. It was great fun organising people from different churches to be involved with outreach in the town and another huge learning curve for me. Jeanette (now Darren's wife) designed the logo and we asked Andy Hawthorn from 'The World Wide Message Tribe' to speak in the evening at the Heritage Centre. These were exciting times as God was training us for great and mightier plans in the future.

During this time my home church didn't hold an evening service so some of the bus team took the opportunity to visit other churches in Macclesfield. This proved an invaluable way to meet people and invite them to get involved with different events we had planned for the town. Little did I know that one of these projects would lead me to Uganda.

In 1991 I walked around the town with the mission youth evangelist, Kevin Shaw, and stopped to pray in front of empty shop doors. He wanted a building in which to hold a 'Third World Café.' The plan was to raise money during the few months leading up to Christmas. We acquired the premises of a former paint and DIY store in Queen Victoria Street in the town centre and invited all the church congregations to get involved. The café was called 'Christmas Cracker Café.' We had the best time recruiting people to help clean the place up, build a counter, find tables and chairs, cutlery and crockery, table cloths, and people to entertain the customers whilst they ate their food. Lasting friendships were made as people came and worked together in the café using their different abilities and we raised lots of money for Third World causes. As I also worked in the town centre it was my job to coordinate the different shifts and look after the café door key.

One day a lovely Dutch lady called Maria Maw came to me and asked if she could borrow the key whilst the café was closed. Her intention was to make food to sell the following day. Originally from Holland, Maria had been living in Macclesfield for six years having retired from the hotel and catering business. She was working part time as a companion to an elderly lady and also cared for several other elderly folk whom she visited and ran errands for.

The following Easter, Maria went to Spring Harvest in Margate and whilst there she went into the mission tent because she knew it would be lively. As she listened to the speaker she suddenly heard a little voice saying:

"Get up and go!" She thought she was hearing things. The speaker continued and once again Maria heard: "Get up and go!" She dismissed it thinking: *I am too old anyway*. At that moment a man who was sitting at the back of the stage stood up, took the microphone and pointing to the audience said:

"And if you think you are too old, you are not!"

Maria realized it was God who had been telling her to 'get up and go' but she had no idea where God wanted her to get up and go to! She met with the speaker after the seminar and he encouraged her to pray at home with people from her own church to seek out God's intentions. She wrote many letters to missionary organisations and one came back from the Baptist Union Seminary in Jinja, Uganda, stating that they were looking for someone to set up a library there, a project that was expected to take about three months. Maria knew in her heart that this was the direction she'd been waiting for.

In 1991, at the age of sixty-five, Maria sold her car, packed most of her belongings into the loft of her little flat in Macclesfield, renting it out to provide a small income, and off she went to Uganda to begin work at the Baptist Union Seminary, collating over two thousand books. This brought her into contact with people working with 'Youth With A Mission'. On her return to England, she went on the discipleship course at YWAM in Kings Norton.

In 1992 Maria suddenly appeared on the doorstep of the shop where I worked.

"Where have you been?" I asked.

She told me she had been called by God to go to Uganda and in the next breath she asked me to go with her as there was so much work to be done. I knew when I was in Ghana that God had given me a great heart for Africa; I had wondered then what it was all about, and now I knew. I felt my heart leap! I prayed about it but felt God say that stability for my daughters was most important at that time, and so I had to wait.

A few months before Maria went back to Uganda, my mother died suddenly. It was a tremendous shock; she was very healthy or so we thought, but she died of a thrombosis. Mum had a huge influence in my life; she had a terrific spirit of adventure and was by nature very spontaneous. She and I were similar in so many ways and had many a stand-up argument because we both thought we were right!

Mum enjoyed typing, or should I say thrashing (because she wasn't gentle on the keys) on a portable typewriter, and loved a game of Scrabble, so after her death I asked Maria to take the typewriter and Scrabble game to Uganda to teach the children English. I also gave her a huge bag full of old Christmas decorations from my days in the pub.

During the next three years I studied the Bible. I went to many conferences, met lots of people, and drank in as much as I could. I was so hungry for the word of God.

One Monday, in September, 1994, Maria suddenly appeared again in the shop I was managing. Happily it was my lunch break so we went to a small café where we chatted about her work in Uganda. Maria handed me a video explaining that it showed her home in Africa with some of the Ugandan children she cared for. This meeting changed the direction of my life and I shall never forget the week that followed.

That evening, I knelt down to put the video in the machine, switched it onto 'play' and didn't rise again till it had finished. I cried all the way through. My tears were not for the poor little children but due to a great sense of yearning. I knew I had something to offer; the gifts and talents I have are all practical and I could see the great need for someone to help Maria to encourage and support the people in Uganda. It was then that it occurred to me that it didn't matter that I had no 11 plus, 'O' or 'A' levels. I had the privilege of education and being stimulated at home and school, unlike the children I saw in the video.

After Bible study the following night, a friend drove me home, and as she dropped me off she said:

"I would like you to accept this. I missed your twenty-first Birthday (many years past!) but I believe you should have this and go to Uganda." With that she handed me an envelope.

I opened it and to my astonishment there was a cheque for £500.

"Are you sure about this?" I said, stunned. I had never experienced such generosity.

"Yes I am. Twenty-one is a very special birthday. You have the key to a new door, God has spoken to me and I feel you should go to Uganda," she replied.

I sat there hardly moving with the envelope still in my hand. "Thank you, thank you very much" I was so grateful. I walked to my front door praising God for this remarkable gift and the obedience of my friend.

The next day Maria popped into the shop and gave me a photograph album containing pictures of the children she was looking after in Uganda. Throughout that week my excitement mounted at the prospect of going there, yet I still hadn't really got my head around it.

"God is sending me to Uganda!" I quipped to a friend the following Sunday at church as I handed her the photo album to browse through.

After the service she tapped me on the shoulder:

"I could hardly contain myself this morning, have you got a pen?" she asked.

I handed her a pen and she wrote a cheque for £100 saying: "I have been wondering to whom I should tithe this money. I believe it should be you. Spend it on the children or anything you feel is needed for your forthcoming trip."

Wow! God does move fast when he wants things to happen! As I stood there with the cheque in my hand, another lady became involved with the conversation.

"When you come back, I will give you half the fare to take you out there again," she said.

My goodness, this wasn't going to be my only trip! I stood there, stunned by all that had so quickly taken place. A gentleman then walked towards us and enquired what was going on.

"You will never believe it; God is sending me to Uganda!" I replied, hardly able to contain myself.

"I would like to support you financially whilst you are out there," he said.

Well! You could have knocked me down with a feather! I was flabbergasted! It felt like I was on a horse; the doors had opened, the horse was just about to bolt and I was having difficulty holding onto the reins. I became much more focused; friends, family, customers at work, and people from other churches all wanted to know about Maria's work in Uganda. Like traffic lights we went from red to amber to green for 'go' in a heartbeat.

The months went by quickly. Maria came to speak at Tytherington Family Worship Church on November 20th, 1994. She showed a small part of the video to the congregation, and asked for help especially in the area of setting up a charity. She explained that many people wanted to help but they needed an organised charity to work through, and she was hoping someone would take her on or that she could come under an organisation that was already established. At the end of the service, a semi-retired gentleman had a word with me. He wanted to fix a meeting for the following Tuesday.

He said, "I am going home to pray. I believe I should help you set up

First Steps

a charity".

We had the meeting and he suggested we had another when I returned from Uganda. Praise God, the seed had been sown! Within a few months I was given the money I needed, had all my injections, checked my passport and bought my air ticket for this new adventure.

"So Christ has really set us free. Now make sure that you stay free, and don't get tied up again in slavery to the law." Galatians 5:1.

Chapter 2

Uganda

It was my birthday, February 28th, 1995 when I arrived in Uganda. God had given me the best birthday present I could have imagined and it was about to change my life. My daughters were now in their early twenties and independent young women. God's timing was perfect.

The first thing I noticed when we touched down at Entebbe Airport was how green everything was: the grass, the trees, the shrubs. Looking around, I saw my first little mud huts, beautiful flowers, and happy-looking people. There was a tractor and some farm equipment in a field that looked as though it had come from the dark ages but at least they were doing the job. Above a little building was a sign, 'Crash Fire Station'.

Thank goodness we arrived safely, I chuckled.

Customs greeted me with a cheery "Good morning, Madam. How are you?" I came to realise this greeting was used all the time and, being my first time in Uganda, I found it very endearing and welcoming. Collecting my bags, I walked through customs and the doors that led to the outside world. I found myself surrounded by a sea of Ugandans all in search of family, friends, or guests they had come to pick up.

"Rhona, Rhona! Over here!" There was Maria waving and beckoning me over. We hugged warmly.

"Welcome, welcome, welcome," she said. She was as excited as I! She escorted me to a funny little bubble car that was very small and belonged to her friend Everit, whom she insisted on calling Everest. I had loads of luggage and I looked at Maria with a puzzled expression on my face.

Uganda

"It will be fine, nothing is impossible with God," she said confidently and, with some firm persuasion, everything fitted in. 'Nothing is impossible with God' became one of the stock phrases throughout the trip and eventually the motto for 'Maria's Care' "...*but with God all things are possible*." Matthew 19:26.

Everit took us to Entebbe Taxi Park and, after Maria had negotiated the price, we got into a taxi or *matatu* as they are called, to take us to Kampala. I hadn't thought it would be so hot. (I can hear you saying: "But it's Africa, what did you expect?" Well! I hadn't got my head around it all!)

During the thirty mile journey we passed such marvellous sights: mud huts along the side of the road of all different shapes and sizes, a large box with live chickens on the back of a bicycle, three men on one motorbike. My eyes were on stalks! We passed a lady with shopping on her head and a baby on her back, signs to various guest houses, and old tyres piled up for sale along the roadside. Ladies were bent double cleaning with small handmade brushes outside their shop or home. People wore colourful woolly hats and garments, some held hands and swung their arms in an easy manner; everyone looked relaxed.

Once at Kampala Taxi Park I couldn't believe my eyes; I was looking at a sea of mini-buses. These *matatus* travel all over Uganda; there were hundreds of them, bumper to bumper, and I had to haul my luggage through the small gaps between them as I raced to keep up with Maria. I nearly lost her at one point; she knew where she was heading but I hadn't a clue. I had two large holdalls, a rucksack on my back and a guitar. I must have looked quite a sight, especially as Maria insisted I wore a straw hat to keep the sun off my head. I felt I looked like Mary Poppins.

We eventually reached the *matatus* en route for Jinja, and hoisted ourselves and my luggage on. Everyone wanted to help but Maria quickly taught me not to let anyone touch the luggage except our conductor, but with so many people milling around I had no idea who he was!

Maria took command: "No, put that down!" I heard her cry as she organised the large bags into the back of the bus. I looked at her with disbelief as we left these precious belongings and started to walk towards the vehicle door.

"You have to trust God," she said.

Sitting just behind the driver, with the rucksack and guitar in front of us on a narrow ledge, I noticed a sign that said fourteen passengers only were allowed on; I looked around and counted sixteen on the bus already, and others were still coming onboard. As we waited, many traders tried to sell us their goods; one came on holding a large board with handkerchiefs, watches, sunglasses, a few old bras, belts, plastic children's toys, even a selection of batteries in a box.

"You buy this one, this one," he said, waving different articles in my face.

I probably would have done had Maria not taken control! Others came to sell local newspapers, or soda bottles and water. Maria suggested we bought water for the long journey ahead. She advised me never to buy anything with a loose fitting lid as the bottle could have been tampered with. Under Maria's watchful eye we also purchased six samosas. Behind me a man had eaten a full cooked meal whilst reading his newspaper and handed the plate back through the window as we left the taxi park! A lady passed with her baby on her back, a large bag on her head and two small children following her. I was agog as I took in these sights for the first time.

The *matatu* continued to fill up with people, the conductor shouted something and everyone moved around.

"Welcome to Uganda!" Maria said and we both roared with laughter.

A young boy got on and sat opposite us on the ledge where I had placed my rucksack and guitar, his bony knees wedged up between me and the lady beside me. Eventually we left with twenty-four people on board! Leaving the park was a feat in itself as the driver wove his way through hundreds of other *matatus* to the main road, and I came to understand that you take your life in your hands trying to cross busy roads in Uganda. Nearly one hundred miles stretched ahead of us from Kampala to Kamuli via Jinja, I knew this was going to be one journey I would never forget.

It took just over an hour to reach Jinja. Along the way we passed houses made from all sorts of materials: mud, bricks, corrugated iron sheets, and wood nailed together at different angles with cardboard filling any gaps either on the side or the roof. Kampala is the capital of Uganda and people there wore many different styles of dress; some wore the beautiful traditional *gomez* dresses (local Ugandan style) some in European dress, and some in very little as the clothes they had on were tattered and torn. I noticed the huge variety of colour; the Ugandan women certainly knew how to look vibrant, especially their head scarves, and they didn't mind what colour went with what! Some people wore shoes, jewellery, and watches whilst others had none. Some sat on the street begging or selling items displayed on bits of paper. Along the main road I could see large eight-storey buildings and a few tall hotels, none of them in good repair. The Ugandan people were only just getting back on their feet again after the appalling atrocities they had suffered under Idi Amin's regime.

The roads were in a terrible state of neglect with pot-holes everywhere, and on the corner of Kampala Road and Parliament Avenue there was a huge manhole open to the sky, several feet wide and deep, with nothing to warn traffic or people that it was there! To me it seemed like an accident waiting to happen!

As we drove along the main road, Maria pointed to various buildings and told me a story about each one. She told me about the time she came all the way from Kamuli to register the school she had set up. She waited for ages and eventually, when she got to the counter, she was asked for papers she didn't have. She returned a few days later with the required documents to discover the office had lost her initial registration forms and she had to start all over again. Maria was sixty-eight years old by now; a purposeful lady with energy and determination, but a very hot and often penniless lady. She really didn't need this lack of efficiency. She was managing on her pension and the little bit of money people who believed in her calling had sent her. I was soon to see just how much she did with the little she had.

As we drove further from the capital, I could see the huge change in the structure of the buildings; they were now low, simple affairs spread out over a vast landscape rather than the big bold buildings I had seen in Kampala. Most people carried their belongings on their heads or in plastic bags. I looked out of the window and saw a bicycle go past with five people on it: a man peddling, a lady sitting side-saddle behind him with a baby on her back, a child on her knee and another on the crossbar. I thought of the weight on the bike. How did the tyres stay up? Can you imagine this in the middle of Manchester? Another bike went past with six crates of soft drinks tied on the back. Another had fourteen trays of eggs tied across with a thick black rubber strap.

I had started reading a book loaned to me by a friend who had been to Uganda, called 'The Man with the Key has gone,' by Dr Ian Clarke, a doctor from Northern Ireland. It expressed the humour and pain of life in Uganda in the aftermath of war and in the midst of AIDS. It prepared me a little for all I began to experience.

As we passed a lady with a baby on her back and a suitcase on her head, Maria said she had probably just given birth and was walking back from the hospital. I thought back to the birth of my own children; the comforts of a five day hospital stay, and then transport home in the car. I thought about all I had in my life and how I should be grateful and not concerned with what I lacked.

I glanced at the speedometer which was showing 140kmph. We passed signs that read: 'Speed kills' and 'Driving on shoulders prohibited' (this really conjures up an unusual mental image!) We saw one petrol tanker in a ditch after the driver had lost control or fallen asleep at the wheel during the long journey from Kenya. After a pretty hair-raising journey we arrived at Owen Falls Dam and drove over the bridge into Jinja.

"Welcome to Jinja, I just love this place!" Maria enthused. She told me how she began work here in 1991 at the Baptist Union of Uganda Seminary. She had been given the task of collating two thousand books to make a library. She had no paper, scissors, glue, containers or pens, yet within a few days she had managed to acquire all the necessary items to do the work. People would come into the room and ask if they could help. Being a very efficient organiser, Maria encouraged them, showing them what she wanted them to do. Some of these people had never used scissors before so this was a new skill they were learning. Many wanted to read the books as they were treasures and hard to get hold of.

Whilst helping these people, Maria asked questions, especially of the younger ones. She learned that many of their parents had died during the war or through disease. In Uganda, if you had no money for medicine, then you simply died. If a mud hut had a bit of material with a red cross covering the door, it was a sign that there was no adult in that home to take care of the children, and friends and neighbours would do their best to look after them.

There were a lot of single girls that came to help Maria and she enjoyed chatting to them; teaching them how to spell, read, and discuss personal hygiene – all the things their parents would have taught them had they been there. Maria had three adult daughters herself so felt very comfortable helping the Ugandan girls. She was asked by the B.U.U. to visit the village of Kamuli two days a week to help a small group of girls and she willingly agreed. When she had first arrived she had said to God: "Please don't ever send me here!" Maria felt it was the back of beyond and she just loved Jinja. She learned a lesson that day that she shared with me: "Don't ever tell God what to do."

After many weeks in Kamuli, sitting under a tree teaching the girls to sew, play Scrabble to improve their spelling, and how to type on a cardboard typewriter, God called Maria to live in Kamuli.

One Sunday, whilst living in a very small room there, Maria felt God nudge her to go to church in Jinja. She walked up to the main road and waited for a bus. She knew that even if a bus arrived straight away she was going to be late. Three hours later she arrived at the little church, deserted except for one woman sitting in a pew.

"You're late!" the woman said in a stern voice.

"I know I am late," Maria replied in the same tone. Walking up the aisle, she approached the woman.

"I need a house," Maria said.

"Where do you need this house?" the woman enquired.

"In Kamuli," Maria said.

"I have a house in Kamuli," the woman answered.

By this time the two women had made eye contact. It transpired that the lady was leaving the area and had a house in Kamuli she wanted to rent out.

Because of her obedience to rise and go to a church in Jinja, Maria found herself moving to a house in Kamuli in 1992.

"If you are obedient, I will bless you." Deuteronomy 28:1-2.

I was astonished at this extraordinary story, and felt so privileged to be travelling with this remarkable lady to Kamuli, but I could see why she loved Jinja so much. The taxi park was much smaller than Kampala and many people knew her and shouted out her name in greeting. Maria was easily recognisable and the people loved her. We changed to another *matatu* and once again we waited. A lady passed by with a box on her head and a live chicken peeping out, I thought to myself: *This is Uganda, full of surprises!* I witnessed a man buy a three-piece trouser suit through the window. A salesman boarded holding a small pot; he did a sales pitch in the local language, pointed to his nose and coughed dramatically suggesting the little pot was a cold remedy. He sold quite a few little pots that day.

The drive to Kamuli was very pleasant. We passed broken down lorries laden with green bananas, known locally as *matooke*. The main transport here was either a *boda-boda* (a man who transported people on a bicycle) *matatus*, or trucks. We very rarely saw a motorbike or scooter. As we approached the village there was a large sign on the left 'Welcome to Kamuli'. This is what I had been waiting for all this time.

I wonder what God has brought me here for, I pondered.

Maria asked the driver to take us down the hill to the gates of the lodge, the accommodation Maria was renting for the children in Kamuli. Maria told me that in the very early days when she had to buy everything in Jinja and take public transport, they looked at her as though she was crazy. The materials she bought included bunk beds!

"Come on, come on, nothing is impossible with God!" she would say, and miraculously everything went on, or in, the *matatu!*

I felt this day was a very special gift from God because it was my forty-sixth birthday. In Psalm 139:15 we are told, *"My frame was not hidden from you when I was made in the secret place. When I was woven together in the depth of the earth, your eyes saw my unformed body. All the days ordained for me were written in your book before one of them came to be."*

We jumped off the vehicle to the sound of the children's voices.

"Welcome back, Maria!" they cried as they laughed and joked, and helped us unload the bags and shopping Maria had bought. It was dusk by now so we quickly stored everything in the respective rooms. Maria introduced me to all the children and the staff and they sang to welcome me. As I walked into my little eight foot by seven foot room I started to laugh; the Christmas decorations from the pub I used to run in England were now strung up across my room. I felt at home. A large card on the table bore the words 'Happy Birthday' in large letters. The children called me to eat. We sat in a little makeshift dining area and ate cooked red kidney beans with greens called *dodo* (very much like spinach). After that they brought out a bright pink birthday cake with candles, which had been cooked in an oven in the ground. Everyone sang as I blew them out. What an incredible first day! Each day held new experiences and I was so thankful that I had chosen to follow God's call to come to Uganda.

Over the next few days, I got to know the people who lived with Maria in the lodge and was shown around the compound. Maria had moved here from the little rented house where she first started. Many teenagers had come to her with young children and asked her to look after them; consequently she now had thirty-eight orphans in her care.

The boys slept in little rooms on one side of the compound and girls on the other. I witnessed a small boy with big determination wheeling a wheelbarrow containing a jerry-can full of water and tipping it into a large cleaned-out petrol barrel. It must have weighed about the same as a huge sack of potatoes. The children did all their own washing and helped to prepare food for each meal. They peeled sweet potatoes and dug up groundnuts that they had planted and grown themselves. This was the first time I had ever seen peanuts, as I knew them, grow. They shelled peas, soaked kidney beans, picked *dodo*, and washed and cooked it. The children all helped the matron, Aunt Rose, who was looking after their daily needs.

Water was scarce and very precious; we washed in our own plastic bowl in our room and put the water into a bucket that was left on the little step outside our doors. Each day someone was allocated to collect it to feed the chickens and water the plants. Maria devised a water catchment system; she attached guttering to the fascia boards so that when it rained the water ran into the gutter, down a pipe, and into a huge clean petrol barrel. This might sound like common sense to you, but no one in Kamuli had gutters, and Maria didn't really have the money to splash out on such an extravagant item, but it proved invaluable. The children and people around Maria were learning all the time.

Maria had many bright ideas and acted on them – nothing was impossible! She thought the children should learn how to play netball and asked me to bring some deflated balls from England. She approached me one day with a task to do:

"Rhona, will you go and help the children erect a netball stand in the ground?"

Apparently, a few weeks previous, the netball stand had been put up, but it was so high that Maria had it taken down and had about a foot sawn off the end. Now we had to erect it again. Armed with a bowl, a stick, water, cement, sand, and washing up liquid (only because I had seen builders in the U.K. use washing up liquid when they mixed cement) we walked over to where Maria wanted us to place the pole. The children helped me dig a hole and then fetched little stones. We stood the pole in the hole and some children held it in place whilst others put stones carefully around the base. One boy mixed the cement, sand, and water as instructed, and then I added some washing up liquid. I am sure that made all the difference!

The children, all thirty-eight of them, had a part to play! We let go of the pole and prayed it would stay up, that the cement would set and there would be no rain that night. Praise God, there it was the next morning – solid as a rock! The children had a wonderful time playing netball with only one pole; they practised as much as they could so that they would win matches at school.

Maria asked us to buy vegetables and bread in Kamuli and the children wanted to show me the town. As we walked along the road each one insisted on holding my hand. Children we met ran out calling: "Maria, Maria," because I was one of only two white women in the village where they obviously thought every white woman was called Maria. We passed lots of little half-built houses, mud huts damaged by the weather, and old ladies selling tomatoes or tiny bananas that lay on small, broken, wooden tables under trees. As we passed through the town people waved or hailed: '*Jambo*', which means 'Hello'.

Some local children were terrified as I passed the end of their garden; they had never seen a white person before. I stood still and offered my hand to them. Often they would take a little step towards me, eventually becoming bold enough to shake my hand. We had so much fun! Some children held out their hands as I sang the rhyme: 'Round and round the garden like a teddy bear,' and as I tickled them under their arm they laughed with real joy; it was a whole new experience for them. In town we visited the bakery which sold bread and delicious little victoria cup cakes, but there was little else on the shelves.

I dressed at 6am the next morning whilst it was still dark. Maria was in a hurry as we were to go to Kampala for a meeting with Peter, her lawyer, regarding the lodge and how she could register as an NGO (Non-Governmental Organisation).

On the way to the taxi park, Maria took me to see inside the telephone exchange sited in a large container next to the post office. She knocked on the door and a very sleepy man beckoned us in. He had slept the night there on a mat under the table. The exchange must have come out of an old office block from fifty years past. I took photos of the switchboard operator who wore earphones and sat opposite a tangled web of telephone wires with lots of little plugs at the end of each. Apparently the exchange wasn't working that day due to the lightning and thunderstorm that had taken place during the night. That was it, Kamuli was cut off. We hadn't yet reached the age of mobile phones.

We had a long wait in the taxi park. Maria explained this was a frequent occurrence and settled down to read the book she had with her for times such as this. The *matatu* to Jinja eventually left at 7.30am. On the way we were stopped by the police who asked everyone to show their I.D. Our companion, Pastor Herbert, had forgotten his and the policeman wanted him to get off the bus.

"He is with us," said Maria, "If he goes, we all go."

Eventually the police got fed up with this silly game and let us all continue the ride. Maria was a role-model for me and others around her; she always did what she believed to be the right thing to do with sheer guts and determination.

As we drove along the road, I saw children going to school carrying chairs or bricks on their heads, bundles of wood for the school cook, and books secured with string. In the distance, I saw a half-built classroom and realised what the bricks were for. A huge lorry full of *matooke* passed us and we saw beautiful girls along the road wearing lovely bright-coloured wraps. A large coach passed by with at least sixty people on it with luggage hanging out of the windows and on the roof a stack of mattresses, a wooden bed, live goats and chickens, plus jerry-cans swaying precariously as the coach sped along. What an unbelievable sight! I suppose if you are moving house in Uganda that's the only way to do it.

Little mud huts stretched as far as the eye could see, all at different stages of repair. We didn't hear thunder but the flashes of lightning lit up the sky and made an awesome sight on the horizon. In Jinja we bought hot chapattis wrapped in newspaper for breakfast. I could smell the wood burning on which the local food was cooked: chickens, fresh bread, and popcorn.

In Jinja, we changed *matatus* and continued the journey to Kampala. We passed wooden shops with very little on the counter; just a few passion fruits and bananas. Some goats wandered freely by the side of the road whilst others were tethered up by one leg. A man carried a 'Singer' sewing machine on his head and placed it under a tree; another carried long pieces of wood tied across his bike; every time a vehicle came he had to stop and move his bike sideways to avoid a collision. Many women with babies on their backs were hoeing and digging in the fields. Maria pointed out the tea-growing plantation on one side of the road and sugar-cane on the other. People walked with baskets full of tea leaves on their heads to have them weighed; their clothes were sodden from the waist down as a result of their work along the rows of wet tea bushes.

Once in Kampala, Maria led the way up long, winding roads walking behind vehicles and crossing over a few times. I nearly lost her because I had my head down looking out for all the pot holes. Finally we reached the BUU (Baptist Union Uganda) office where we met Michael, the director, and his secretary. A long discussion ensued about the future of Maria's work and how she should carry on. She had only a small amount of money and was finding it very difficult to make ends meet. We didn't resolve anything as the BUU didn't have funds available to help her. Pastor Herbert was still with us as we took a *matatu* over to the other side of town.

On the way, I saw, for the first time since I had arrived in Uganda, another white person.

At the university complex, we visited Helen, a lady who was very sick and needed medicine which Maria provided. She was delighted to see Maria and we all went for lunch. We were served chicken and as the visitor, I was given the neck and giblets, a considered delicacy. I thanked them very much and asked Pastor Herbert if he would like to eat it. Thankfully he was delighted! I went to the toilets and laughed at the sign on the door: 'Please flush toilet. Use cistern or water in bucket outside.'

Once again we were off at break-neck speed, I could hardly keep up with Maria and she was twenty-four years my senior. It was the middle of the day and very hot. What do they say? 'Only mad dogs and English men go out in the midday sun.' Well, they're right!

Our next visit was to Peter, Maria's lawyer. Maria told me how kind Peter had been to her. He saw her as a true missionary; living and working with the people, and had previously taken her into his home to meet his family and stay there for a while.

Maria never wasted time or an opportunity to buy essentials so we called in at a stationery warehouse. She was very good at finding a bargain and if one store seemed too expensive she would say so and march out and straight into another one.

"Best price?" Maria said, pointing to the paper.

"4,500/- Ug shillings," (about £3 in 1995) replied the shopkeeper, a far better price than before, so Maria bought four reams and filled a basket with other stationery materials. We turned a corner and Maria bumped into a friend who 'just happened' to have the two books Maria needed and some exam papers.

Wow! What a God incidence, I thought, although I did feel like a donkey being loaded up. We left all our purchases in a small room by the main taxi park.

"You have to trust the Lord and these people." said Maria.

Before I left England, I was asked to visit Jessica whilst in Uganda. She was a lady who was involved with the Gideons, an organisation which distributes Bibles. We had agreed to meet at a small guest house near Nsambya Hospital. In full sunshine and under a cloudless sky, Maria and I walked up a huge dusty hill, asking people where this guest house was and nobody had any idea. Maria was becoming particularly thirsty and my concern for her grew. Eventually a man directed us to a convent where we could rest and have a room for the night. At the reception Maria sat down and repeatedly asked for water, but the receptionist was intent on us filling in some forms. When it looked as though Maria was about to pass out, she received a glass of water.

We were shown to our rooms and as Maria fell on her bed I explained to her my grief. I felt so down-hearted; I had letters, money, books, and greetings to give to Jessica and I had failed to deliver them. We prayed and I went to my own room. Here there was a ready made bed with clean cotton sheets, the walls were painted cream and a metal stand with three coat hangers stood in the corner. I was thrilled to have such comfort.

A knock on my door roused me. "You have a visitor," the man said.

I could hardly believe my eyes, there was Jessica standing in front of me! I opened my arms wide to welcome her, grinning like a Cheshire cat! After that I burst into tears. How God hears and answers prayers! We exchanged so many stories; she told me how many thousands of Bibles she had delivered and I was staggered. Darkness fell and she left with all the gifts I had brought for her. How I praised God for allowing her to find us. It transpired that Jessica had asked many people en route if they had seen the *bazungu* who were looking for her!

After showering, I bathed my badly blistered foot, shared a meal with Maria, and retired to bed, grateful that I had accomplished what I had set out to do that day. *"For we are not our own masters when we live or when we die. While we live, we live to please the Lord. And when we die, we go to be with the Lord. So in life and in death, we belong to the Lord."* Romans 14:7-8.

As I drifted to sleep that night, I recalled that a few weeks previous I had bought a lottery ticket for £1 and had no peace about it. A national lottery company in the UK had just announced the millions people could win and I had been tempted. During the night, I had such an interesting dream that I wrote it down and shared it with Maria the next morning.

In the dream, I was in London walking up the steps from the tube station when a man approached me and asked if I would like to buy a lottery ticket, I only had a £20 note. He said he could change it so I bought a ticket. He gave it to me and went to the back of his scooter, opened a box and came back with an envelope that I thought contained my change. He drove away and I opened the envelope to find a selection of used envelopes with corners removed where the stamps had been. I was dumbfounded. I turned to see Bob and Mo, my friends from church walking towards me. They asked if I was all right. I explained to them what had just happened as I was furious at being so stupid. Then I woke up. The dream was so real I asked God what it was all about.

"You will have all the money you need, trust me, don't doubt. I am very rich and will provide for you". I thought how God had met all my needs in the past and spending money on the lottery was such a waste.

Maria was thrilled with my dream. "This answers my prayer," she said. "I have been on my knees asking God what I should be doing and this confirms what I have been feeling. Praise the Lord! He answered two in one." She never did explain to me what she meant, but I think it was along the same lines of trusting God to provide.

On leaving the convent Maria and I had our photo taken, with me wearing my straw hat. This photo would be in the first charity leaflet for CRU when we set up in 1996.

We returned to Kampala Taxi Park, collected the goods we had left there the day before and boarded a Costa bus to Jinja. The bus should seat twenty-five but as usual there were many more passengers. At Jinja we transferred our entire luggage to a private vehicle. Once again many people called out to Maria; she had really made her mark there. She directed the driver to the house of her friend Ingela, near the Busoga Guest House. Ingela, the wife of the Director of YWAM, served us a light lunch and invited us to stay the night.

That afternoon Maria took me to Main Street.

"Come inside and look," a shopkeeper invited, and we entered his little shop called 'Exclusive Boutique'. Inside were dresses, shoes and bags hung from the ceiling, and Maria bought me a Ugandan straw bag. I felt I had arrived! I already had the straw hat, now the bag to match!

We passed many small shops with very little on the shelves and the outdoor market was just the same; stalls with just a few vegetables and fruit, second hand clothes, table cloths and bedding.

It was in Jinja market that I saw a street-entertainer for the first time. He was a funny looking man with a huge wig. He blew a whistle and gathered people around him by telling jokes and beckoning the children over. I have never seen anything like it before or since. He placed two coke bottles on the ground six feet apart and balanced a pole on the top, then limbo danced under them with everyone clapping and cheering him on. I took a picture which he was not happy about, so I gave a donation as he passed his hat around. We jumped on a *boda-boda* and returned to Ingela's house, where I enjoyed playing with her children. There we made plans for a trip to Bujagali Falls the next day.

The next morning we drove out towards the Owen Falls bridge and followed signs to Bujagali Falls and on to a rough marum road. Major roads in large towns and cities usually have tarmac but, once beyond the city limits, most road surfaces are made of marum; red soil rolled hard by the traffic and bountiful with ruts, cracks, pot-holes, puddles and the occasional stream crossing them. We travelled past very basic mud huts. The grassy bank dropped away from the road and we could see lots of little mud shops in the dip. The only way they could be reached was by crossing a plank of wood from the road to the shops. I saw washing hanging out over bushes and thought about all the dust that we and other road users made. I wondered if it ever looked clean.

The Call, the Cost, the Choice

The view of the Bujagali Falls that opened out in front of us was spectacular, breathtaking. A woman with a baby on her back was making her way up the steep slope carrying a jerry can full of water on her head. Two children tried to carry one between them but it was so heavy they had to stop and tighten the vegetable bung in the top to prevent the water spilling out. A cow wandered about grazing on the little bits of green grass.

We carried our picnic box down the steep track. On the way local children ran in front selling mats for 200/- Ug shillings (less than 10p). We bought ten mats, a pineapple, avocado pears and soda. We didn't have a care in the world as we ate our picnic, wandered down to the side of the falls, and later played ball with the children. There was no one there but us; no tourists, no noise, and no buildings, just the gushing water, the birds singing and children enjoying themselves. It was heavenly. I snapped away with my camera as a reminder of this wonderful interlude in the day.

By mid-afternoon, we were back in the vehicle and on our way home. Maria and I collected all our goods: ten mats, four boxes of computer paper, a bag of maize, a sack of rice, and the basket of stationery materials. Ingela dropped us at Jinja Taxi Park and the journey home to Kamuli in the *matatu* was as much a squash as ever. I offered the driver one of the mints I had in my pocket.

"What's this?" he asked.

I told him it was a mint. I don't think he was any the wiser but he ate it anyway and smiled.

As we drove along the dusty road, there were goats tethered to little bushes and many children in bright-coloured uniforms walking home from school along the verge. The vehicle stopped and a woman got off, gave a message to another lady then jumped back on again. *What timing!* I thought. With no phones for miles this was the next best thing.

On reaching Kamuli, I could hear Maria having a long, loud discussion with the conductor about the price he was going to charge us for the luggage.

"We are not selling it! We are looking after your children. Orphans!" she said, poking the man in the chest.

We stopped, our goods were unloaded and there we stood at the side

29

of the road surrounded by our luggage as they drove away. I have no idea what arrangement Maria and the conductor came to in the end but she looked pleased. I took a few bags and placed them on a passing *boda-boda* and we arrived to a great cheer from the children at the lodge. They had really missed us and been worried as we hadn't returned for two days.

Maria greeted the children and then called a meeting for all over twelve-year-olds, gathering them together like a mother hen would her chicks. I took photos of her under the Freedom Tree, drinking tea and telling them all about our two-day adventure. She then caught up with what had been happening in the school and lodge. Later all the children ate their meal whilst sitting under a few bamboo mats draped over an array of wooden poles.

Maria and I sat in her little room, while a thunderstorm broke overhead. She has a great gift of making a place look homely with scatter cushions, a calendar, and photos of her family on a little desk, candles, and a clock next to her bed. Flowers and plants in old, washed-out paint tins added to the ambiance. She had her bathing area outside next to her room; a very small area where she placed a plastic basin of water on the floor and washed from top to toe. We ate our meal and discussed how she was going to manage the school.

Maria told me how the lodge and school began. After she and her group of teenagers cleaned and decorated the rented house they moved into it in 1992. Maria began teaching the young girls to sew and type on a cardboard typewriter and other basic skills. "When I walked along the street people would shout, 'Maria, Maria I want to go to school,'" she recalled and so, in 1993, Maria set up a school in the old cinema. She remembered three tall boys who attended primary year 7. She had been surprised to see them there but found out later that it didn't matter what age you were, if your parents couldn't afford the money to send you to high school you stayed in primary.

A woman at the council offices gave Maria the permit necessary to establish the primary school because she could see how smart and well-dressed the children were. A few weeks' later local people began arriving asking Maria to look after children whose relatives had died through sickness or during the war. She always had huge challenges to tackle; so many children wanted education that she realised there was a need for the school to have larger premises to accommodate them all. Once again Maria called upon the Lord, and once again he answered. A man who owned three long buildings paid Maria a visit. Two of the buildings were divided up into sixteen little rooms; the other building had four rooms in it. The man was seriously ill and needed money for hospital treatment so he rented the premises to Maria at an agreed price. Maria moved some of the furniture in to the place she called 'the lodge'.

"This was a vision from the Lord; a man came out of the blue and I just did it!" she said.Some time before, government officials had visited the local primary school in Kamuli. They told the children that if they couldn't pay their school fees they'd have to leave immediately. About two months before I arrived in Kamuli, more than two hundred and fifty children, teachers and parents came to Maria and pleaded with her to establish another school. Mrs Rebecca and Pastor Herbert were two of these people; they became integral to the work at 'Maria's Care'. Maria really didn't know where to begin; she already had thirty-eight children to care for and only one small kitchen, two latrines (one for each sex) a small pension, and a little money from friends who believed in her work. Suddenly she was going to have over two hundred children and seven staff.

She decided to build a mushroom (small round classroom) in the lodge grounds. She also organised a lean-to (a roof held up by two poles) for the older students, against the wall of Pastor Herbert's Baptist church. A few teachers were willing to help and the children settled down to their lessons. Maria also organised the building of a little kitchen at one end of the lodge grounds and a covered dining area. It was very small at the beginning but as the project grew so did the dining room!

"God did this, I didn't ask for this to happen. He just did it!" Maria kept exclaiming! She was always obedient and would say; "If God wants it doing I will do it. Nothing is impossible with God."

We talked for a long time of the possibilities, problems and difficulties Maria faced with the school till in the end we decided to pray and leave it with God. It was such a huge project on its own, never mind with the orphanage as well. I left Maria and walked back to my room. As I opened the door, a little frog beat me to it and with a hop skip and a jump disappeared under my bed. I sat down and wrote my diary. The thunder and lightning had stopped. A dog barked. I could hear the children's quiet voices and a child coughing in the distance. Whilst I sorted out the medical supplies I had brought with me from England for the mission hospital in Kamuli, I could hear the drip, drip, drip, of water coming from the gutter into a petrol drum, and the crickets nearby making a riotous noise. My experiences in Uganda thus far had given me much to think about. My reading that morning had been Philippians 4:19,*"And this same God who takes care of me will supply all your needs from his glorious riches, which have been given to us in Christ Jesus."*

Early one morning, at 7.30am children started to arrive and soon over two hundred children were milling around in the lodge compound. By 8.30am no staff had arrived. Maria was very anxious as the school had only been running a few weeks and she was insistent that we always started with an assembly. Eventually she led the children in singing and a Bible reading. As she taught the children explaining the passage to them, the teachers began to drift in.

Maria called a staff meeting under the freedom tree with Mrs Rebecca, Pastor Herbert, and the other five staff. She was angry with them, telling them they had to be on time for school in future and how important it was to start with praise and worship. She said she would close it down if they didn't comply.

I, who had been in Uganda just ten days, got the shock of my life when Maria rose to her feet, looked at me, pointed her finger and said: "You deal with it," and walked off.

I hoped the shock I felt didn't show on my face. I sent a quick arrow prayer to God "Help! What do you want me to do?" I heard a voice in my head say: Encourage them. I took a deep breath: "I would just like to encourage you all. I am sure it must be difficult for you having just started this school. Why did none of you arrive at 8 'o' clock when school begins?"

Some of them looked down at the floor and others took a sideways glance one to another. Eventually a couple of them pointed to their wrists and said: "We have no watches."

Ah, good point, I thought. How was I going to help them solve this? We discussed where they all lived and the best way they could support one another to make sure they all arrived early enough to do the assemblies. Mrs Rebecca suggested they took it in turns each day.

I asked Mrs Rebecca if she was qualified to be the headmistress.

'Yes' was the reply.

Good! I thought.

I asked all the teachers what subject they taught and if they had the right qualifications to teach.

"Yes, madam," they said.

Great! I thought. We were on a roll. Then I asked Pastor Herbert if he was happy being the deputy head.

"No," he said, "I am a pastor."

Ah, I hadn't expected this to be his answer. I took another deep breath: "Will you support Mrs Rebecca till we find someone to fill your place?"

Thankfully, he agreed, although added that his commitment could only be occasional as he had his parish duties as well, which I thought was fair enough.

We spoke for a while and I explained to them that Maria had been under a lot of strain. I gave them a picture of how I saw what had been happening to her:

"Imagine this empty plate; this is Maria's life here. Then she takes on thirty eight young orphans. She needs staff to help; she starts a typing school and has older students coming for lessons. She is dashing backwards and forwards to Kampala with papers because she knows the school has to be registered before any exams are able to be taken. Then you come and ask if a primary school can be started here and two hundred children arrive with no teachers to start the day. Can you see why her plate is overflowing and she can't cope?" They all nodded. I told them I would go and talk through all we had discussed with Maria. They all shook my hand and thanked me very much.

Thank you God! I thought. I had just been thrown in at the deep end... and swam!

This was all recorded and I went to Maria's room with the list. It was clear that Maria was faced with enormous responsibilities. Had she taken on too much? We drank tea and discussed how something had to give before she cracked.

We decided to walk to her friend Glenda, a doctor's wife. She and her husband Marcel had been working in Kamuli Government Hospital for a few years and Maria had gone to visit many times when she was exhausted and in need of a break. They had a little house at the bottom of their garden and Maria would go there and read or just sleep. Glenda welcomed us and went off to make some ground coffee and pancakes for breakfast, which I have to say were delicious! I gave her the medical supplies for the hospital that I had brought from England with which she was truly thrilled, and Maria went off to the little hut for a few hours to read, sleep, and pray.

Glenda's husband, Marcel, arrived home from the hospital quite shattered. We talked about the appalling conditions in the hospital and ways we could try and help one another. He wanted clean water, and we thought of how we could get wells dug and ways to pump it to the hospital by hand or with solar pumps.

Maria and I then had to leave to go to Busoga High School which was preparing for a visit the following Saturday from an American team called 'True Love Waits.' We had a meeting with the deputy head and discussed all the necessary arrangements. We had a three mile walk returning home in the heat before we could rest when suddenly a *matatu* came past.

"Thank you, Lord!" cried Maria.

Twenty minutes later the bus stopped and unloaded us and a huge amount of goods. I took photos of a beautifully-woven basket containing an enormous dead fish about four feet long on the back of a bicycle. To everyone's amusement, I photographed a man strapping a goat and hen to his bike; the livestock didn't seem perturbed by this as though it happened to them all the time. He was soon on his way, peddling down the road, hen and goat in situ! I praised God for all that he was teaching me about life in Uganda.

Back in Kamuli, Maria and I walked to the old cinema building previously owned by some Asians who had fled the country during Idi Amin's regime and had never returned. Maria had started a library there, a little nursery and a crèche; but the library wasn't looked after properly by the locals so Maria stopped. She had left behind some of her tables and chairs which would now prove useful at the school and suggested we return to pick them up, I readily agreed not realising the only transport we had were bicycles.

We arrived at the cinema with three bikes and lots of helpers. They were very excited as we removed tables, chairs, a clock, six wall shelves, a desk and many books. I took photos of this venture and the children were nearly hysterical with laughter at the pantomime it all seemed to be. Everything was balanced (I can't say carefully) on top of the bikes and wheeled back to the lodge. Maria was very pleased because she had wondered how she was going to achieve this mammoth job.

I walked back with Godfrey, a lovely young man whose mother had died. Maria had told her that she would look after Godfrey to the best of her ability. (He is now a teacher in Kamuli). At the lodge the smell of the cooking fire lingered in the atmosphere. It was dusk; the sun was setting, the sky was beautiful. Tables had been set for a meal alfresco in the lodge compound. It looked scrumptious: rice, mixed beans, bananas and pineapple. We sat down and I had to laugh as we ate the food; little chickens ran free in and out of all the bedrooms, mine included. Now I know the true meaning of free range chickens!

In the evening, I went with Maria and Godfrey on the bikes to visit Maria's little dream house. She needed her own place near the lodge but far away enough from the children to rest, relax, and be at peace. It would cost about £35-£40 a month to rent and we needed to see if it was still available.

After such a wonderful day, I felt exhausted with all the walking, negotiating, travelling, and organising, and thought about how Maria must feel having been up since dawn. We were all in bed by 9pm that night. I read a small portion of the Bible and praised God for his love and protection. *"Love is patient, love is kind. It does not envy, it does not boast, it is not proud. It is not rude, it is not self-seeking, it is not easily angered, it keeps no record of wrongs. Love does not delight in evil but rejoices with the truth. It always protects, always trusts, always hopes, and always perseveres."* 1 Corinthians 13:4-7.

Early next morning I could hear lots of people running around and a few hushed voices. Then it went quiet. There was a thud again and the running resumed. It was so early I went back to sleep. I woke again to the sound of knocking at my door.

I pushed the mosquito net aside. "Yes?" I called.

"Come and see the white ants, Rhona!"

I put my skirt over my night dress and picked up my camera. A huge toad jumped out of the way as I stepped outside and although it was barely light I could see the children running wild all over the place. They were catching huge white ants in a sheet. I took photos as they screamed with delight.

"Whatever are you going to do with them?" I asked.

"Fry them and eat them!" they replied with glee in their voices.

"Mmm, very nice," I replied, laughing as I walked back to my room.

Maria always encouraged the children to help with the washing: "This includes you boys, you won't be eating breakfast or going to school if the washing isn't finished," she shouted.

Everyone ran in different directions. I laughed as Maria sat in her chair surrounded by forty little empty seats. Slowly the children finished their tasks and one by one they came to join us for prayers and Bible study. I was reminded of the text in Luke 24:32, *"They said to each other: "Didn't our hearts feel strangely warm as he talked to us on the road and explained the Scriptures to us?"* And I thought to myself how true this was.

After we had committed the day to the Lord, eaten a tasteless burnt porridge and the children had gone to school, Maria and I read the Bible together and prayed before she left to have a meeting with the probation officer. Maria had been meeting him for over two years and needed papers signed in order to become a NGO

At the school I went into the sewing class where some girls sewed up the two slits in my skirt as my knees kept peeping out. In a small room nearby, six girls were learning to type and I became tearful when I saw my mother's typewriter being used. I opened a cupboard and found some Bibles falling to pieces, their backs hanging off. Maria explained later that the combination of heat and cockroaches eating the glue in the spine meant that whole sections, as well as individual pages in the Bible had fallen out. We took the boxes of Bibles outside and I taped them back together again.

Mid-morning, with a gorgeous smell of food cooking, I looked across to see Aunt Rose wearing the apron that I had brought her with a bath-hat on her head to prevent the smoke sticking to her hair, whilst I sat with Christopher, the accountant, looking at all his books and cross referencing the different amounts. I asked many questions. He had a lot of exercise books and a very simple but good accounting system.

When Maria returned from the probation officer, she was really pleased as he had given her a letter, the one she had wanted for the last year. Now she only needed one more. She explained that he was coming to inspect the place at 2.30pm. A quick tidy up was done. 2.30pm came and went. No probation officer.

Maria did have another visitor though, Astrid, whom she hadn't seen for a long time. Astrid was a VSO (Voluntary Service Overseas) lady from Holland involved in agriculture and had been engaged in obtaining equipment for the lodge. Maria never missed an opportunity and asked Astrid about the possibility of being collected the next day to take food and water to Busoga High School for the 'True Love Waits' meeting. Astrid agreed.

"Praise the Lord!" Maria said, "God moves in mysterious ways."

The children were walking around eating the fried flying ants. They had taken the wings off and fried the bodies. They offered some to me but I declined, saying:

"I know they are a special delicacy, so you share them with your friends." Phew! I got out of that lightly. What a coward!

Maria and I sat down to a late lunch of soup Aunt Rose had made with bits of unrecognisable meat floating in it.

"What's in this?" Maria shouted, "Have you killed that chicken that was running round my room?"

Rose replied that the chicken was safe, and we never did find out what was in that soup.

An hour later than expected, the probation man arrived; Simon, a very nice gentleman about thirty years of age. He gave the compound a thorough inspection looking in on classes, and was very encouraging speaking highly of Maria's work. He had been asked by the government the previous December to write a report on all the places in the district that cared for children, and this included Maria's work. He had the report with him and allowed us to make a photocopy. He signed the visitors' book and told us that he had some supply teachers coming to the area and would recommend one of them coming to the school. Maria was thrilled.

Early that evening Aunt Rose took me and my bike with a punctured tyre into Kamuli. I recorded voices in the marketplace and bought a pair of flip-flops for myself. There was literally nothing else for sale. As we walked, Rose told me about the close encounter with death she had when robbers came to a house her husband was guarding. Sadly he was killed but Rose escaped with her daughter. At the same time, Maria had been praying that someone would come and help her. Then she met Rose who needed work and shelter. God showed his concern for both women and answered their prayers. I clicked away with my camera taking photos as we walked along; one in particular of a lady sleeping under a tree with her baby; on the small sheet she sat on were some meagre bunches of bananas for sale.

Later that evening in my room, I opened my suitcase, knowing that my ten day trip to Uganda was nearly at an end. There would be little to pack; I was leaving most of my clothes behind for Maria and the staff as they were desperate for anything to wear. The crickets were making a racket, the little frogs were hopping about, the smell of smoke hung in the air and it was dark and still really hot. I looked around my room and asked myself: What next? God had obviously brought me to Africa for a purpose. I took a stroll in the compound thinking deeply about what that might be. I was thrilled that the netball pole was still standing up and the washing line was mended.

Whilst sitting with Maria later and drinking coffee, she told me about all the difficulties she had faced during the months before I had arrived. Talk about living on the edge! At one time she had only enough money to pay the lodge's rent, buy food, or pay for the children's education, but not all three. She called everyone around her to pray underneath the freedom tree and because the children were desperate for education, they were prepared to sacrifice food to pay for it. The very next day a miracle happened when Maria was told that there was some post for her at the post office; she went and found an envelope containing money from a friend who believed in her work. I say this because many people thought she was quite mad to give up everything in England and step out in blind faith at sixty-five years of age. But she knew God had called her and nothing was going to stop her being obedient.

"Praise the Lord for answering our prayers" she said. They had food and shelter for another month.

"For your Father knows what you need before you ask him." Matthew 6:8.

Maria was shattered at the end of a very busy day. It seemed to me that she was mentally and physically exhausted and there was so much planned for the next day. As I got into bed, I recalled the morning's Bible reading how God is faithful, and the only one who can give us assurance of security and excitement for the future when we give him control. The next day Maria called the children to look at the beautiful sun rising in the sky. The children washed their sheets, some made breakfast, and others put jerry cans into the wheelbarrow and wheeled them to the water barrels.

Whilst dressing, I could hear Maria telling the children a Bible story, with background noises of the cock crowing and the birds twittering. She explained how God is power and the Holy Spirit in us is his power helping us in everything. They prayed, then sang a song to the tune of the 'Quartermaster's Stores.' It was so funny to listen to them as I knew the words to the original song.

I read my Bible study for that day from Exodus 14:13–15, *"But Moses told the people "Don't be afraid. Just stand where you are and watch the Lord rescue you....The Lord himself will fight for you. You won't have to lift a finger in your defence!" Then the Lord said to Moses: "Why are you crying out to me? Tell the people to get moving!"* Only as I write this down years later do I see what God was saying to me back then.

Astrid arrived mid-morning and we filled the truck with food and water to last the day before driving the fifteen minute journey to Busoga High School. Some of the children jumped into the truck to come with us and I hitched a lift with Godfrey on his bike. As we arrived at the school it seemed that the birds were singing God's praises, and the air was cool after the rain the night before. The children arrived and assembled expectantly as the 'True Love Waits' team set up.

We had all moved under a flame tree and sat on the benches that had been set up there. The choir had a drink of water and began to sing; it was very moving. We prayed and had a wonderful time of praise and worship. The team from America introduced themselves and spoke from the Bible about salvation.

They performed a powerful drama for the students showing how easily HIV and AIDS is spread through casual, unsafe sex. If one man had sex with one woman who had previously had sex with three men who had each had sex with two other women and so forth, then all those people could be carriers or infected with the disease. The drama ended with the young man falling for a lovely young virgin girl, sleeping with her and her subsequent death through AIDS. It got the message across. The children learnt that condoms are not 100% safe, they were taught to make sure they weren't out of date, that they were put on properly and then disposed of carefully, to always wash their hands after sex, or better still – abstain in the first place!

The team had a big impact on the students and gave out hats with 'True Love Waits', written on them. In the evening we all enjoyed a good meal; we sat in a large circle to sing and had a super time of praise.

My stay in Uganda was coming to an end and I wanted to visit Glenda. Godfrey took me on his bike and on the way I fell off backwards because he suddenly stopped to let the girl he was carrying on the crossbar off. He lost his balance and I landed in the bushes! He was mortified and quickly rushed to help me up. I remembered hearing a famous lady on the radio once say:

"If you fall down, don't try to regain your dignity too fast. Get accustomed to your surroundings, take your time and get up steadily."

"It's OK, Godfrey," I said, "I'm getting accustomed to my surroundings."

He gave me such a strange look. Eventually I allowed him to pull me up. I felt fine because my body had had time to re-adjust. That lady gave very good advice. I had banged my head and had a cut on my right ankle. Godfrey kept apologising but I told him I would live and that it could have been a lot worse. He was so ashamed that he had dropped a *muzungu* (me).

Glenda welcomed my arrival. Her husband, Marcel, was busy typing a 'thank you' letter for me to take back to England. He was frustrated because the computer was playing up and he had three nurses calling him to visit sick patients. He was also furious with a situation he was facing; a woman was bleeding badly after just giving birth and, although her husband was a good blood-match, he was refusing to give blood thinking that he would die. Marcel persuaded him in the end but it was touch and go for a while. Eventually Marcel appeared with the letter, apologised for the delay, and thanked me for all I was doing. He had to rush as the nurses all had different patients who needed attention.

"Go, go," I said. "Don't worry about me, you have so much work to do, God bless, bye." He shot off on his bike.

"Wow! Look at daddy go, he must be going one hundred miles an hour!" shouted his children.

I must admit he did move fast. *We have no idea what these doctors and nurses go through, no idea at all,* I thought.

Godfrey appeared to take me back to the lodge.

On the bike!

The Call, the Cost, the Choice

Once there, everyone sang as we walked together to the taxi park. Two children held my hand all the way. I felt sad but also knew this was just the beginning of something, although I had no idea what. It was like a parade when Maria and I left with the children shouting and waving to us.

We arrived in Jinja after a wonderful journey up and down the hills along the straight road. We stopped to let people off, to collect water, to pass notes and money, even give messages. I was beginning to understand the phrase 'jungle drums'. It was happening in front of my eyes. A huge amount of luggage was on this vehicle, another house move I think. There was a bed, bags of linen, a box of food, plastic bowls, jerry cans, and a live goat. I kept feeling feathers tickling my ankles; I looked down and saw two chickens under the seat.

We left my suitcases at the home of Maria's friend and jumped on a *boda-boda* to the Busoga Trust Guest House. I was shown to my room with one bed with a four inch mattress and bedding. There was also a mat, two hangers, a light bulb and, yes, I did have curtains and a key in the door. Maria gave me her mosquito net and I managed to hang it sideways from the one and only hook on the wall. In the evening she and I went to the Sunset Hotel situated on the edge of the Nile. There we saw a magnificent view of the sun setting. We ordered our drinks and a special fish dish that Maria wanted me to try. By 7.10pm the sun had set and it was dark. I ate my meal listening to Christian music in the background. It was all so special to me. I thought of all the people who had made my trip possible: personal friends, people from different churches, customers from work.

It was pitch black when we left the Sunset Hotel and we wondered if we would get a *boda-boda* back to the guest house. Maria spoke to the gate-man who took us scrambling through the bushes. As there weren't any fences we went across the back gardens of big houses and past some little shops. People looked up in disbelief as they sat around open fires and saw us walking from the pitch black into the light. The gate-man at one hotel shouted something and two *boda-bodas* arrived.

Miracles do happen; we both said 'Praise the Lord!' It was really very funny. *What a way to finish my trip!* I thought to myself. I did pray for protection all the way back though because it was so dark and we were riding side-saddle through the back streets, onto the main road, then off again and through the bushes.

Uganda

Back at the guest house we had coffee in the lounge whilst the main gates were locked at precisely 8.30pm. The Ascarie (security guard armed with bow and arrow) pulled the huge iron security door shut between the bedrooms and lounge and we all went to bed.

That's us, all safe and sound, I thought. I was in my room ready to write my diary when I suddenly realised I had left my bag in the lounge along with my passport, money, pen and paper. The lounge was left open at the front for the Ascarie to shelter at night. What was I to do? If I tried to pull the iron door open I might set an alarm off, or get shot as an intruder! My imagination ran overtime. Eventually I opened my door and tip-toed towards the main bedrooms ready to call out to the guard.

Just at that moment a young Englishman popped his head out from behind his door and came to my rescue. He laughed when I told him my predicament, opened the iron door, and retrieved my bag. His name was Marcus from Eccles in Manchester. He was just 19 years old and had worked hard to pay for his trip to Uganda. He was in Jinja working in a lovely school but felt he was being wasted as the children had good teachers and really didn't need his help. I told him all about Maria's school and he was really interested. We exchanged addresses and I suggested he should contact Maria himself. I found out weeks later that he did in fact contact her and stayed for a few months in Kamuli helping the children with their work. How God brings good situations out of bad ones! *"And we know that in all things God works for the good of those who love him, who have been called according to his purpose."* Romans 8:28.

Next morning, we walked to the home of Maria's friend who offered us a warm shower each which we accepted and thoroughly enjoyed. All we had in Kamuli was a plastic bowl and cold water to wash in, so this was heaven! She even had a toilet with a proper seat! We had been used to latrines so this was sheer luxury indeed. By 10.15am we had arrived at the taxi park with my luggage and left for Kampala twenty minutes later when the *matatu* had filled up.

In Kampala we stored my luggage under a desk in the office of the bus depot and prayed it would be safe. From there we went to Cresta Towers where we were to have a meeting with a man from the Gideons organisation but he didn't turn up, so we had a meal in a nearby café, counted our money, and discussed what I needed to do once back in England. We finished lunch and walked to Peter Nyombi's office; Maria's lawyer. He was very pleased with the letters of recommendation Maria gave him, and made copies for me to take back to England, showing people that Maria's project was in the process of becoming an NGO.

In due course, we collected my luggage and struggled down the busy, steep steps to the far side of the taxi park and boarded a *matatu* to Entebbe. Once there we walked to the beautiful Victoria Hotel. The view was stunning; beyond the golf course we could see Lake Victoria. Maria and I talked more about our achievements whilst I had been in Uganda and Maria's dreams and visions.

It was nearly dark when I left my luggage in the porter's room for the night and we visited the house of friends of Maria; Andrew and Greta Nunn. They had offered us a bed for the night and, even though Greta was unwell, still she welcomed us and made us feel at home. I thanked God that I had been well all the time I had been in Uganda because I'd eaten so much unusual and curious food. It was a beautiful house and they were lovely Christian people. God was so good to meet all our needs like this. *"And my God will meet all your needs according to his glorious riches in Christ Jesus."* Philippians 4:19.

We spent two wonderful happy and relaxing days with Andrew and Greta discussing our thoughts and dreams for the future. We even had the opportunity to have a delightful swim in the pool at Lake Victoria Hotel. This was the first time I had seen such clean water. We slept well and I woke on my final day in Uganda to the sound of children singing on their way to school. I thought about all I might say when I got back to England.

I read Psalm 8:1-9, *"O Lord, our Lord, how majestic is your name in all the earth! You have set your glory amongst the heavens. From the lips of children and infants you have ordained praise because of your enemies, to silence the foe and the avenger. When I consider your heavens, the work of your fingers, the moon and the stars, which you have set in place, what is man that you are mindful of him, the son of man that you care for him? You made him a little lower than the heavenly beings and crowned him with glory and honour. You made him ruler over the works of your hands; you put everything under his feet; All flocks and herds, and the beasts of the field, the birds of the air, and the fish of the sea, all that swim the paths of the seas. O Lord, our Lord, how majestic is your name in all the earth!"*

I sat and thought about the incredible words I had just read. How privileged I was to have my own Bible to guide me when so many people in the world had to share one, ripping it in half so one person could have the New Testament and another, the Old. How I had taken it all for granted until seeing the situation for myself in Uganda.

After breakfast, we prayed together committing the day to the Lord, and set off for Entebbe Airport. The road was dreadful with pot-holes where the tarmac had completely gone. On arrival, I handed Maria an envelope containing money for two months' rent for the little house we had seen the week before. It had no running water or electricity but she desperately needed a place she could call her own. I knew she could spend this money a hundred times over elsewhere but I believed this would fulfil her dream; somewhere to seek God away from the daily work and frustrations, somewhere to shout 'Help!', and somewhere to reflect and rejoice in all God was doing. A place she could offer to other missionaries to come and rest and be at peace, in much the same way Glenda's house had been respite to her.

I checked my bags in at the airport and paid the tax necessary on leaving Uganda. Maria was convinced I would be back to help her next year.

Maybe I will, I thought, but I knew I had a huge task ahead of me to set up a network.

As I walked towards the plane, I saw all the passengers' luggage lined up outside on the runway. I had to point mine out to the airport porter who took my bags and put them behind a line.

I remember thinking, *So this is the security measure in place!*

I boarded the plane and looked at the crew in amusement; I realised I had seen them the day before around the pool at Victoria Hotel.

We all look different with our clothes on! I laughed to myself.

The plane engine revved up, we taxied along the runway, and I looked out of the window at the lush green palm trees, the red dust, and blue sky with white fluffy clouds. I saw huge letters that had been written in green grass on the hillside, ENTEBBE.

Yes I am leaving, but I don't think this is the end of this project. This is just the beginning; I wonder what God is going to do? I mused.

Then I remembered what God had said to me when I was converted on May 14th, 1987:

The Call, the Cost, the Choice

"You think you have had an exciting life so far. Just wait till you see what I have in store for you." This was it! I knew this was the beginning of the exciting project that he had in store for me and it would go on and on.

We had a good flight to Brussels and then on to England. I arrived wearing my straw hat, flip-flops, and a long skirt. What a sight! I felt exhilarated but extremely cold.

Chapter 3

Setting up the charity

On my return from Uganda in March, 1995, I was able to share with my church the work that Maria Maw had started in Kamuli, how desperate her situation was and how much she needed our help. Gerald Moss, a retired business man, was listening to this message. He asked me to write my vision down and said he might be able to help me. We shared our thoughts and he suggested we invite friends to a meeting with no strings attached, to reveal our vision to them. We did this the following month, and after sharing with them we asked if they would like to be involved. To my great surprise they all said 'yes'!

Much later in the year I received a letter from Maria part of which read: 'The country has gone mad, prices have tripled. I have managed to pay school fees for the primary children and three months' rent. Praise the Lord, Love and God Bless,

I am worn out, Maria'

Over the next twelve months, Maria and I continued to do what we believed God had called us to do. I had been sent back to England after that first visit with instructions from Maria to raise money to build a school and orphanage in Kamuli. It was a huge struggle for both of us. Little did we know God had other plans. While I was fundraising and trying to set up a charity, God sent an Asian family to give Maria three dilapidated warehouses in Kamuli. *"For my thoughts are not your thoughts, neither are your ways my ways," declares the Lord."* Isaiah 55:8.

Later, Maria told me the story:

"A vehicle pulled up and three people got out, one asked if I was a charity.

'I suppose so,' I replied. The Indian lady introduced herself as J.J. Madhvani, along with her mother and brother. She said she had some premises in Kamuli that they would like to give to me. If I would just like to get in the car they would take me to see them. I thought this was a real answer to prayer until the driver turned left, so I shouted:

'There is nothing down there!'

He continued to drive, however, and five hundred yards further we came to a broken gate. We piled out and in front of me were three dilapidated warehouses.

I did not shout: 'Praise the Lord.' I shouted: 'Oh no, not three more headaches!' "

She had already battled through so much in the last four years but, Maria being Maria, she grabbed the baton and ran with it. This is a lady that leads from the front, a great role model for all of us; so she carried on regardless of all the problems. Within a few months, she managed to reorganise the place with boys' and girls' dormitories, a school office, main hall and classrooms. With very little money, she got the basic materials and with a local builder and carpenter, she managed to make the place habitable.

One day she arranged the children and staff into a long line leading from the lodge to the gates of the new compound, later to be called 'Maria's Care.' They all helped pass furniture, bedding, plates, crockery and all the kitchen equipment along the line to the new building. Both Maria and I could see the grace of God at work; the warehouses could have been anywhere in a fifty mile radius of the lodge, but they were right on her door step. Even though the photos Maria had sent me of the three dilapidated buildings looked awful, I could see the fantastic potential and the vision Maria had for the place.

Back in England, it took a long time to set up the charity. Papers were submitted and rejected for one reason or another; it was disheartening. Up to that point, the committee and I were the only ones that knew of Christian Relief Uganda's (CRU) existence so I suggested a date to launch our Trust and we set the date as Saturday, April 23rd, 1996. We arranged the table and chairs in the church hall, and as we sat down ready to pray before the meeting, Sue, our secretary, said:

"I had a letter this morning from the charity commissioners." We all looked at her with enquiring eyes. "And," she continued, a smile forming across her face, "they have granted us a charity number!" A great intake of breath was heard as we all took in what Sue had just said.

Setting up the Charity

I was overjoyed along with all the other members. "Wow! Isn't God good? We aren't launching a trust; we're launching a charity!"

We all had different gifts and talents to offer the board and so 'Christian Relief Uganda' was born. We could see how God had encouraged us to keep going and not give up at the first hurdle, both for us in England and Maria in Uganda. We believed with passion that the work in Uganda was in his heart as well. He needed people like us to support Maria and the destitute people there. This was his project that he was entrusting to us. What a privilege and a responsibility to be called by God.

It tells us in Psalm 139:16, *"All the days ordained for me were written in your book before one of them came to be."*

Chapter 4

Maria's work in Kamuli

The SOS to me from Maria read:

"Unbelievable! God walked into the lodge in the form of three Asian people offering three huge properties. I need volunteers, carpenters, builders, electricians. Oh, Rhona, is it not wonderful? Please tell your people; please ask them to pray that we are doing it all wisely. I need you desperately to keep me calm and give me guidance."

It was in September, 1995, as I was walking through the shop where I worked, that I was reading aloud those words from Maria's letter. She had made quite a few requests.

"How on earth am I going to find people like this?" I questioned, just as Gordon Birch walked through the shop; He was working in the flat above and needed some milk for his brew.

"Whatever are you talking about, chuck?" he asked.

I explained to him that I had received a letter from Maria asking me to find someone who could do a bit of plumbing, electrical work and building.

"This will be fun." I quipped.

An hour later, a little voice piped up, "I think I'm your man. I wouldn't mind going to see what it's like and it's got to be better than painting over graffiti on shop windows." It was Gordon.

"Well, if you are serious, my friend Barbara and I will be going in February next year. Let me know when you get your injections."

I left it like that because many people had told me they would like to go to Uganda and I never saw them again. The following Friday, Gordon reappeared,

"You're on; I am starting my injections next week." I was flabbergasted.

With a smile on my face, I talked a little about how basic it was in Uganda and how uncertain I was as to what Maria had in mind. Gordon seemed undeterred. He smiled back.

"We'll see," he said.

Plans were put in place. We had flights to go to Uganda on Friday, 9th February, 1996, and over the next few months we worked towards this date. Barbara and I were collecting donations and goods to give to people in Uganda, whilst Gordon was busy renovating property for one of his family. The day before we were due to fly to Uganda, I arrived home from work to a message on my answer phone:

"Please ring the travel agent."

I rang only to be told that Sabina Airways were on strike. I couldn't believe it. I went hot and cold, my mouth fell open, and I couldn't speak for ages. The travel agent asked if we would consider going next Tuesday but that was impossible as too many arrangements had been put in place. (This was prior to e-mails and mobile phones. We had no direct way to contact people in Africa; even emergency faxes depended on electricity being available in Uganda at the right time in the right place). He said he would see what he could do. I went into a state of shock and decided I had to praise God in all circumstances. I prayed and asked God for help so that all three of us would travel together the following day as planned. After half an hour, the agent rang back. The Manager of Sabina, a friend of his, had been wonderful; he had booked three seats for us from Manchester to Heathrow where we would then change airlines. He was booking us on a new airline called Alliance Airways.

I rang Gordon and asked: "Do you want the good news or the bad news first?"

"Go on," he said, "What's happened?"

I explained the situation; the bad news was we were not flying with Sabina; the good news was we didn't have to leave at 3am in the morning but 1pm in the afternoon!

"Great" he said, "I have time to paint a few more doors in the flat I'm renovating."

I praised God for sorting everything out and giving me a peace about it.

On the morning of Friday, 9th Feb, 1996, several people phoned and said they would be praying for us. And we really needed prayer. The phone rang once more; it was the chairman of Rotary, Maurice Glynn.

"Hi Rhona, when do you go to Africa?"

"In 15 minutes!"

"My goodness!" he exclaimed, "I had better come straight away; I have just typed all the documents for you regarding the equipment Zeneca are packing right now for Uganda." He arrived forthwith with the documents and told us the assignment would be flying out in a few days and would arrive in Uganda on February 13th. Can you believe it? Maurice thought we were going the following week and rang on the off-chance I would be home for lunch! Another God incidence, I thought. This is surely the beginning of many little miracles we might be encountering in the next two weeks.

Barbara and I picked up Gordon and headed for the airport. Before we even left we knew we had far too much luggage; all we could do was pray. Sabina had faxed their office in Entebbe so Maria wouldn't be waiting all night for us in Uganda. At Manchester Airport, I was apprehensive with a hundred and one things dashing through my mind but I was also very excited. We collected our plane tickets and then weighed in. I took a big deep breath and sent another arrow prayer to God. The luggage weight limit was twenty kilos, and the dental equipment alone weighed twenty-five. Sabina had given us an extra allowance of five kilos each which gave us a total of seventy-five kilos between us. Our entire luggage weighed in at one hundred and twenty-six kilos. I really prayed God would blind the eyes of the baggage handlers so they wouldn't see the weight. We got over this first hurdle as most of the BA passengers to Heathrow were on business with only hand luggage, but the girl at the desk warned us that we were overweight and she had no idea what would happen at Heathrow. I prayed they wouldn't weigh our hand luggage! We had no idea what we would do if they refused to let us take the entire luggage to Uganda. I envisaged us leaving it at the airport and letting someone take it to a charity shop. We had a choice; pray, or leave some of the goods in England.

Once at Heathrow, I had an inner panic and prayed. I really tried to trust God with the luggage. The silly thing was that our own personal luggage would probably only come to about four kilos. Everything in the bags was for other people, various hospitals, the orphanage, and the new school in Kamuli. My knees were knocking and my tummy was turning over as I approached the Airport check-in desk, attempting a smile at the man sitting there. I lifted the suitcases and placed them on the scales at the same time trying to tell him about all the last minute changes we had made and how all the things were going to an orphanage, hospital, dental unit, and school in Uganda. The weight clocked up. He smiled and said:

"Oh, don't worry about that, I've got my wrong glasses on today," He passed the whole lot! He didn't ask one question, not one! We were on our way, my heart was leaping and I was close to tears. He asked for our passports and handed us our boarding tickets.

"I hope you have a wonderful trip," he said.

"Thank you." I replied. I couldn't believe it; our second miracle, Praise the Lord!

We arrived in Entebbe at 8am. Maria's friend, Everet, whom she still insisted calling Everest, was waiting for us. He signed our yellow card to say where we were staying. We were nearly through customs when an officer shouted after us. He asked Gordon what was in the black box he was carrying.

I stepped forward, pointed at Barbara and said, with as much authority as I could muster in my voice:

"This lady is a dental hygienist; the box is full of dental equipment."

He nodded, shrugged his shoulders and said: "You may go now," and waved us on. We were all through. Praise the Lord. Again!

Outside, Maria was waiting for us and, after introductions we exchanged some money as we had to pay for the pre-booked accommodation even though in the end we hadn't slept there. The exchange rate was 1,500/- Ug shillings to £1. Maria negotiated a price for a *matatu* to take us all to Kamuli, including a stop in Jinja to pick up two dogs, one of whom was promptly sick. They became guard dogs at the compound. It was a long, hot, hair-raising journey, which took over four hours. A couple of mini buses pulled out in front of us and we had to do an emergency stop.

"Welcome to Uganda!" I exclaimed to Barbara and Gordon.

The Call, the Cost, the Choice

On the way, the driver stopped and said we had to re-negotiate the price as he had used over half the petrol. Maria was having none of it and told him we were only ten minutes away, so he continued. When we arrived at the lodge, the children were so excited they jumped up and down as they greeted us. Barbara and Gordon were surrounded and we were ushered into a little mushroom-hut with a straw roof where we all drank cool juice.

I looked around and saw so many changes: different areas had new buildings, parts of the ground that had been bare before now had grass and flowers, another example of how Maria's marvellous talents helped to make a place a home.

Maria then took us to see the new school. Here we were at last, walking down to an enormous compound with not a tree in sight, towards three huge warehouses that we could see from the road. I understood what Maria meant when she wrote to ask me for a man who could do lots of different jobs. I also realised how much work had already been done before we arrived. We looked around; Maria had been busy having doors and windows knocked through and some of the brickwork needed urgent repair. In the main hall, a desperately unsafe balcony had been erected. She had taken five days off to come and collect us from the Airport, and returned to discover some jobs she had allocated hadn't been done, whilst others she hadn't spoken of had been. Within days, Gordon was busy with various projects in the compound, including the prompt removal of the balcony.

We went in and out of classrooms; some had a few desks in, others had none. As we walked and talked, I noticed how spotless everywhere was. The grass had been cut and bricks placed sideways to define the path, but there was still so much to do. We went back to the lodge to pray and to ask God if we should get the school ready or leave it for the staff to do. A few minutes later, the secretary, Beatrice, came to see Maria, saying that there was a lot to do over in the school and she would go and do it.

Wow! That was a quick answer to prayer.

After lunch, we went over to Maria's new house. Barbara experienced her first ride on a *boda-boda*. She wobbled a bit and nearly fell off (made a few funny noises!) but soon got the hang of it. This was the little house I had seen with Maria in 1995, and now she had made it home. There were three rooms including a bedroom with coordinating curtains and cushions, locally-made chairs, table and bookcase. The kitchen was basic but adequate and led out to a small yard in which she had sown some seeds and lovely flowers had grown. It all looked so colourful. There was a small, round dining area attached to the back of the house, covered in dry grass. It was quite charming to sit there having afternoon tea, a good British habit. We certainly needed our siesta. Behind the house, in the boys' quarters, lived a young man called Bodo; he was a medical student doing a thesis on malaria and the mosquito.

After our evening meal, we discussed the plans for the following Saturday, 17th February, the date set for the official school opening. I was to be guest of honour. I asked Maria why she had chosen me.

"Because I want you to talk to all the parents, teachers and staff about the fundraising involved to sustain this huge project," she said.

The next day we walked to the local baptist church where Pastor Herbert lived and preached. I felt like an explorer as I tried to remember the way. We turned left out of 'Maria's Care' gates and followed some of the children; we passed the end of the road where David, the carpenter, lived and then passed a little maize mill. At the crossroads, we turned left again past a huge piece of land with signs promoting a new hospital. The local people said the signs had been there so long they would believe it when they saw it! As we walked along people happily greeted us: *"Jambo! Jambo!"* they cried with delight.

On arrival, we saw many of our children from 'Maria's Care'. They had been there since 9.30am attending the Bible study before the service. Beatrice led the service in a most humble way with no regard to any interruption of people coming and going, the goats bleating, hens clucking and pecking around, and the cock crowing right next to the little building. Just before noon she finished by singing a song. There were about fifty people in the congregation and it appeared that as the service went on more and more people arrived. They placed benches in the front and then sat down. It was only at the end of the service I realised the congregation hadn't grown but that all the people had come from the back to the front because the sun had moved and they would have been burnt sitting in it. You live and learn.

I thought how wonderful it would be in three or four years or even ten if we could build a guest house in Kamuli; maybe have our own *matatu*, and full involvement with the school, hospital, dental clinic and orphanage. It would be good to have a simple but hygienic place up and running. I believe we all have a human right to be educated and our basic needs met.

We had brought with us from England a cake-board, a '60th Birthday' sign, balloons, poppers, and a candle that said '60' on it. When we arrived at 'Maria's Care' I handed everything to Aunt Rose to make a special cake for Gordon's birthday. Back at Maria's home, we met Dan, the electricity man, and Christopher, the bursar for Maria's school, which was to be called 'Kamuli Parents' Baptist Primary School'.

The sun was shining the day Maria went to buy school books and paint for the T.S.O.L.S. (Training School of Life Skills); this was another project Maria had set up specifically for older students who hadn't had the opportunity of further education. The teachers were paid but the students only had to make a small contribution towards their food and uniforms. Maria instructed Barbara and me to take the primary school assembly and gave us a list of thing she wanted us to do.

Afterwards, we travelled by *boda-boda* to Dr Marcel and Glenda's house. Barbara and I sat side-saddle on the back of the bikes, Barbara looked very confident but she assured me it was all a front. We laughed and giggled because the drivers couldn't get going. We were sure it was our weight!

Marcel was about to dash off to a conference for many of the consultants from all the mission hospitals in Uganda. Apparently the hospitals were in a financial mess and they needed to discuss the way forward. There was a remarkable tropical storm whilst we ate a meal with Glenda and Astrid. We had to move inside to talk as the rain made so much noise. The electricity went off and we lit lots of little candles. I thought of the people in the hospital who were possibly in the middle of an operation; it was so dark, how would they cope?

When the storm died down, we were escorted around the hospital grounds and wards. I took photos of the box of Johnson & Johnson examination gloves that we had donated; the hospital had such a short supply of sterile gloves that they washed each pair after use, rubbed them in dusty chalk, and hung them up around the windows to dry and be used again. When I explained that in England we used them only once before throwing them away, they were stunned. There were no curtains between the beds allowing privacy and just one portable screen for the whole hospital.

We saw two tiny babies head to toe in an incubator that was made from a wooden box on a small stand with a pig bulb underneath it. The babies had different coloured blankets so the mothers knew which baby was theirs. Sadly, we passed by a side room in which we saw a stillborn baby wrapped in a pink sheet. Over at the nurses' school, the midwife was teaching a group of young student nurses; Barbara and I learnt so much by listening in to the question and answer session.

In one children's ward, the sister told us it had a fatality rate of nearly 100%. I couldn't believe my ears. These children often came in with typhoid, meningitis and other diseases that proved fatal. I was quite bewildered by all I had seen; I have never been good with blood and sickness.

On the way home, we met a very happy Maria; she had been to Jinja and managed to buy the paint and books needed for the new school. We knew that this was an incredible achievement because shops usually didn't have much stock.

The next morning we met a very unhappy Maria. She had overslept. She made a list of all the jobs she wanted doing, and we had a rather heated discussion about the posters and signs she wanted making for the school opening day.

That day we were able to spend some time at the new school. I was very impressed with the standard of work. I noticed on the blackboard some complicated algebra. The school curriculum was set out in a series of books for the teachers to follow; unfortunately however, the teachers did not have most of the equipment they needed. I wondered how the children managed to grasp what a magnet was and how it worked when they had never seen one. Barbara and I worked hard all day; we cut paper, glued and stuck teaching resources, and made posters. We covered things with sticky back plastic I had brought from home, and Mrs Rebecca helped us to make a huge sign: 'Kamuli Christian Community Youth Centre.'

Late in the afternoon, we sat in the lodge with Gordon and two visitors, Stewart and Rodney, eating peanuts. One of them jumped into a water barrel and had a bath. He smelt lovely but Maria was not amused and went mad because water was so precious.

By 7am the next morning, Maria had already gone to the taxi park. She had pushed a note through our door listing our daily instructions:

The Call, the Cost, the Choice

Cut out A.B.C. (alphabet) from card for the primary school.

Make banners and flags for new school ceremony.

Write the sponsors' names on the boards to go above the classrooms.

Make playdough. (We decided to make this nearer the time or it might go hard).

Over at the school we gave little soft toys brought from England to the children in the crèche. They were delighted and hugged and kissed them. One little boy held his clown up and talked to it; he was so sweet and really cherished it. We soon discovered the children weren't the only ones to enjoy the toys; the mice and rats would rip them open in the night and take the stuffing for their own use if ever they were left on the floor.

I went over to Mrs Rebecca and gave her a letter from the headmaster of Henbury High School in Macclesfield. She was thrilled to bits and kept hugging us and thanking us for the chalk, pens and calendars, donated by the school. Various organisations had sponsored classrooms to be furnished, so we spent time making signs to be displayed above each classroom door:

Tytherington Family Worship

Tytherington Cubs

St Peters Letchworth

Henbury High

Copeland

Uppingham

Benllech Camp

I.Sinnet Lawson

We had fun trying to find enough straight pieces of wood to write all these names on.

I wrote one sign in deep red: 'SICK ROOM.'

In the evening, we walked into Kamuli and tried unsuccessfully to phone Jessica and Nelson, the Gideon Bible representatives for Kampala. We got back home just as Astrid, whom I had met the previous year, arrived. She had come to borrow Bodo's bike. After introductions and a chat, Astrid asked Barbara if she would go to Busoga High School and talk to the students about cleaning their teeth and preventative measures against tooth decay. Although Barbara wasn't geared up to do this, she made a choice and agreed to go. This was the beginning of Barbara's dental ministry in Africa.

After breakfast, we walked to the T.S.O.L.S. and collected a parcel I wanted to give Jessica and Nelson if God would help us meet them.

Barbara and I were going on our own expedition to Kampala; a three hour journey squashed in a *matatu* with the usual bound up chicken under my feet. Thankfully, it didn't make any fuss, and neither did I. We managed to ring Jessica and Nelson from a payphone in Jinja and left a message that we would be in the Sheraton Hotel at 2pm. We had no idea who would pick up the message or when.

In Kampala we found a small bank where we could change some currency. We were ushered into a very small dark room and directed behind the counter where five women were counting and weighing money on rather sophisticated scales. Initially, I was amazed there wasn't a screen between us and the bank clerk until I noticed the armed guard sitting quietly in a corner.

Very subtle, I thought.

We were then escorted into an even smaller room and we both began to wonder what we had got ourselves into. The room had a desk with a window and four little holes cut in the glass, just enough to put our hands through with the money we needed to change. We were safe, and so was our money.

Out in the sunshine again, we took our lives in our hands as we headed towards the Sheraton Hotel, crossing roads and dodging in between moving vehicles which seemed to come haphazardly at us from every angle. Motorbikes and bicycles would appear from nowhere to add to the confusion. In the end Barbara grabbed my arm and led me across the road waving her hat in the air to stop the traffic, as she had decided no one was going to squash us. We roared with laughter. What a sight! It worked every time after that.

We had lunch in a restaurant bar called 'Strike.' As we ate our salad which would have fed at least four people, we felt a little guilty knowing that there were starving people not far away. We walked to the hotel and prayed we might meet Nelson and Jessica; they arrived at the same time as us. With the help of others in the Gideon movement they had delivered two hundred and fifty thousand Bibles to various clubs, hospitals, hotels, prisons, barracks, offices and schools in just one month!

The Call, the Cost, the Choice

We handed over the supplies we had brought with us: belts, shoes, a watch, soap, toothbrushes and paste. It was like Christmas morning! I had even packed a hearing aid – with no idea why I was taking it – but God obviously did. Jessica and Nelson were thrilled with it as they knew someone who desperately needed one. Back in England, I had looked at the little box containing the hearing aid and wondered what I was going to do with it and who on earth would want one when I got to Uganda. Clearly someone's heart's desire was being answered.

Looking around, I started to think about the great potential for small groups of people to come out and have the 'Ugandan experience' for themselves.

"Wouldn't it be great to bring people out here to experience Uganda?" I said to Barbara.

We met up with Maria and went to the education offices at Cresta Towers where she needed to photocopy papers and documents, before disappearing upstairs to see someone about registering the different classes in her school. Barbara and I sat 'people watching.' It was so interesting to see how many different characters passed by; all colours, shapes and sizes. Several European businessmen looking rather hot and sticky in crumpled shirts and trousers went past, and I considered how Barbara and I must have looked as we had been out in the heat and travelling in a hot *matatu* since 8am.

When Maria reappeared she was steaming! They had lost all her papers and she had to come back the following week.

We walked to the craft market behind the National Theatre where there were over thirty little stalls selling all sorts of knick-knacks, plus sodas and clothes. Maria particularly loved to shop and we all thoroughly enjoyed ourselves buying several mats, trays, and fruit bowls – all for under £10. What a bargain! Maria spotted a green dress covered in embroidery that she took a great liking to and thought it would do well to wear at the official school opening. Barbara and I agreed it suited her and bought it for her as a treat.

Then we were off again, hiking up and down the road in and out of zooming cars and bikes. Maria never ceased to amaze me; she would pray, step out, and off she went! She decided we should stop and have some ice-cream, so we ordered blueberry, and when it came it was literally blue and stained our lips that colour too.

There was one item on our list that I held little hope of finding. You have to remember that Uganda was just picking up after years of war and trouble, and people were still apprehensive of coming back and settling. Many were still nervous about setting up home and investing in businesses and shops so I really didn't think we would find Velcro. O ye of little faith! Maria went into a shop that was just about to close and there it was! I was astounded! Matthew 7:7 sprang to mind, *"Ask and it will be given to you; seek and you will find; knock and the door will be opened to you."* I couldn't believe it – and they only charged Maria 35p a metre!

It was getting dark as we left Kampala Taxi Park and sped along the road towards Jinja, passing candle-lit mud huts, bonfires surrounded by groups of people, a few shops still open, cafés with people sitting outside, a few bars and a bustling open market. In Jinja we were directed to the centre of Main Street where we boarded a *matatu*, whose driver was trying to drum up business:

"Kamuli! Kamuli! Kamuli!" he shouted.

I thought this was great fun and joined in. He in turn thought this was hilarious too. Gradually, the vehicle filled up and the local people cheered as we left Jinja for Kamuli at what felt like a snail's pace behind many huge lorries groaning their way up the hills.

In Kamuli, we had a fifteen minute walk ahead of us back to the lodge; thankfully, Maria had taught us not to go out without a torch. Bodo was waiting up for us and we told him about our exhausting day. To this day, I have no idea where Maria gets her energy from – she had been up since 4.30am.

Maria had much on her mind including the official school opening the next day. Barbara and I went back to the lodge and continued with the tasks we had started a couple of days previously, including a plan of the school.

Gordon asked for two signs to be written:

SUPERVISORS WORK AREA and NO UNAUTHORISED PERSONS ALLOWED.

Maria wanted signs for the front gate:

TRAINING SCHOOL OF LIFE SKILLS

VACANCIES

SEWING

COMPUTER

BUSINESS STUDIES

Where would we get wood long enough for all these words to make the signs? Incredibly we did. While I worked on them, Barbara went with the dental equipment to Dr Stephen at the small local government hospital in Kamuli. I was glad she felt confident to go off on her own.

Gordon and Dan spent time with a very dead electricity box; they wondered if there would ever be life in it again. Miracle of miracles, between them they had a plan and a few hours later we had electricity.

As I said earlier there wasn't a tree in sight. Well, there was now! Maria had asked some of the lads to dig trees from around the lodge and plant them in the compound for the day; after all we needed colour and places to hang the banners. We managed to find a pole on which to tie the Ugandan flag; I have no idea if we put it up correctly, but no-one complained.

Children ran everywhere as jobs got done; desks were hurled out of classrooms while the floors were all brushed and washed. There was a buzz of activity in the compound: some children were removing stones so the floor in the dining room could be laid the following week, others were cleaning and sweeping the huge dormitories, Aunt Rose was busy with her little helpers preparing food. The sponsors' names were put on top of pictures on the wall in the main hall, and Barbara ran around with a staple gun re-fixing anything that wouldn't stay up because the glue dried up so fast!

With all the last minute things in place, we walked to the local market. While we were there, the weather suddenly changed for the worse and everyone made a dash for cover. We took shelter in the Nile Hotel, a little shack with corrugated sides and roof. We sat on upturned crates and watched the huge hail stones hit the ground. The weather in Uganda can change incredibly quickly, depending on the month.

Maria explained that she needed thirteen prizes to give to students who had performed well in school for the next day. We opened a box donated from England and counted; and yes! You guessed it! There were thirteen diaries. Perfect.

Maria was delighted with the prizes and put on a music tape. At once she started to laugh, clap, and dance around. On the tape, the children were singing about the right they had to feel the wind on their faces. I realised that the children were the purpose of this trip. They were God's gift to us.

Many people had been invited to the school opening: officials from the Welfare, Health and Education Department of the council, lawyers, missionaries, teachers, local people, and of course the pupils and their parents – those who had them. I was guest of honour; I still hadn't taken that in! Maria had briefed me; she wanted everyone to know how the money was raised and how people supported the work God had called us to be involved with in Uganda.

God's timing once again was perfect; I had attended the first Kamuli Primary School PTA meeting with Maria back in Feb, 1995, and now I was at the opening of 'Maria's Care' in February, 1996. I am humbled to think this was all in God's hands and he chose me to be present for the official school opening. What a privilege! *"You saw me before I was born. Every day of my life was recorded in your book. Every moment was laid out before a single day had passed."* Psalm 139:16.

I woke early on Saturday, February 17th, 1996; the big day had arrived. Over breakfast, the idea emerged that we needed a plaque to commemorate the official opening of the school. Barbara and I both looked up at Maria's curtains.

"That's it." Barbara exclaimed as we got a chair and took the curtains and pole down. We asked Bodo to be the official photographer at the unveiling and I wrote out what should be written on the plaque:

K.P.B.P.S

Was officially opened

By Maria Maw

On Saturday, February 17th, 1996

We walked into the school hall and looked around for somewhere to place the plaque and curtains, Barbara spotted the blackboard painted on the wall, and we agreed it was the ideal spot.

The two English students working with Maria at the time, Rodney and Stewart helped emormously. How they had met and signed up to work with Maria I will never know, but there they were and, bless them, proved very useful around the compound. With their help, we put the curtains in place over the temporary plaque, and Maria didn't walk in on our surprise!

The Call, the Cost, the Choice

Rodney had written everything on the plaque except the name of who was opening the school; he had the chalk and I prayed he would have written a name in the space by the time the curtains were pulled back during the ceremony. A more permanent plaque was made later.

The invitation was for 2pm – 5pm: Maria, Barbara, and I showed guests around the school, and the pictures of all the sponsors on the main hall wall. The atmosphere was electric as children played the drums and African music echoed around the compound. I wished I had a camcorder with me to capture all the excitement and fun of the day.

At 3pm we were ushered into the main hall. Pastor Herbert escorted me to my seat next to the President of the Baptist Union of Uganda, along with Barbara, Maria, and Mrs Rebecca. The hall was packed; people had come from miles around. As well as Maria's missionary friends, there were people whom she had met over the years since she first came out to Africa. Some had come from Kampala and the local council. They all looked wonderful in their bright-coloured Ugandan outfits that they wore especially for this occasion. We realised that many had also come to enjoy the food afterwards.

It was a marvellous day. The programme ran smoothly, the children danced and sang, and Maria, Mrs Rebecca and I handed certificates to the children who had helped build the school. Maria gave the diaries out to pupils who had passed exams, and one student, Annette, was given a watch because she got a credit in First Grade in Year 5.

It was my privilege to ask Maria and Mrs Rebecca to come and unveil the plaque and to officially open the school. I threw an arrow prayer to God hoping the right name had been written in. I stood next to them as they opened the curtain just in case the pole fell off the wall.

Maria's name was there! Hallelujah!

There was great excitement; people clapped, shouted, ululated, whilst others stamped their feet and sang. Then I escorted Maria over to the door where we had attached the red ribbon (a bit of forward planning; I brought it from England). She took hold of the scissors, Moses from the BUU prayed, the audience shouted and clapped. It was super.

We escorted people all over the compound and they chatted about the weather in England at this time of year. It's funny how people always talk about the weather. We all enjoyed eating the food: chicken, mandazas, and samosas that the English and Swedish guests had contributed to the table. We ate very well.

At 6.30pm, everyone who was left helped to clear up. By 7.30pm we had finished and then enjoyed an hour of praise and worship. The children sang a song I had taught them during my last visit; 'Blessed be the name of the Lord, The name of the Lord is a strong tower.'

I spoke on Proverbs 3:5-6, *"Trust in the Lord with all your heart and lean not on your own understanding; in all your ways acknowledge him, and he will make your path straight."*

Praise the Lord, the whole day was wonderful.

I had my first restless night after that and woke early. God had laid so many plans on my heart and mind. I had a choice to make as I tossed and turned in my bed. When Barbara woke, I told her how I had been thinking of bringing people out with me to Uganda in the future and how I would organise it. She thought it was a great idea and we said we would go to various hotels with our idea and find out the prices of rooms. This was the very beginning of what turned out to be an amazing vision for the future.

We read our Bible reading for that day which proved appropriate, about leaving the past behind and moving to make a new start. It fitted in well with all Barbara and I had discussed. It is incredible how God speaks to us through his word if we are listening and want to hear. *"Forget the former things; do not dwell on the past. See, I am doing a new thing! Now it springs up; do you not perceive it?"* Isaiah 43:18-19.

We left Maria to have a 'quiet' morning. That's a joke! It's never quiet when Maria is around; she is a character larger than life. Rodney and Stewart walked with Barbara and me to Kamuli Pentecostal Church. We went to the industrial coffee site and through the large open gates and there, in the far corner of the compound, was a warehouse. In the front porch were four benches. That was it, our church for the morning. I wondered how Rodney was feeling because he had told us about this amazing 'wild on fire' church that people had recommended to him. The church had been running for six months and had twenty-eight in the congregation. People started to arrive and we joined in singing and praising the Lord in different languages. 'Jesus Christ is Lord. He is Lord.' We sang and prayed for an hour and I must admit it was brilliant.

The pastor stood and welcomed all the visitors. Rodney shared a personal testimony about growth. He had come to realise that he was not there to change Africa but that he wanted Africa to change him. He believed God had called him to the mission field and wanted to show him how to pray for Uganda. He knew he had to seek God for direction in the future when he returned to Scotland.

The pastor then shared the word with us. He read from 1 John 3:1-3, *"See how much our heavenly Father loves us, for he allows us to be called his children, and we really are! But the people who belong to this world don't know God, so they don't understand that we are his children. Yes, dear friends, we are already God's children, and we can't even imagine what we will be like when Christ returns. But we do know that when he comes we will look like him, for we will see him as he really is. And all who believe this will keep themselves pure, just as Christ is pure."*

Then he gave his testimony. Before he was a Christian, he was always drunk and pretended to know God, until one day God came and embraced him. He cried as God said to him:

"James, I love you. You are my son,"

He couldn't deny the love of God and became a Christian.

Another minister, Pastor Gabriel, spoke on the love of God, and the importance of preaching the cross of Christ. He gave the example of the sign for 'minus':

"This negative sign is us separated from God," He said. "Then Jesus came and made the 'plus' sign in our lives, which is the positive. Jesus' death has given us eternal life; this is the plus in our lives, to be with him forever in heaven."

Wow! I know where I am going to be! Praise the Lord.

"And through him to reconcile to himself all things, whether things on earth or things in heaven, by making peace through his blood, shed on the cross. Once you were alienated from God and were enemies in your minds because of your evil behaviour. But now he has reconciled you by Christ's physical body through death to present you holy in his sight, without blemish and free from accusation if you continue in your faith." Colossians 1:20-23.

I found the whole sermon inspirational.

The pastors asked us to go forward and laid hands on us. We shook one another's hands and said the grace together. I had a huge lump in my throat when two little girls came up, shook my hand and went down on one knee. I couldn't handle it; I felt so humbled that they should do this for me.

The next person to shake my hand was Pastor Gabriel; as he hugged me I burst into tears. I told him we were all equal at the foot of the cross and that people from every nation who loved the Lord would one day be together in heaven.

I dried my tears. I was so pleased we had come to his church.

As we left I noticed people carrying benches out; they strapped them on their bikes and pushed them home. It suddenly dawned on me that twenty-eight people wouldn't have managed on four little benches.

What commitment, I thought. They had to bring something for all of us to sit on.

The following day we were to go to a fishing village. This was a compulsory trip. Maria said so.

We packed a picnic, sunglasses, hats, cream, and extra camera film. At just before 9am, we were all set to go to Bukungu. We walked down the road and passed the premises of David, the carpenter. He was very proud of the building and gave us a guided tour, introducing us to all his staff. He explained to us how he had lived in a room 8 foot by 6 foot with no roof for a whole year, but in that time he had built the workshop around himself. He made all his own tools, including a circular saw without a safety guard in sight. I was thankful we didn't have a health and safety man with us.

He and Maria shared a great trust in each other as was obvious in their conversation together.

He took us into the house he was building for his wife and five children. There was dust everywhere. The lounge measured about 18 foot by 12 foot and there was another room that the whole family slept in whilst the house was being constructed. I could hardly believe anyone lived here. Since then I have seen much worse.

We thanked him and walked up to the lodge to meet Gordon and Rodney. In one classroom I presented the pupils with a huge box of stationery materials donated by the Tytherington Family Worship Sunday school. We had a great time together before going to the taxi park to meet Maria and to embark on what proved to be the most hair-raising bus journey I have ever had.

The Call, the Cost, the Choice

It began when I climbed aboard a dilapidated *matatu*, the worst I had yet to travel in. It was ready for the scrap heap. In England it would have been banned from going on the road. MOT, what's that?

Rodney, Gordon, and Maria sat on the back seat, where we could only see the tops of their heads as they were so low down, due to the fact the seats didn't have much filling in them. Gordon thought the side of the bus was about to fall off; it was barely welded on. Half the windows were broken and there was rust everywhere. The door wouldn't close and the conductor was holding onto a window frame with no glass in it. We had to laugh. What else could we do?

Maria and Gordon put their feet up on the spare tyre that had been pushed in from the back of the vehicle. Barbara and I sat in front of them with part of it under our seat. The bus filled up with twenty-two adults and three children (I counted!) when there should have been fourteen people only including the driver. We were convinced the whole floor was going to drop out. It took three people to push start the bus just to turn a corner and stop for petrol. It was an absolute scream and we had to cover our mouths as the fumes threatened to make us high even before we began the journey.

The vehicle had to be push started once more. There was no ignition key and wires hung dangerously down from underneath the steering wheel.

As we set off Maria suddenly shouted: "He's going the wrong way for Bukungu, I do hope we are on the right bus."

That did our confidence the power of good, as if the bus wasn't bad enough.

We rolled a few yards to the air pump; the bus so full its tyres needed re-filling. We expected them to burst with the amount of air being pumped in.

It was Gordon's turn to shout then: "No, no, oh no!. You don't need fifty pressure. You only need thirty – thirty five!"

The driver paid the attendant and off we went, thankfully in the right direction.

We eventually left Kamuli Taxi Park at 10.45am. Bump, bump, bump we travelled over all the pot holes. The sky was blue, the birds sang. And so did we:

"We're all going on a summer holiday. No more worries da-di-da..."

We laughed at everything; it was such a surreal experience.

Five minutes into the journey, we were stopped by three armed guards. I desperately tried to look serious but I was nearly hysterical with laughter. I put my hand over my face and kept my head down.

They wanted to see everyone's I.D.

Great! We didn't have any on us. (Actually I was astonished that they didn't confiscate the bus instead!) We soon realised they weren't interested in us. There was one chap on board, though, who spent ages trying to convince them that he was on the way for an interview and didn't have his I.D. on him. I calmed down and prayed God would soften the hearts of the guards. He did, and they let him continue his journey.

Praise the Lord we were off again. Thankfully, we were on a hill going down, so no push was needed, No engine either. I thought. We freewheeled down the hill to the bottom and then the engine kicked in, and we juddered our way up the next hill.

On each side of us, we passed tiny villages with just six or eight mud huts, a few trees in a clearing and bushes with beautiful flowers. A man rode his bike carrying a rolled-up corrugated tin roof about twelve feet across. Another man struggled along the road with thirty or so bricks tied to the back of his bike.

The journey into the back of beyond was so bumpy that the spare wheel which had started under Maria and Gordon's seat was now under mine and Barbara's, and it seemed that they too were getting closer to us. We suddenly realised that their seat wasn't attached to the floor and was gradually moving forward. We howled with laughter – they had about six inches leg room. Eventually people got off and we had a reshuffle.

As we drove along there were fewer villages, with mud huts further apart. We stopped at a clearing where people had set up market stalls. Maria explained that the clothes sold on the market were from various charities. People wore many different styles of clothes; some in Western outfits, and others in their beautiful *gomez* dresses with turbans tied on their heads.

Once again we were off freewheeling down a hill.

As we continued towards the lake, I saw more people pushing loads on their bikes along the road. Some had animals strapped on the back;

others were pulling cows or goats, or carried chickens in open wooden boxes.

A vast selection of coloured materials was also being sold from a stand by the side of the road. The little children looked so cute, but most of them had few clothes and even less had shoes. Women working in the fields outnumbered the men, and as I stared, I noticed a man acting as a live scare-crow. He sat in the shade of a small shelter covered with a straw roof, guarding a paddy field. Whenever a bird came, he ran out and scared it away. We passed a school and the children waved to us; they wore bright yellow uniforms and looked like little canaries.

We had been travelling for an hour and a half, up and down hills and overtaking loaded lorries travelling at a snail's pace, when our *matatu* made an awful noise. Gordon thought it probably only had two gears, (at one point he wondered if it had a gear box at all!)

After two hours and a considerable distance, we eventually arrived having paid about £1.35 for the privilege, and after being cramped in the same position for so long we fell off the bus.

The lake stretched as far as the eye could see. I remember thinking: *This is a photographer's paradise.*

As my eyes scanned from left to right, I could see many Ugandans going about their busy lives: a man was rolling dough ready to make chapattis, women and children collecting water in jerry cans. Gordon reckoned a full can probably weighed about half a hundred weight (fifty lbs). Another man sat drying fish which looked hard and white that he had caught from the lake that morning. A pregnant lady passed us with a bag on her head and two in her hands, I thought of the strain on her body.

I was dying to go to the toilet, but no one spoke English and so, after pointing and making noises to a Ugandan woman, she directed me to the small latrine at the back of her house. It was made of woven branches with gaps through which I could see everyone going past (and I suppose they could see me) whilst I squatted down, but this just added to the whole extraordinary day.

The local children followed us wherever we went; we felt like the pied piper. We walked down to the edge of the lake and watched bales of cotton being unloaded off a boat and onto a wagon. At lunchtime, the children watched fascinated at the *buzungu* sat eating their picnic, I felt as though we were on show at a zoo and it was probably just as funny for them to watch.

A man came over and asked us to sign the visitors' book and we obliged. We asked if we could hire a boat and go out on Lake Kyogo (pronounced Choga) to see the fish being dried further out on a pontoon. The lake looked magnificent with beautiful flowers bobbing on the surface. I later discovered that these water hyacinth had been introduced to the lake and had eventually covered it completely, which in turn became a disaster for the local fishermen. The whole lake had to be reclaimed from the flower but some still flourished.

We all climbed into a handmade dug out boat, which wobbled from side to side, and we looked anything but dignified as we clambered over the little wooden seats. Maria did extremely well, with a hop skip and a jump she was sitting down before any of us.

At this point, I had no idea that crocodiles lived in the lake, if I had known that there's no way I'd have gone out on it.

As the men rowed us out to the pontoon we sang songs, until they suddenly stopped and decided to haggle over how much we were paying for the trip. Their English was so poor that we couldn't understand one another, but eventually Gordon and Rodney said they would sort it out when we got back to dry land, which they did. I felt rather embarrassed as all we were haggling over was the equivalent of about 35p each.

For the return journey to Kamuli, our driver put two live wires together under the steering wheel and we were off. On the way we saw herds of goats, a cow with huge horns, chickens and turkeys, straw and elephant grass tied to the back of bikes, and enormous sacks of maize bumping along on the back of scooters. It was an incredible sight.

We arrived back in Kamuli with sore bottoms, noses full of petrol fumes and what seemed like half of Uganda's dusty roads on our clothes and in our hair. We felt and looked a right mess but we had had a wonderful and very different day out. One I shall never forget.

Barbara promised me she would wash my hair outside in the back yard with the hosepipe. I was really looking forward to this and suggested we put on our swimming costumes and make a meal of it. Just the thought was a joy.

We arrived back at Maria's and went to our room where Barbara armed herself with shampoo, comb, towel; all the necessary equipment to be my hairdresser. I put my filthy hair under the hosepipe and turned on the tap waiting for the sheer delight of cold water running over my head and face to clean and cool me.

Nothing.   Nothing!   Not a drip.   The water was off.

We couldn't believe it, we had forgotten that in Uganda sometimes there is water or electricity and sometimes there isn't. Not to be dissuaded, we dragged the jerry-can and plastic basins from our room and got on with the job. It was lovely, but not as exciting.

Early the next morning, I walked down the garden towards the latrines. I passed the gardener who was clearing the path, passed the pineapple bushes and banana tree. I could hear the congregation from the church next door singing in their own language a song I knew "...every knee shall bow, every tongue confess that Jesus Christ is Lord..." There was the most wonderful fragrance of Jesus: the singing was beautiful, the birds were chirping, the crickets were clicking their back legs together, somewhere a cock crowed, people in the garden chatted to each other, and I could really sense the presence of God.

Later that day, Barbara and I walked to the clinic, where she was to meet Dr Stephen about a dental unit in Kamuli. She handed the key and black dental box to Richard, the public health dental assistant. There was a great sense of excitement as they opened the box and Barbara took out the contents: instruments, anaesthetic tubes, gloves and needles, so many things that would make his life easier.

Richard explained to us the conditions in which he was working and what was expected from him. He was the only dentist for miles around, and had an enormous workload that far exceeded a dentist in the U.K. who would be responsible for eight to ten thousand patients. Another charity had bought Richard a bike to help him get around. He often had to cycle over twenty miles just to see one patient. Dentistry is a new up and coming profession in Uganda and Kamuli was fortunate to have him there. He had been working for three years without any pay from the government. Dr. Stephen said most people worked for about twelve months without pay but three years was ridiculous, so Richard was taking his case to court in Kamuli.

Dentistry, however, is low on the government's list of priorities. There are at least ten killer diseases taking precedence. Dental patients have to contribute money towards treatment, but it's never enough. Ignorance and fear play a big part in the Ugandan people's understanding; consequently by the time they visit the dentist the condition is usually severe. Richard believes that if he can gain their confidence and educate them in dental hygiene, they won't need to have teeth extracted every time.

Early in the afternoon, we travelled in another run-down vehicle to Busoga High School. We met the head who escorted us to a classroom with more than forty teenaged pupils. She introduced us both to the students and then Barbara made her presentation about cleaning their teeth, plaque, and the prevention of tooth decay. She explained that they didn't have to fear the dentist; that if they went regularly then they wouldn't have to have teeth extracted. (At this stage we had no idea that most of these students hardly had enough money to have a meal each day never mind disposable income to have a check-up at the dentist).

At Kamuli Boys' School, there were hundreds of primary-aged boys in the main hall waiting to hear Barbara tell them how to clean their teeth. They gave us a slow hand clap as we followed the head up the steps onto the stage. Once again, Barbara gave a thorough presentation, gearing it towards these young boys.

Later we were taken to Kamuli Girls' Boarding School in a large truck. We were invited to sit on clean sheets in the front whilst the Head and two students jumped in the back.

I can't imagine this happening in England. I thought.

We received a warm welcome and were directed to a field where about two hundred primary-aged girls stood under trees. They clapped as we took our places on the seats provided behind three tables. Each time we had been introduced with the words: "We are very privileged to have these ladies come all the way from England because they love and care for us so much."

Barbara later gave the dental posters she had used in the presentations to Richard for his clinic.

Maria had arranged a leaving party for us that evening and many people we had met during our two week trip had been invited. The food was delicious, including a cake Aunt Rose had baked for my birthday (a little premature as my birthday was still several months away).

We managed to celebrate in style before the heavens opened and everyone got soaked. The electricity went out so we lit candles and hurricane lamps. The party finished at 9pm and we said our goodbyes. After packing most of our belongings, we fell into our beds, exhausted.

I woke early and stayed in bed, praying for guidance for the future. I thought through how I would go about setting up trips for people to come and experience all the wonderful things I had in my own visits. I wanted to share the sights of Uganda that had inspired me: the plantations, the little fishing villages, the waterfalls, the source of the Nile, the people, and the vibrant colours of this country, the azure blue skies, the red earth, and the verdant lushness of the trees and plants.

I had fallen in love with Uganda!

I remembered the scriptures that said God will bless those who are obedient to him. *"And we know that in all things God works for the good of those who love him, who have been called according to his purpose."* Romans 8:28.

We ate our breakfast and quickly put the luggage into Dr Stephen's truck before driving to a petrol station. Whilst the tank was being filled, a woman came over and washed the windscreen. When Dr. Stephen paid the assistant, he was given a free packet of 'Omo' washing powder. We reckoned this was a hint as the vehicle was rather dirty.

On the way to Jinja as we passed a clinic, I quickly took a photo of the sign which read: 'Machete Clinic.'

"I wouldn't like to go in there with a headache," Gordon quipped.

On our journey to a guest house in Entebbe where we would stay for our final few days, we talked about the plans we had to get the container of goods sent from AstraZenica in England, out of customs.

I thought about God's perfect timing in so many things we had done over the last few weeks; even the fact that Dr Stephen was taking us straight to Entebbe instead of us having to use the three *matatus* again that we did at the beginning of our trip when we went to Kamuli.

At Entebbe Airport, Maria and Stephen headed towards the cargo sheds, while Barbara and I went into a large snack bar. At first there were only a few people sitting there, but within five minutes, over a hundred Entebbe ground staff filled all the tables. Praise the Lord we had already ordered our food.

I noticed the man sitting next to me reading my diary as I wrote it. We got chatting and discovered that he worked in an office upstairs. He said he would help us clear our box of goods.

Maria had gone with Stephen to get clearance for the box; he had said that clearance could take anything from thirty minutes to three hours or days, and he knew the shed would close at 5pm. We were ever hopeful that God would open doors quickly as Maria had eaten only a small cake all day and was getting very restless.

As we waited, we prayed and asked God to help to get the box out soon, for Maria's health and strength, and for hearts to be softened. Barbara went for a walk; we had seen some stuff released to a white man and thought it might be our turn soon. At 3.45pm Barbara came back and we sat down to read from the Bible, John 14:1-14, specially thinking about... *"You may ask me anything in my name, and I will do it."*

We were wondering why the consignment hadn't been released and tried to figure out what God was doing. We knew it would be in God's time. Barbara looked over to the main gates and said:

"Oh look, another *muzungu*; if she is looking for the young man we saw earlier she has missed him by two hours." As the lady walked closer, Barbara spoke again:

"I think that's Tracy, the lady who was in your lounge in the U.K. three weeks ago."

We met Tracy in England through a mutual friend telling her we were going to Uganda. Tracy is a dentist who asked Barbara if she would take the black box with instruments to Kamuli.

"It is Tracy!" I cried, and Barbara ran over very excitedly and greeted her warmly.

Just to think; this is what God had been planning all along. We sat and discussed the work she had been doing and the crate she had just got out. A man approached us, and 'guess what?' it was the same man we had seen two hours ago and it was Tracy's husband, Michael.

It turned out the book I was reading 'The man with the key has gone' was written by Dr Ian Clark who not only lived in the same district as Tracy and Michael but was in the same house group in Aylesbury. They were all working at the same hospital in Kiwoko, Uganda. We were flabbergasted. What an end to our day! Maria and Stephen appeared saying the clearance office wouldn't release their box till the next morning.

The following day we met Maria in the customs office where four men were sitting at a desk. One called David was reading the newsletter concerning the charity we had set up. The other man, Fred, was being shouted at by Maria. In the end, Maria said she was fed up and told us to take over.

Barbara and I chatted to the men, praying for their hearts to be softened. They started giving us figures of 165,756/- ug = about £110, to release our container of goods. We were shocked; people had donated these goods and this was more than the contents were worth.

Everyone left. David started asking me questions, for instance, was I married? I told him I had two lovely daughters. I asked him how many children he had, and he answered "eight". I laughed, said goodbye and went rapidly out of the door, walking quickly to catch up with Barbara and Fred, the other clearance officer. We continued walking and Fred said he could reduce his agency fee from 50,000/- to 30,000/- about £20. Things were looking better. We met Maria who was exhausted and suggested we went into the airport restaurant and had some food, Maria really needed that; she had been like a little wilting flower that had suddenly been watered; she bounced back up and was in full bloom again.

At 7pm, we went back to Lakeside View Guest House in a taxi. Barbara saw a 'Rotary' sign by the roadside and said, "You know we had a letter from the Rotary, I wonder if they could help now?" I kept quiet and thought about what she had just said. I picked my moment and when the taxi driver stopped to buy some water I asked him if he knew any Rotary men in the area.

The lady serving him replied, "Yes, we do, Dr Emmanuel Tumusiime-Rushedge. He lives within walking distance and he is the president of Rotary," She suggested we wrote him a note and they would take it to him. Barbara found an envelope and wrote:

"Dear Dr Emmanuel Tumusiime-Rushedge, Can you please HELP?" A few minutes later a car came along the drive. The driver introduced himself, he was Dr Emmanuel Tumusiime-Rushedge. It was quite amazing! He told us he was in the middle of a Rotary meeting when he got the note. He dropped everything and came to see what he could do to help. What a wonderful example of coming to help some ladies in distress.

He asked for all the details and told us to get the papers from the clearance office the next day. He explained that we should have spoken to them earlier as they had lots of Rotarians who worked in the clearing offices. He drove us to a hotel with a newly-formed beach; sand had been flown in from abroad. We thoroughly enjoyed our time with Dr Emmanuel but the tiny lake flies drove us mad.

We arrived back at the guest house and discussed the things we had found out and the way God had planned the events so delicately was quite unique, a huge learning curve for us. What an incredible day!

Next day, I held onto the fact that what God had started he would continue to bless. We knew we had to go to the airport and get the papers for Dr Emmanuel. Maria went to Victoria Hotel to swim as it was supposed to be our day off. Barbara and I started walking to the airport and it took us thirty-five minutes to reach the clearance agents' office no 83. The men were really surprised to see us; we explained that we needed the Rotary papers, leaflets and letters, and were told they had been sent downstairs. A man was sent to get them from customs.

We waited and waited. Barbara eventually got fed up and said: "I have a feeling the papers might still be in this office."

Whilst we sat there, we realised the desk that the papers had been put in wasn't there anymore. It was a strange feeling to think that within eighteen hours the office had changed. When David got back, we asked him where his desk had gone; he pointed to a desk upside down on top of a cupboard. It turned out that his desk had broken and they had pushed it out of the way. I climbed on a chair and opened the so-called locked drawer upside down and retrieved our papers. Barbara had been right; they were still in the office. I put the papers in my bag just as Fred and David said they needed more money to get the things cleared. I had had enough! We had given it all to God, this was our day off. We walked out of the office, back to the airport and jumped into a taxi back to Lake Victoria Hotel. Maria tried to ring the D.E.D to arrange transport for the large box to be picked up from customs the next day. Unfortunately, the phone and fax machine were dead: "Oh Lord we are counting on you to do something," she said.

Two hours later, Maria tried again; still no connection and the office closed at 5pm. It seemed that we would not be successful that day.

Then Barbara said, "I think this is the doctor coming."

I looked up and there he was, smiling like a Cheshire cat. He explained that he had had a very good meeting with his men. He needed to get hold of the past president of Rotary because he had some money left over from the last year. He needed a letter from Maria to give permission to the president of Rotary to dispatch and deliver the consignment. I was ecstatic inside. Praise The Lord! He had come through for us again. What he had started he had finished; this was his answer to our prayers. Maria wrote the letter and handed it over to Dr Emmanuel.

The doctor was a most interesting character; he drove us back to the guest house where we said our goodbyes and he left. We were thrilled, shattered but very, very happy. Talk about God putting the icing on the cake, he had taken it out of our hands and we had a free day to look forward to.

The next morning, we went to Lake Victoria Hotel and relaxed by the pool; I climbed to the top of the diving board and took some photos of the golf course overlooking the lake. The sun was yellow, the sky blue, clouds white, trees green and the ground red. I thought again: *This is a photographer's paradise*. Around the pool stood tall, elegant palm trees in good condition, the hedges were covered in bougainvillea flowers and the smell of food being cooked wafted across. I thought that everything we had experienced had been so worth-while. We had done a lot and we had learnt so much more.

Soon it was time for us to leave and we drove to the airport by taxi. Gordon never did return to England to live; he set up home in Jinja and is there to this day. Various people came to see us off. We sat and ate pancakes and ice cream for the last time then went through to board the plane. It cost us £14 airport tax to get out of the country. We thanked everyone for the most amazing time, got into the plane and flew to Nairobi then on to Brussels and Manchester. We had just left 80-90 degrees. We landed where snow was on the ground and the temperature below freezing.

Barbara and I both had had a remarkable time. We realised there was so much more we could do in the future, but for now we were looking forward to Maria coming home for her seventieth birthday and the launch of CRU on April 23rd.

I wondered what God had got in store for us in the future.

When Maria became very ill in September, 1996, I wondered if the Lord was going to pass the mantle on to me.

Chapter 5

Learning to trust God

By the end of November, 1996, I had boxes and boxes filled with donated clothes, books, stationery, hospital equipment, spectacles, knitting wool, toys, etc. A nurse even rang to see if I could use a trolley with glass shelves and a weighing machine for new-born babies in Uganda. Maria had taught me never to say 'no', but I did start to wonder how on earth I was going to get all these goods there.

The following January, I sat in my lounge and looked at over fifty banana boxes filled with donations; over to the right there were sewing machines and behind me were a few huge tents and a camping stove. There were boxes of shoes and football boots, hospital equipment, a sterilizer, medical supplies, latex gloves, crepe bandages and hundreds of packets of plastic syringes. Maria had requested a hi-fi system with speakers and a microphone, a twin-tub washing machine and other items. They were all in my lounge after people had responded to an article in the local newspaper. I had a big lounge but even so I had to put more boxes in the downstairs cloakroom and porch.

It seemed that, after each speaking engagement, I was given either a portable typewriter or hand sewing machine. So many people had things in a cupboard under their stairs or in the loft that they 'knew would come in handy one day.' This was the day!

One evening, I remember saying to God: "Lord, I really don't mind using my home like a warehouse, but I don't need these things and they do in Uganda. How are you going to help me get it all out there? In Jesus' name, Amen."

The very next day, quite out of the blue I had a phone call from one of the local Rotarians:

"Hi, Rhona, I believe you have some things that need to go to Uganda."

The Call, the Cost, the Choice

With great excitement in my voice I said: "Yes I do."

He went on to say he would get a van and he could take it to a friend of his who flew things out to foreign places. He said he would get back to me when he had a date.

I came off the phone and cried: 'God you have done it again!'

I remembered reading in Matthew 17:20, *"I tell you the truth, if you have faith as small as a mustard seed, you can say to this mountain 'Move from here to there' and it will move. Nothing will be impossible for you."*

Well, that's what I had, 'faith as small as a mustard seed,' when I asked God to sort it all out for me. Why should I be surprised?

There was so much planning to do. The year before Maria had been ill and flown back to England, where she was recuperating in a retirement home in Macclesfield. When I visited her, she was surrounded by elderly people who needed full-time care. She sat me down and proceeded to talk to me in such a business like way, I just laughed! She told me how much money was needed for each orphan in the compound at 'Maria's Care'; what school they should go to, personal requirements and uniform needed, and wages for the staff.

I wrote all her requests down, and organised a committee meeting. Maria wanted all these things done yesterday, but a letter would take at least eleven days to get to Uganda and the same for a reply. The telephone wasn't much better as electricity in Kamuli was appalling and the telephone exchange was something out of the ark.

After the committee meeting, I tried sending a fax to Kamuli; this was also a hit and miss affair. I had to word the message carefully otherwise the whole village would know the details.

After one Sunday service in my home church, two Rotary men asked me to sign some documents regarding the transfer of goods to Uganda. I thought it was marvellous that they had put themselves out especially for the sake of the people there. I knew that I and two others were going to Uganda in February; no promises were made by these men, but they said they would do their best to have the cargo coincide with our trip.

The day arrived. In January, 1997, I was on my own in the house when a van appeared. Two men asked me if they could load the donations into the van that was going to Uganda.

Learning to trust God

I don't know how we did it but we did. We manhandled every box, sewing machine, typewriter etc on our own. There were tons of donations. The Rotary man arrived; he couldn't believe his eyes. We continued to chuck things in the van: tents, a camping gas cooker, and two trolleys. I remembered my fold-up bike in the shed. I had tried to ride it on many occasion and found going up the slightest hill exhausting, so I threw that in the van too. At last my lounge was empty. I had a feeling I should have done an inventory as we put the goods into the van, but it was a bit too late for that.

I prayed and left the container in God's care.

At the same time Maria was feeling a lot better. She suddenly said she felt God was calling her back to Uganda to finish what she had started out there. *O my*, I thought, I really didn't think Maria was well enough. I remembered the time I walked with Maria holding onto my arm into her house and after only a few minutes she would fall down in a heap on the floor.

She would say: "Rhona, what have you put in my tea?" We always had a laugh about it, but I knew she wasn't very strong; she was always full of surprises, however, and we had several discussions about when she would be returning to Uganda. One day she suddenly bought a four-wheel scooter, booked a flight and arranged to meet me in March at Entebbe Airport. That was that, sorted!

On February, 19th, 1997, Judith Rowe, a health visitor, Ann West, an assistant teacher, and I all set out on a trip to Uganda. This was yet another time when I prayed for the luggage to get through check-in. Once again God came up trumps. I wore two shirts, two skirts and carried a jacket. The four suitcases and four large holdalls all had donated goods in them. In the early days there was so little in the shops in Uganda that anything we took was welcomed with open arms. We had a good flight, and friends of Maria's from Banana Village, a tourist enterprise, sent a vehicle to pick us up from the airport. We stayed there overnight and then changed our money the following day and arrived in Kamuli, hot and tired.

This was the first time I had been to 'Maria's Care' without Maria being there. It was a strange feeling. I was also putting into practice ideas I had said I wanted to do in the future, such as taking groups of people to experience Uganda.

We stayed in the little house next to the Maramu Conference Centre in Kamuli, a distance from the main school. Each day we walked to 'Maria's Care' and met Kate, a lady who was working on her own in the nursery there for children under five. She was very pleased to meet us as she desperately wanted the company of *bazungu*. She was doing a fantastic job, considering she had had to start from scratch. She told us how the house was full of rats when she arrived; it was frightening to say the least. I had no idea how she had managed to stay and thought she was brave indeed.

This trip proved to be a huge eye-opener on more than one occasion. It soon became apparent that the staff found it difficult to cope without Maria who was the solid rock everyone had come to know and rely upon in the compound.

We tried to join the pupils each day for praise and worship, and, as we watched the different teachers in their classrooms, we realised they needed more help and resources. Judith and Ann decided to spend some of the money they had raised on a new nursery floor.

I was busy in various educational meetings held by the local council men in our hall. I was learning all the time how the country looked at life. They discussed the way they wanted children educated, and some gave their testimony of how they managed to get school fees. One man told us he bought a pig; after it had bred he sold some piglets and used the money for school fees. He wanted the local children to think for themselves. I wondered where he got the money from to buy his first animal. Many of our children didn't have anyone who could even help them onto the first rung of the ladder.

Another job which Judith and Ann supervised was painting the dormitories. The ceilings were very high so one of the older boys made a ladder whilst another one piled beds on top of each other in order to reach. Health and safety wasn't in it!

On my birthday, Judith and I took a couple of the boys into town to buy some paint. We chose the paint and brushes, and then went to Kamuli bakery and treated the boys to a soda. I didn't realise at that moment how the shopping time was being drawn out, and we walked slowly back with frequent stops as the paint was quite heavy.

We eventually returned home and the main hall had been transformed. There was bunting and Christmas decorations up everywhere. The tables had been covered with beautiful coloured cloths (I think the sheets had been whipped off beds) paper plates and food were in place, there was even a birthday cake with candles.

We had a real party, and then the delicacy that had caused them so many problems arrived; jelly and custard. We had a fridge that had a mind of its own, the jelly wasn't setting quick enough and the custard was very difficult to make. Ann dished it out and by the look on the children's faces you would have thought we were poisoning them! I blew the candles out and everyone sang 'Happy birthday.' Later we all sang and danced to the music on the rickety wooden stage. All in all we had a fantastic party.

The next few days were taken up being driven miles into remote villages to visit animal projects. We distributed clothes, food and gifts to families. It was always hot and occasionally we forgot to take water with us; we were so concerned about the donations that we forgot about our own needs. One family we visited had nine children; most of them had extended belly buttons. Judith told me this was due to the way the umbilical cord was cut when the baby was born, and could be dangerous in later years.

I had been given hundreds of balloons which we inflated and enjoyed the fun as the children played with them. They rarely had balloons and even their popping caused shock and delight,

We arranged the children into lines and played balloon races with them. The balloon had to pass over one person's head then through the next one's legs and so on. Happy chaos ensued as everyone laughed and confusion reigned.

The next day I took Judith to meet Mary, a midwife at the local hospital, who gave us a grand tour. Some beds were occupied by women who had delivered babies or were waiting to have them. As we looked about us, we saw how basic everything was. Each woman had to carry all the bedding and everything she needed from home for the baby, bearing in mind she would be nine months pregnant and probably coming some distance, on the back of a *boda-boda*.

The wards were badly decorated with paint peeling everywhere. Paint was chipped off the metal beds and helpers had to sleep on mats under them. (When Maria had once been ill, Mary slept under her bed for a few days to look after her) it was just how they did it in Uganda; the nurses attended to all the medical needs and helpers attended to the patient in every other way. Some windows had a net curtain loosely strung across it, others had nothing. There was only one privacy screen to share between two wards. One mother sat on a floor mat bathing her newborn baby in a bowl of cold water.

We must never forget how blessed we are in England, I thought. I found the whole experience quite depressing.

Some women found it hard to scrape the money together to pay for treatment in hospital. I have heard of cases where pregnant women have walked all day to the hospital, and if their baby wasn't due when they arrived, they would sleep under a tree in the hospital grounds until the baby was ready to be born. These women only had enough money to stay in hospital for one day.

We walked around the wards then, through a door, we saw lots of pregnant ladies queuing outside a room; we walked across an open passage and a nurse escorted us into the small room. As Judith knew what she was doing, the nurse asked her to take the ladies' blood pressure, height and weight. I was allowed to write down, in a little book, whatever Judith told me.

Judith was in her element so after a while I left her and walked back to 'Maria's Care'. She returned an hour later grinning like a Cheshire cat. She had helped to deliver a baby girl and was asked to name her. I have been to the maternity hospital many times and never seen a baby born. I believed this to be another God incident especially to encourage Judith.

The next day I took her to the mission hospital, and we couldn't believe our eyes when we saw one of the women from the day before still in labour. We discovered she had been transferred on the back of a *boda-boda* from one hospital to the other because of medical complications. She had been in labour for over seventeen hours and was now in the mission hospital to have the baby and complete the rest of her treatment.

As we walked round the hospital I was amazed how many bedpans were strewn on the ground outside. There were some wards I didn't look in. As we passed the burns unit, I decided this was one of those wards I wasn't brave enough to visit. Judith was a trained nurse though so she was able to chat with staff and doctors quite happily.

I learnt that everyone had to pay for the treatment and their prescription. If they really couldn't then there was a way to be subsidised.

We looked in the hospital's main dispensary, I couldn't believe how little there was on the shelves. Once again I thought about the amount we wasted in England. We saw hundreds of latex gloves that had been worn during operations in surgery hanging on window frames drying, ready to be used again. The wards were just as dilapidated as in the other hospital. By 1pm all the patients had been seen and the place was nearly deserted. As we walked out of the hospital we saw families sitting under the trees cooking meals. One lady caught my eye; she was beautiful and had just had a baby. She was lying sideways on the grass in a bright coloured *gomez* dress. I took a few lovely photos of her with the baby and supporting family.

The following morning I went to our own school assembly and presented a wind-up radio to the head teacher. She was thrilled and wound it up for us all to listen to the music and then the news being read. (The following year I enquired how the radio was faring to be told they had sent it away to be made into a battery one! It's never been seen since!)

In the afternoon, I rode for an hour and a half on the back of a motor scooter to Nawaikoke College with the headmaster, Mr Abwa. I had donations for the college from St Peters in Hale, England.

I was ushered into his office, which consisted of a table and chair and a pile of books in the corner. The main reception room had two tables and chairs, with more books piled high and next to them was a box of chalk (this was to last the college a year). Underneath the table was a kettle, and paper.

As I walked around, I realised the college was a work in progress, being literally built round the students. Some rooms had wooden doors and window frames in, others didn't. The students carried their own seat from class to class. There was only one classroom that had desks, and some rooms didn't even have a proper floor, but broken bits of brick waiting to be cemented in; the students didn't care as long as they had a teacher and blackboard. In the same classroom there was only a three-quarter sized blackboard and I commented upon this, only to be told that there weren't enough old batteries to take the black acid out of to paint it fully. I could hardly believe what I was hearing.

I was shown around the college grounds too where the builders had dug over thirty feet down for the new latrines they were in the process of installing. Then we walked across a field towards a small green building, Mr Abwa unlocked the door. Inside was a man grinding maize;

he explained to me that they needed another attachment so they could take the husks off the maize. I wrote his request down.

After I had said goodbye to all the staff, we left and headed towards St Peter's High School in Namwendwa. I had some donations for the staff there. As we approached, a few pupils looked very suspiciously at me and I wondered why. As I got off the bike, Mr Abwa explained to me that all the pupils in the immediate area had been given vaccinations by a group of white doctors and nurses, and it had just been announced on the radio that one child had died. Now everyone was suspicious of anybody in the area who was white. He said it was a good job I was with him.

Thankfully, the staff welcomed me, I signed the visitors' book and the time I had with them went very well. We continued on our journey, this time to Mr Abwa's family home.

"We are going to have to run," he shouted.

I thought he meant we would be getting off the bike but he put his foot down and we flew across the top of the pot-holes and badly-made roads. Eventually, we arrived outside his little brick house and ran inside just as it started to pour down. He had seen the rain coming, that's why he had rushed. The Ugandans are very good at reading the signs in the sky; every cloud means something to them.

As I entered the house people were flying around everywhere trying to retrieve as much as possible from outside; bowls, jerry-cans, food, benches and washing came in. We had thunder and lightning right above our little house with the rain hitting the corrugated tin roof and making such a din I couldn't speak or hear anyone else speaking. After a while, I noticed people coming in the back door with benches which they placed in lines in front of me.

I hope they're not expecting me to do a presentation, I thought to myself.

Six beautifully dressed ladies sat in front of me; I smiled, and they smiled back. Eventually the rain subsided. I was told that the lightening had struck a banana tree and it had fallen onto the house next door. It had been demolished so the residents had brought what they could to this home. This is how it is in Africa.

We had a lovely time together; we chatted and I gave out the donations to the family, from the congregation in Hale, and ate the delicious food which had been prepared by Mr Abwa's wife.

Just before I left, one of their daughters came with some gifts for me: a full stalk of bananas, five fresh eggs in a plastic bag, and a live chicken. I thanked them very much and wondered how on earth we were going to carry this lot back to 'Maria's Care' on the bike. Thankfully they found a small box, put the chicken in and put the lid down. One of the girls had a sharp knife and cut a hole in the top of the box and the next minute the chicken's head popped out. We decided to put as many bananas as possible into my large rucksack that had contained the donations, and the eggs into Mr Abwa's bag which he strapped to his chest. He suggested I covered my head as the road would be dusty but the only thing I had with me was a blue surgery cap, it looked hilarious! I got behind him on the bike; the box with the chicken in was handed to me, so now I was ready to go. I took a photo of the extended family and they took one of me as it was something I really wanted to remember.

It was quite late as we rode back to Kamuli when suddenly the bike started to splutter. We dismounted and Mr Abwa investigated whilst I went for a walk and thought about what might happen if it got dark and we couldn't get home. In those days we didn't have mobile phones and we were miles from a petrol station or garage.

I reckoned the local people were hospitable so I would probably end up sleeping in a mud hut for the night. As I looked through the trees I noticed a 'Coke Cola' sign. I pushed the branches and leaves out of my face and found the tiny shop that was selling sodas. The lady wouldn't let me move till I had drunk the contents of the bottle. By the time I returned to Mr Abwa the bike was working again, thank the Lord. Some men had come to help him; they tinkered with the engine and pushed the bike a few hundred yards, I leapt on again quite relieved that we were on our way once more. We arrived in Kamuli just as darkness settled.

Judith and Ann were relieved to see me as I handed over eggs, bananas, and the chicken to Aunt Rose. The children were all excited because they had been helping to decorate the dormitories, so I went to admire their handiwork. Judith explained that the minute the paint cans were empty the children wanted them; they wasted nothing.

We settled down that evening and made up lots of little bags of gifts for the children who lived in 'Maria's Care.' Judith and Ann had bought lovely green fabric for the students to sew and make little bags to put donated gifts in. For the girls we had little combs, vaseline, soap, hand cream, pencils, crayons, rulers and pencil sharpeners. The boys had similar toiletries and stationery but there were also ties or belts for the older lads and dinky toy cars for the younger ones.

After school the next day, we called the young girls into the main office and gave out the little green bags. They were thrilled to receive them; some tipped the bags all over the table as they sorted through the various items. They kept saying: "Thank you, thank you."

Then we called the boys in and gave them their bags, they were so excited and ran back to the dormitories to play with the little cars.

We then asked the older girls to come in and, after giving them each a bag, Judith emptied a sack of bras onto the table; the girls had their blouses off quicker than we could say 'Jack Robinson'. They tried different bras on; if it didn't fit they would offer it to another girl, and so it went on till everyone had a bra, except one girl. Ann came to the rescue; she slipped her bra off through her blouse sleeve and gave it to the young lady without one. Everyone was happy.

There was a knock at the door, "Madam, could we please have a car instead of a tie?"

We realised that, although we had thought the older lads would like a tie or belt, they didn't. They had never had a toy car to play with so this is what they wanted. Thankfully, we had a few cars left and managed to share them around. I realised just how much we took things for granted.

We were due to leave the compound the next day. That evening, we had a wonderful party in the main hall with all the staff and children. We ate lots of food and listened to music; different people sang to us and we all danced. The following morning we packed our luggage and made our way to the taxi park.

The journey from Kamuli to Jinja was the usual hairy experience and there we changed *matatus* to head to Kampala. I wanted Judith and Ann to enjoy the ice-cream Maria had treated Barbara and me to the year before, but after walking round in circles in the hot sun for far too long I realised I was lost and reluctantly gave up the search.

Judith and Ann took the *matatu* to Entebbe alone as I needed to find a place to sleep before meeting Maria who was flying back to Uganda from England the next day. I walked with them to Kampala Taxi Park, saw them both onto the right bus and we said our goodbyes. The *matatu* pulled away leaving me standing there not knowing in which direction to go. There was nobody in the whole of Uganda whom I knew.

Nobody.

The people Maria had introduced me to had all since left.

I wandered around praying God would show me a hotel I could afford. With the little money I had I bought a loaf of bread and a bunch of bananas. By now it was getting dark, (just what I didn't want) when I saw a sign: 'Grace's Guest House.'

This will do, I thought, and walked in and along a narrow passage to the reception desk. Fortunately, they had a room available and I was escorted along another passageway and through a door into a small room. I shut the door and felt a tremendous weight lift off my shoulders and great relief that I was safe. There was a single bed next to the wall and an en suite bathroom. It was very basic but all my own, with a proper toilet and a seat. Yippee!

I ate a couple of bananas, went for a drink in the little bar by the reception then headed to bed.

The next morning I woke early, mainly due to the noise in the thoroughfare outside my bedroom window. I had breakfast, paid my bill, and asked for directions to the taxi park since I was completely disorientated.

I knew I had so much to do before meeting Maria at 12 noon.

The *matatu* took me as far as Entebbe Village where I had to get a *piki-piki* to the Airport. My task then was to find the Rotary man called Nelson and retrieve the container that had been flown over. I didn't have any more details.

Gosh, I thought, *I don't have much to go on!*

I stood on a small hill opposite a huge office and looked through the barbed wire gate; I wondered how many men were called Nelson. It must have been breaktime because hundreds of people from the airport offices suddenly swarmed past me, I looked longingly for a clue.

Please Lord, I said. *Let me find Nelson.*

As a businessman walked past me, I plucked up courage and said:

"Excuse me; I am looking for a man called Nelson who belongs to the Rotary club." There, that was that, I had nothing else to offer.

He put his head to one side and said, "My name is Nelson."

The Call, the Cost, the Choice

I was just about to shriek: 'Praise the Lord,' when he carried on:

"I don't belong to Rotary, but I think I know who you want."

My eyes opened wide as I followed him up some metal steps outside the large office buildings, went inside and climbed up another flight of stairs. He knocked on a door and asked for Nelson.

"Sorry," the lady replied. "He has gone to meet a *muzungu* from England."

I just knew the *muzungu* in question was Maria. Nelson escorted me all the way to the arrival department in the airport. Hundreds of people were there waiting for their friends, relatives, missionaries and business partners.

We turned a corner and suddenly I was being introduced to another Nelson. I couldn't believe my eyes or ears. The customs man called Nelson had done his very best to help me find the Rotary man called Nelson. I praised the Lord for answering my prayers.

I said goodbye to Nelson from customs, and stayed with Nelson from the Rotary club. He told me he was in the Gideon movement. (There are 'Gideons' all over the world; they distribute Bibles to people in offices, schools, old people's homes etcetera). I was thrilled; here I was with a Christian brother looking after me, another God incident. I felt God was working overtime on my behalf.

I was on the top floor in Entebbe Airport and looked through a little gap between people as they pushed one another to see out of the window. I gave up, and sat down with my small rucksack and bag with bread and bananas in.

I listened to an announcement. "We are sorry, but due to a technical fault, the 12 noon flight from Heathrow will not be landing."

Everyone was shouting and running all over the place. In situations I have no control over, I go limp. *Well there is nothing I can do,* I thought to myself.

I read my book for about half-an-hour. People around me had seen me sitting still and asked if they could leave their bags with me till the plane came in. I had no problem with this as I wasn't going anywhere. Different people came and talked to me and I had many good conversations. Nelson had gone back to his office, and said he would be back later.

Then the announcement came that we were all waiting for.

"The plane originally from Heathrow will be arriving shortly."

It was nearly 4pm by now; I had a banana sandwich and waited.

At last something was happening. Everyone raced to the window, everyone except me that is. I still had all the bags around me. A huge crowd had gathered so I really didn't mind sitting in my seat away from people getting crushed.

A man came rushing up to me and said: "The plane didn't land."

I asked him what he meant. Apparently the plane had a problem with the front wheel and they couldn't risk landing. Once again, I stayed seated. I scratched my head and wondered what I should be doing. It was getting dark; I hadn't anticipated waiting this length of time and had nowhere booked for the night. Just then Nelson reappeared with a white man.

We were introduced: "Rhona, this is Brian Gould from England."

I burst out laughing: "Brian," I said shaking his hand. "We spoke on the phone a few weeks ago."

Brian lived about thirty minutes away from my home in England, but we had never met. He was on a Cidoonc trip and had a meeting that night. When I woke up that morning, I hadn't known a soul in Uganda but now I knew two. I was thrilled.

Nelson said I should wait for Maria and when she arrived we were to stay with him and his family as they lived quite near. Another answer to prayer.

I did wait. For three hours. Eventually a much smaller plane arrived.

By the time Maria landed, got through customs and out of the airport, it was nearly 9pm. She was exhausted and I comforted her with the news that we had a bed for the night. It was gone 10pm when we eventually arrived at Nelson's home and even though the family had cooked a meal for us poor Maria was in no mood for eating; she just needed her bed.

I really enjoyed the food as I was fed up of bananas. We both slept well that night.

Because of the problems with the various planes, Maria's luggage plus her four-wheel scooter had been detained. British Airways told Maria they would put her up in a local hotel. That was music to Maria's ears, although with all the hassle that was the least they could do.

The next day, with Maria safely installed in Lake Victoria Hotel, I went to meet Nelson in the customs office. When I arrived, I was introduced to a young man called Fred who was going to be working with me till we got all of our goods out. I had no idea what sort of day this was going to turn out to be. (Thankfully, I still had a few bananas left and half a loaf of bread).

After endless phone calls and running around, we found where our container was stored. I was escorted down to the customs office where about thirty people were waiting by a door to go in. I was taken past all these people, a man with a gun opened a door for me and I went into another room.

There I met a very brash and stern female customs' officer. I wondered why she was like this with me, I hadn't done anything. She was shouting and bossing people around in the most aggressive manner.

I was given three large pieces of paper with all the details of my consignment on. I followed her through to what looked like a large airport hangar. Inside there were hundreds of boxes, all shapes and sizes. They had a system, I am not sure how it worked mind you, but all I knew was it wasn't my turn. I was asked to go away and come back later. How much later, I had no idea.

Thankfully I had arrived early in the morning so I waited a couple of hours and returned at 10am. Once again I was asked to leave. At noon I tried again. All I kept thinking was that today was Friday, and if the container wasn't opened and released by 5pm it would cost a fortune to be held in storage over the weekend.

The cross customs lady called me over and pointing to my five boxes said sternly:

"What's in there?"

I explained to her some of the items that I could see.

"About a dozen pairs of shoes." I said.

She went mad.

"What do you mean 'about a dozen'? I want to know exactly how many pairs of shoes there are."

She went on and on. Everything had something wrong with it. I hadn't got the serial number for the bike written down or the style number on the sewing machines. I didn't know how many pairs of spectacles there were, or the serial number on the medical trolleys. I had no idea what was in some of the boxes for the hospital or how many bandages had been packed. It was a nightmare. All the time I was praying for a breakthrough with this woman. I prayed and prayed, there was nothing else I could do.

In my head I repeated the verse in Philippians 4:6, *"Do not be anxious about anything, but in everything, by prayer and petition, with thanksgiving, present your requests to God."*

(I later read verse 7 which also proved true. *"And the peace of God, which transcends all understanding, will guard your hearts and minds in Christ Jesus."*)

Nelson from customs had given me his assistant, Fred, for the day and we stood together writing down every item that came out of the five huge six foot by six foot cardboard boxes. These were not only filled with very small things like shoes, spectacles, and crepe bandages but also thousands of small polystyrene bits that cushioned the goods.

We took my bike out, then the two trolleys with glass tops that had been carefully wrapped, books, material, stationery, tents, medical instruments...and so it went on. I noticed the twin tub that was sitting neatly in a corner covered with white bits, and next to it was the hi-fi system that Maria so desperately wanted. We repacked everything and climbed down from the high platform that the boxes stood on.

We took the paper with all the items on it to the main office only to be told to go and work out the cost of all these goods so that the tax could be worked out.

Help! Tax! I hadn't bargained for this, I had very little money.

Fred and Nelson's secretary worked on our papers for over three hours; they looked at the list and then consulted a huge book. Each item had a tax price next to it. I wandered about, inside then out; there was nothing I could do except pray.

It was encouraging for Fred to know I was there. They worked very hard, knowing I wanted an answer and every now and again they would tell me how they were getting on. I bought drinks and food for them, which I hoped help them concentrate.

Time dragged on, I had no idea how long this was going to take and I must have looked at my watch a hundred times trying not to be anxious but praying like crazy that we would get the consignment out that day.

"Let's run." Fred shouted, as he picked up the papers.

We did.

We ran along the main office passage, down the metal steps and across the forecourt, through the gates and past the main airport terminal, passed huge buildings and hangers. We eventually arrived at the customs offices, where Fred guided me through a door, passed a guard with a gun and into a large office with a pool of ladies typing on portable typewriters.

I was asked to stand and wait, and then I was ushered into a smaller office and told to 'Sit, Madam.'

The Asian man behind the desk looked at me; without speaking he held his hand out for the papers I was holding, and then he read them. He kept looking at me over his glasses; I had no idea what was going to happen next. My heart was beating fast, I was hot, the palms of my hands were sticky and perspiration ran down my forehead and neck. Under my breath, I was praying all the time, God was certainly teaching me to be patient.

What else was he trying to tell me? I thought.

He was teaching me perseverance. "*...and let us run with perseverance the race marked out for us. Let us fix our eyes on Jesus...*" Hebrews 12:1.

A door opened and in walked the cross customs lady.

That's blown it. I thought. *Whatever does she want?*

Fred kept looking at me, I still didn't know why we were in this office, I knew it was all terribly official and decided it was probably best to keep quiet.

"Are you a registered NGO?" the Asian man asked.

"Yes," I replied.

I held the paper out with the NGO details on; he didn't take my paper.

"Are you a registered charity?"

"Yes, we are," I said.

After scrutinizing the custom papers, he stamped them and handed them to me.

I was told to go.

Where to? I wondered.

Fred told me what to do; he guided and directed me around the office. I praised God for Fred, he really knew what he was doing and the people respected him. I looked at my papers. They had been stamped twenty-two times. It was now 4.45pm. I knew the huge warehouse doors would close at 5pm and all my boxes would be in there for the weekend. We had to run. Just at that moment the cross customs lady came over to me and asked if I had been given tax exemption.

I had no idea.

She grabbed the papers from me. "Yes, you have," she said with a smile on her face.

I'd not seen her smile before. I thanked her, grabbed the papers and ran. I had had no time to think about how we would transport the five boxes to Kamuli; I had been totally engrossed in getting the paperwork sorted out.

We ran fast and got to the warehouse at 4.50pm. To my horror, I could see some of the workers taking their white coats off and hanging them up. My heart sank. As we approached the building, I saw four people waiting to look at the papers. Talk about the Lord moving in at the eleventh hour. We rushed through and got four more stamps on them, then as I started to walk into the customs warehouse I saw a man putting his white coat back on again. He used his key to unlock the fork-lift truck and swung it around towards my boxes.

I looked to the heavens, *Thank You, God!*

"Where is he taking them to? I haven't organised a vehicle!" I spoke to Fred about this and he pointed outside. I could see a small green truck; I was amazed and slowly walked outside. Sure enough all the boxes were being loaded onto this open topped green truck. I had no idea where this had come from (and still don't to this day).

As I stood there with a frown on my face, a large Ugandan lady approached me and asked what the matter was. I explained that we had five huge boxes and I didn't think they would all fit on the truck I was pointing to.

"Madam," she said sweetly, "Go and sit down; you are going to give yourself a headache."

She was right. I did as I was told and sat on an old bit of metal just inside the main doors. I watched with amazement as the fork-lift took each box and loaded them one by one onto the truck. With all five boxes loaded, the man took off his white coat, hung it up and walked past me, I thanked him so much for taking time to transport the boxes. He smiled and then the two huge customs doors were shut and padlocked.

As we drove out, I glanced back to see the gates also being locked. I was thrilled and humbled too. God had done what I had asked and he came through for me.

We drove to the hotel where Maria was staying. By the time I had told her this incredible story and had a drink, it was nearly 7pm and getting dark. I handed her the papers and told her to talk to Nelson about the cost of getting the boxes out; I knew it must have cost someone several hundred pounds including the hire of the truck. I didn't want to cause anyone else to have to pay and didn't want to go back to England leaving a debt, though how we would reimburse the cost I wasn't quite sure. I never received a bill so to this day I do not know who our benefactor was!

I left Maria at the hotel and sat in the front cab with the driver to my right and Fred to my left; he wanted to come for the ride as he had never been as far as Kamuli. I thought he was mad, knowing the drive would be well over four hours. We discussed the day's business and how amazing it was that we got everything through by 5pm. Then we shared a few pieces of bread that I still had (It was a large loaf!)

As we drove through Kampala, we saw workers going home and people still shopping. Uganda livens up after 7pm; food was being sold and people sat on the ground selling books, drink, food, watches, and clothes. I could see the little paraffin lanterns placed on the ground near the goods. We drove out of Kampala along the main road through traffic lights that didn't work, passed more street sellers and out along the road full of pot-holes. It was dark, the moon was thin, and we didn't have much light as we crossed the Owen Falls Dam towards Jinja.

Suddenly, the driver slammed on his brakes as a policeman waved us down. Our driver wound the window down, and greeted the policeman politely.

"Papers," ordered the policeman.

The driver turned to me: "Papers, he wants the papers."

I smiled, not realising the seriousness of this and said: "I don't have the papers, we left them with Maria."

I am sure the driver's face went pale, even for a Ugandan. He had to explain to the policeman that Madam didn't have the papers. I saw the policeman rub his hands together as he told the driver to pull over.

I sent an arrow prayer to God.

Help!

I climbed over Fred who was rooted to his seat, and jumped down from the cab. It was pitch black. I could see paraffin lights being held up in the distance as I followed the policeman. We approached the flickering lights and I realised they were being held by a patrol of armed policemen and women.

About eight of them crowded around me, I swallowed and tried to compose myself. I wasn't frightened exactly as God has given me such a heart and love for the Ugandan people, but I didn't quite know what to expect. There was a warm breeze blowing and I could hear the waterfall in the distance. An armed policewoman slowly walked up to me (nothing is done in a hurry in Uganda). I looked at the gun that was slung over her shoulder.

"Good evening," I said.

The policewoman looked me up and down: "I understand you have no papers."

"No I don't," I replied.

"Where are they?"

So in two seconds flat I told her the story:

"Well, you see, Maria, who lives in Kamuli was due to return from England at 12 noon. The plane couldn't land so then she was due to come at 4pm, but the plane had a problem so she eventually arrived at 8pm. She was bringing her four-wheel scooter but each time the plane failed they couldn't transport the scooter so now she is in a hotel in Entebbe and will be coming with the papers soon." I was waving my arms around as I spoke. (I realised afterwards that this woman wouldn't have known what a four-wheel scooter was)

She kept looking at me, probably in disbelief at this mad *muzungu's* story. Ugandans speak English slowly and deliberately yet I spoke so quickly it must have sounded like double-dutch to her.

Her eyes were wide open and she raised her eyebrows:

"When will Maria be coming this way again?" she asked.

Off I went again: "Well, it all depends on when the plane carrying her scooter arrives. I have no idea," I said.

She frowned and eyeballed me. By this time I was standing with both hands turned up and out waiting for her to answer me. I looked at her, she looked at me. I had no idea what she was going to say or do, I wasn't thinking anything, I am sure my mind went blank.

I glanced around at the sea of black faces, and guns with shadows dancing on them from the paraffin lights; they were looking at me and my interrogator.

There was complete silence for at least a minute then the policewoman lifted her arm and said:

"You may go, Madam."

This was music to my ears; I didn't need telling again, I turned around and briskly walked towards the truck. At that very moment, Fred jumped out and walked towards me, I waved my hands in front of me and said:

"Get back in the cab, we can go."

The driver revved up and we were off. We drove for about two minutes in silence when the Ugandan driver said in a stern voice:

"Madam, never travel without papers again."

I realised he had been terrified; I had never experienced a Ugandan raising his voice at me before. I said we would be O.K. now and I was sorry for not having them with me.

We drove at top speed to Kamuli without talking or stopping for petrol. As we approached 'Maria's Care', I wondered how we were going to let anyone know we were arriving. We drove up to the big blue gates and, because of the noise the truck had made along the road; four faces appeared through the door in the gate.

I was so pleased to see them; they jumped into the truck and accompanied us down the road to Maria's house. It was 10.30pm and everyone was in bed, but when we pulled up outside the house two of the young boys who lived behind it came running out and let us in. They had heard the truck coming and curiosity had got the better of them, fortunately.

The boxes were so heavy we had to open them whilst they were on the truck and individually unload the goods out one by one. I organised a chain gang and directed the contents into separate areas in and outside the garage: school equipment, medical supplies, household goods, clothes, shoes, books, typewriters and sewing machines. The twin tub and speakers were put straight into the house along with a few boxes of kitchen utensils.

It was gone midnight by the time we finished. The girls gave the driver and Fred food and drink. They both refused the offer of a bed for the night and said they wanted to get back to Entebbe; I couldn't believe that they preferred another four hour drive, but they said they were used to travelling that sort of distance. I thanked Fred for taking care of me all day and the trouble they had both gone to and, after a quick handshake they shot off into the night.

I slept well after an astonishing day, and once again I thanked God for his protection and intervention in the customs offices and on the way home.

I also realised that when we are doing God's work he is faithful. He does look after his children, he does supply all our needs, his promises are true.

I woke the next morning to children laughing; I looked outside and saw a couple of young girls having a wonderful time with what looked like snow all over the garden. They had never seen or felt the polystyrene bits before, and had collected some, which were now in piles around the garden. One of the girls was moving the bits between her fingers feeling how smooth they were; the other had some in her mouth. I called to her and suggested it wasn't a good idea to chew it; this made no difference, I could tell it was a very different texture from anything she had experienced before.

With no way of communicating with Maria, we just had to wait for her return.

Amongst everything in the garage, I found some bright coloured material and my own sewing machine. We needed new covers for some of the chair cushions, so I set my machine up and cut the material out. Whilst I sewed, the children played next to me pretending they were flying in an aeroplane. I kept asking them which part of the world they were going to next, London? Rome? Paris?

After making the cushion covers, I had a bit of material left, I made little bags and the children collected polystyrene bits to put inside. Once I had stitched the ends up the children played with the bags for hours, throwing and catching them with their friends all over the garden.

It was two more days before Maria returned in a truck with her four-wheel scooter, along with two boxes of accessories and a battery for it.

When we tried to assemble all the pieces, we realised the instructions were in Japanese.

Great! I thought. *We got it all this way only to find we can't put it together.*

After much guess work, Maria sat on the scooter, prayed, and pressed the switch.

I do wish I had been holding a camcorder to record the children's faces, and Maria's as she shot backwards. The children jumped in all directions, just like water when you jump in a puddle. Maria eventually found the switch that mobilised the scooter to go forwards and there was also a speed dial she could set: slow, medium, and fast. Whenever she set it on fast, I couldn't keep up with her, or hear her. She would say something and overtake me before the end of every sentence.

Once she was up and running with her scooter, she was able to do so much. It was kept in the garage along with old beds, boxes, and a toad in the pipes. This toad would suddenly croak in the middle of the night or early in the morning and because it was in the pipe it echoed. On several occasions I nearly jumped out of my skin.

We both had great fun distributing the goods to various places. We took the equipment to the local hospital, plus the two trolleys and instruments which were very much appreciated in maternity.

The school head was presented with scholastic materials, and each of the teachers with new shoes.

We saved some of the clothes till we had the chance to visit people in the remote villages.

Maria set up the twin tub in her house and everyone was in awe of it. No-one had ever seen a washing machine in Kamuli, let alone owned one. Water was a valuable commodity so Maria rigged up the pipes in such a way that most of it was saved to water the plants after washing.

Many times I looked round the compound, and wished we had the money to paint the outside walls. Maria told me that education was far more important than paint and that God would provide the paint when he was ready. I realised that the things we think matter, don't. The children needed to be clothed, educated, and fed. They would always tell Maria though when money was tight that education was their priority; without it they knew they wouldn't get a job.

Learning to trust God

I had learnt so much in just a few days about trusting God, obedience, and not stressing but accepting his peace. I have often said to people "I grew up in Uganda." This is a clear example of what I mean. God has taught me so much in my time in that country.

Chapter 6

It takes a whole village to educate a child

It was late 1997 when I started to think about going to Uganda once again, this time for five weeks. Once the dates had been booked, I went around doing presentations and asking for the usual donations of toiletries, clothes, shoes, bed linen, etc.

I had met Richard Jones, a farmer, whilst giving a talk in Oswestry; he offered to put my boxes filled with donations in the milk tanks he was exporting to Uganda. The containers went by boat so could be filled with any weight and he had a consignment due out that February which coincided with my planned visit; this was an offer I couldn't refuse. I dashed to Tesco's and got eight banana boxes to start with; eventually I had fifty one boxes packed with donations, including another sewing machine.

During the next few weeks, I wrote a detailed list of all I hoped to accomplish in Uganda during this visit: photos to be taken, projects to be started or finished, and people I needed to visit. I was asked by other people in England who had a charity or NGO in Uganda to go and visit their projects too, take photos and give letters out.

I packed four days in advance, a miracle for me. Then unpacked and packed again because the suitcase was overweight. I made more and more lists: don't forget the clock, brush, malaria tablets, passport and tickets. Maria had sent a list of all she hoped I would bring: bath mat, little kettle, string, on and on it read. I packed everything and locked the case.

This was the first time Maria had suggested I packed my waterproof-boots; I did think about wearing them on the plane...then thought better of it. I took my jewellery off; when travelling I only wear a pair of plastic earrings and a watch. Eventually I got into bed at midnight; I was as excited as a child on Christmas Eve. I set three alarm clocks to make certain I didn't oversleep.

I was ready by 5am that morning and checked that nothing had jumped out of my handbag overnight.

My daughter silently drove me to the airport; like many she was not at her best in the early hours. I walked straight to check-in; I always hate this bit, and prayed with every step.

A tall, distinguished-looking man walked behind the check-in desk and looked at the screen just as I put my huge suitcase on the scales. The check-in girl looked at the weight, then at me. I continued and placed a bag full of soft toys for the children, on top. I handed a letter to her from Sabina with details of what I was going to do. The tall man never looked at me; he just studied the weight on the scales. My head spun.

"Let it go," he said to the check-in girl.

My heart skipped a beat; I gave her a half-hearted smile and picked up my ticket. In my head I was shouting *Praise the Lord, Praise the Lord.* The gentleman walked back to his office and that was that.

"Enjoy your flight," the check-in girl said, handing me my boarding cards. I knew I most certainly would after that good start.

Other passengers looked so elegant in their tailored suits and leather shoes whilst I stood there in my two skirts, two T-shirts, cardy, and with my carpet bag, but it didn't matter; I was happy and dressed for my own destination.

I put my hand-luggage on the conveyor belt, and then it happened, not for the first time.

"Whose is this luggage?"

"It's mine," I owned up.

"What is the canister?" They could see it through the X ray screen.

"It's the tent waterproof spray," I said.

I was waved on. Last year it had been the electric light bulbs, the year before the wind-up radio and another time when Gordon came with us it had been his hammers, handsaw and building equipment.

Kamuli Telephone Exchange 1995

What a way to travel! Maria was 71 years old

This is why we call the project "Maria's Care".

The Grand Opening of the Primary School. February 17th, 1996

Under the Freedom Tree at the Lodge in 1995
Aunt Rose addresses Maria and a group of teachers.

Rhona eating fried
grasshoppers!

5am at the Lodge. The children catching flying ants - a delicacy for breakfast.

Maria and Rhona with the children outside the little round clinic at Maria's Care in 1996.

Rhona with some of the children before going to collect water.

Local children with very heavy jerry cans after collecting water.

Intepid Explorers!
Maria and Rhona outside the Catholic Seminary in Kampala

Children at the school

The Call, the Cost, the Choice

Once on board, I prayed for a good touchdown, safety for the next five weeks, and for my family and friends. Hopefully, the rains in Uganda had died down and I wouldn't have to use the waterproof boots.

We landed in Entebbe late that evening and, as I got off the plane, the heat hit me. I walked to passport control and asked the lady to stamp five weeks on my passport.

"We are only stamping four weeks on passports now," she replied.

"Oh no, I really need five weeks, I am staying in your country five weeks," I said shrilly.

She asked me to explain my visit and then stamped my passport.

"There you are, thirty-five days."

"Thank you so much, God bless," I replied with genuine relief.

I sailed through customs as four officers were discussing what to do with another lady's luggage, and out through the exit into a sea of faces.

Maria waved me over:

"Welcome, welcome, welcome to Uganda!"

In the next breath, she was telling Ugandan porters to leave my luggage alone.

I met Jemima who owned Banana Village, a new tourist venture she and her husband James were running. We loaded her car and drove along the slippy mud roads; apart from car head lights it was pitch black.

Jemima escorted us to our accommodation; two round houses called *rondavels* with huge king-size beds, a bathroom, dressing table, and mirror, I wondered where they had got the furniture from. The two windows facing one another had nets on and lovely blue Laura Ashley curtains tied back, pure luxury. Maria and I spoke a while and then hit the hay.

I later discovered I was sharing my room with some cockroaches that dashed under the bed when I put the light on to use the bathroom. I was delighted to see a proper toilet, sink, and shower, until I realised they were not attached to the water mains. Next to the sink was a huge plastic container with water and a plastic cup for washing and flushing. But at least I had a basin and a plug that fitted.

I had forgotten the African sounds: the crickets rubbing their back legs together, the monkeys screeching in the trees, the dogs whimpering and donkeys neighing in the background. A hen suddenly started to crow, it was far too early for this and quite unnecessary, I thought. I could hear the African music in the distance and soon drifted back to sleep.

I woke happy after a good night's sleep until I remembered that I had to wash in cold water. Maria and I breakfasted together in the warm sunshine, and caught up with each other's news.

We discussed with James the animal projects we had in mind and he suggested we went to visit a man in Masaka who had a site incorporating all the animals we were thinking of having ourselves. James suggested we bought goats as they needed little attention; apparently hens needed a lot more looking after. This trip to Masaka would be an answer to my prayers for us to see how the animals were managed. I also knew that not far from the farm was a national park with zebras and hippos:

I do hope we go, I thought to myself.

The next day was hot indeed, nearly 90 degrees, but even so Maria suggested we went for a stroll. I needed my sunglasses, hat, and sun cream so I went back into my little dark *rondavel* and put the cream on, grabbed my hat and gloves and off we went.

Well, not exactly.

In the dark I had gone to get the sun cream and accidently grabbed a tube of tomato puree.

We eventually set off, both of us still laughing. We could see Lake Victoria in the distance but had no idea how to get there. We came to a path which went down a shaded avenue, the trees enveloping us as we walked and talked, and found ourselves right by the water's edge. The view was stunning. We could see right across the lake, still with great clumps of water hyacinth bobbing on top, to the other side. Fishermen in handmade dugout boats were going about their business, whilst other people cleaned their bikes or did their washing at the edge of the water.

After a bumpy ride in a Land Rover, we arrived back at the gates of Banana Village ready for our evening meal. We drank our passion fruit; the world looked a wonderful place from where we were sitting. I thought about the people we had passed who were finding it difficult to put a meal together for their family that night, others had been begging all day for school fees, and shopkeepers were trying to make a living. It seemed a topsy-turvy world to me.

The electricity was off so we ate by candlelight. We could hear people talking in the distance and the sound of the crickets was deafening. We went to bed early.

"Happy birthday to you!" Maria sang the next morning as I opened cards and presents I had brought with me from England. We had breakfast together and I gave Maria the dress her daughter had made her; she was thrilled and did a little twirl for the camera.

We celebrated Nancy's birthday that day too; she was Dick and Ivy's daughter. Dick and Ivy are from America and have lived in Uganda for many years; they were in Uganda in the 1980's when all the fighting took place. They were given a few hours to pack and leave the country with their children. Their own children have since grown up and they adopted some Ugandan children who lived with them in Kampala. Dick was a pastor of a large church there. They threw a party for Nancy and generously included me in the birthday wishes.

Early in the afternoon, Nancy suggested everyone should put their swimming costumes on, ladies to the right behind some rocks on the beach and men to the left on a little hill. I hadn't thought about packing my costume as it had been raining just before we left but I was very content sitting in the sunshine with a gentle breeze blowing and watching everyone having races in the water, guests laughing and Nancy having so much fun. Maria thoroughly enjoyed herself, and Nancy looked radiant.

We were dropped off at the main road and our feet had only just touched the ground when Maria flagged down a passing *matatu*. We went straight to Lake Victoria Hotel where Maria was hoping that her niece, Clare, would be, waiting to fly back to England. We found her sipping tea and joined her with her friend for an evening meal.

We took a private hire car back to Banana Village and got hopelessly lost.

Maria gave the instructions:

"Right, right, right," she shouted, then said to me:

"...Or was it left? I think we have just missed the turning."

We drove along in the pitch dark and realised we hadn't a clue where we were and to make matters worse, the driver was becoming anxious.

"Oops, we're lost." Maria said.

I jumped out of the car and asked a passerby where we were, and eventually we arrived safe and sound at the gate to Banana Village.

I fell into bed at the end of a wonderful day and my 49th Birthday. I wondered where I would be the following year for my 50th.

As Maria was not feeling well, she stayed in bed the following morning and I went with Jemima to her little church. It was no bigger than my single garage at home. Talk about no room at the inn!

There were about ten people crushed together on two benches. In front of me, I counted six little boys aged about eight or nine. There was a man on a keyboard, a P/A system in the corner (not that they needed it!) and a lady with a lovely smile stood behind a huge lectern with a Bible open on it. A man to her left was playing a guitar and two people stood in the doorway. Along the side of the room were four benches with twenty eight adults and three children sitting squashed up on them. A lady was peeping through the little window and two people stood in the back doorway. In total there were nearly sixty people in this little fellowship. The praise, worship and prayer were amazing; the spirit of the living God was in that place.

Back at Banana Village that evening, we sat under a full moon and prayed that God would provide a way for us to visit Masaka. It was amazing how God orchestrated our journey.

James knew a man called Fred who worked in Masaka from Monday to Friday, then came home to Entebbe for the weekend. Arrangements were made for us to meet him in Kampala early Monday morning and he would drive us to Masaka. We packed our bags and went to bed early.

We travelled in style in a Land Rover; sheer luxury in comparison to the back of a bicycle side-saddle! At about 6.45am, it started to get light. We could see pupils going to school dressed in red, pink, and yellow school uniforms. Some of them had started walking as early as 5.30am to get there. They had been up early planting crops, washing clothes, and then having breakfast beforehand; this was their culture.

We arrived in Masaka just after 8am in brilliant sunshine. Fred dropped a young lady off with all her luggage; she was going to college and had to take everything with her. She had a tin trunk to keep all her belongings away from the cockroaches that would eat her clothes or the glue in her books. She carried a big red plastic bowl for washing, her bag, a sweeping brush, and a *panga* (machete) for cutting the grass, (everyone is encouraged to play a part in the running of the college). The largest item she had was her mattress and mat to sleep on. Each child had to take all this before they could even begin to study. Other small items had to be bought such as toilet paper, and stationery. Families who send children to high school, college or university often have no money so the whole village helps to support them.

The Ugandans sing a song: "It takes a whole village to educate a child."

We first visited a 'zero grazing' project Maria knew about. I made copious notes and sketches in my diary and, by the end of our little tour; I felt I didn't want any part of this 'amazing' new invention that people were raving about.Cows and goats spent their whole existence, including mating and breeding, cooped up in pens like battery hens. They stood on a slightly sloped cement incline so that all their bodily waste went into a cement trough. Later it could be spread all around the base of banana trees and other crops as fertilizer.

From there we travelled by *matatu* to Lake Mburo National Park. At one point in the journey, the driver stopped the bus and popped into a chemist. We had to wait ten minutes for his prescription to be ready. What a hoot! Can you imagine that happening in England!

He then played a game of 'pass the parcel' using a length of material with the conductor of another bus. As our bus stopped to let passengers off, the other bus would overtake and then vice-versa. They did this for the next hour. Thankfully, the road was straight but I was terrified and prayed the angels would protect us all.

Maria's eyesight wasn't very good and I wondered how she was going to see which stage we were going to get off especially at the speed the driver was going.

Suddenly she cried out: "Here we are. We get off here."

She then bartered with a few men driving *piki-pikis*,(motorised bikes) agreed a price, and we were off again on the back of two scooters. I forgot to check if I had a foot rest and had to travel holding the back of my sandals so I could keep my feet off the ground.

Fortunately, it wasn't too long a ride and we soon arrived at the main gate of the Lake Mburo National Park, where we were shown to two *rondavels*, When I entered I could see the bed hadn't been made.

"Oh, Madam, I am sorry, the room is not dressed properly!"

I thought this was a lovely expression. I sat with Maria until my room was ready, and was delighted with the result. The bed was made with a corner turned back, and a towel neatly arranged on it, a mosquito net was tied above the bed, hurricane lamp in the corner and a few little shelves. What more could I ask for? The restaurant was only a short distance from our rooms; under the canopy of blue sky and white fluffy clouds were seven tables covered with green and white check cloths with chairs neatly placed around them.

We sat down and ordered lunch; a drink and a plate of chips. The drink came straight away and the chips came an hour later. I thought they must have gone back to the main road for the potatoes!

Back at my *rondavel*, I slept for two hours straight. I woke to hear Maria quietly calling me: "Rhona, Rhona come quickly, bring your camera."

It was dusk and the sun was just disappearing, I slowly opened my door and saw the most incredible sight; surrounding us was a herd of about two hundred impala chewing grass.

On the way to our evening meal we passed a man who was stoking a fire under a huge old metal barrel full of cold water that was resting on two small walls of bricks. Maria explained that this was the hot water for our showers and would be ready after we had eaten; I thought this was an ingenious idea. I later discovered there was no mixer tap but I ducked and dived in and out and managed not to scald myself.

After a delicious meal and a hot shower, I fell asleep to the sounds of Africa.

Early the next morning we met Lawrence, our safari guide.

It's quite incredible how we trust people just because they have overalls and green waterproof boots on, I thought to myself.

We walked for about thirty minutes and there in the distance we saw our first zebra, then on a hill two buffaloes and a herd of impala. A vast plain stretched before us and we could see miles and miles of the national park and Lake Mburo. As we continued our walk, we became experts on zebra, hippo, buffalo and impala droppings.

Lawrence pointed to the different places animals had laid and scratched themselves to get rid of tics. At one point, he crouched down and waved to us to do the same. In the near distance was a herd of buffalo with their babies; my heart was beating fast as I quickly took a photo. The buffalo stopped and looked in our direction; it was the only time I saw Lawrence put his hand on his gun.

We heard the story of how Lake Mburo was named (not sure if it's true or not).

Once there were two brothers. One had a dream and told the other there was going to be a flood so he took his family up into the hills. The other brother, Mburo, thought he was being tricked and stayed, but the flood came and he was drowned.

The whole tour lasted for three hours and cost us £4.50 each. I was impressed with Maria's stamina considering she hadn't been well the year before and was now a lady of seventy-two.

After toast, coffee, and a snooze, we set off in a truck for the second half of our Safari but not before Maria had inadvertently padlocked her *rondavel* door, leaving the key inside. The ranger had to use the butt of his gun to break the lock off.

Travelling by truck was an inspirational idea. We could have done another three hour trek but I think it would have finished us off. It was much hotter than the morning and, thankfully, the truck had a tarpaulin soft roof thrown over the top. The trip was wonderful; we drove to the other side of the park and saw eland, topi, velvet monkeys, waterbuck, buffalo, zebra and impala.

We rested a while on a log by Lake Mburo where I took photos of the three rangers, driver and Maria all watching the hippopotamus bathe in the lake. It was a marvellous sight to see these huge animals bathing with their babies. The rangers kept a keen eye on them as they knew they could be dangerous.

One ranger suddenly cried out:

"Look, look!"

Maria and I looked all around and couldn't see anything unusual.

"There! There! Look, a rabbit!" I couldn't believe all this excitement was over one rabbit, apparently they are uncommon.

The bus journey to Masaka and then Kampala the next day had its usual share of chickens, mattresses, bumpy roads, and near misses... and then we ran out of fuel.

"It's a good job we haven't got a hair appointment booked!" I remarked.

Passengers got off and wandered about. I decided I needed the toilet and got off too. A long line of women formed behind me as I ambled along; I realised they were all following me to the toilet and I didn't know where it was. I found a Ugandan lady who was able to direct me, and all the women, to a little round grass hut that served as a toilet. Relief!

People were lined up along the bank on their own or in small groups. I got my camera out to take some shots.

"No, no, no!" someone shouted.

"You get money for this picture?" he asked.

I told him I wouldn't, and in the end he agreed I could take some photos.

Eventually, a private hire car arrived complete with jerry-can filled with petrol, and we all cheered!

Our driver asked a lady to pull a banana leaf from the tree and proceeded to use it as a funnel to pour the petrol into the tank. Within a few minutes, we were all back on the bus and on our way.

You need to have a very good bra on and clench your teeth or you could do yourself some damage, I thought to myself as we drove along the bumpy roads.

In the distance, I could see a gate and beyond that was the most wonderful sight, Lake Nabugabo. As we arrived so did a man with fresh fish on the back of a bike.

"Hello, Maria!" he said.

She was amazed he recognised her. It transpired that in 1994 she had brought a truck full of children here for a few days and had taught Joyce, the manageress, to swim; no wonder he remembered her. Joyce suddenly appeared and ran with her arms open to greet her:

"Maria! How are you?" she shouted.

We signed the visitors' book and Joyce took us to our rooms, they cost the equivalent of £4.00 per night so we decided to stay for two.

We opened our windows to let the fresh air in and unpacked our little rucksacks as we travelled light. Maria put her flask, tea bags, and biscuits out ready to have a cup of tea after our swim. (Some lakes are dangerous to swim in for fear of catching bilharzias disease, but this lake was fine).

We walked out of our rooms towards the lake about twenty feet away. It was breathtaking. I paddled and thought: *If we can experience this on earth then what will heaven be like?*

The Call, the Cost, the Choice

The sun was shining, a breeze was blowing softly, and we needed sun cream on our lily white bodies. The lake was as still as a mill pond; it was so peaceful: just the two of us for miles and miles.

After my swim, I felt chilly so decided to go for a shower. To my surprise, I could see lots of monkeys all around our house. As I got closer, I saw big monkeys with their little babies eating food; the penny dropped as I saw a trail of biscuits coming from our open window. I ventured inside and saw the new packet of biscuits was completely finished. I was mad and went outside to tell them off. The monkeys looked at me squeaking and chatting to one another as though they were laughing at the silly *muzungu*. Maria and I had to laugh too, we made sure all our windows and doors were kept tightly shut after that. I took some photos as a reminder and whenever I see a packet of 'Marie' biscuits I think of those monkeys!

After a good night's sleep, we woke to the sound of 'bang, bang, bang'. I wondered what it was. Apparently the fishermen bang the inside of their boats to wake the fish up and get them moving. I dozed after that but when I did look out of my window again I saw Maria swimming in the lake. The sun hadn't risen and I could just see her gliding through the water; she was having a wonderful time. The birds were beginning to sing, I could hear different animal noises, some I recognised, others I didn't. God's amazing creation was waking up to a new day.

I read my Bible and thought how blessed I was that God had chosen me before the beginning of time to be sitting experiencing this amazing place. Tears ran down my face.

We rested that day by the lake.

Early the next morning, we set off on what was to be another eventful journey, this time to Entebbe to pick up my friend, Sandra, who was on her way to Uganda.

As I got in the front of the car, I could see all the wires hanging under the steering wheel. Fifteen minutes later we stopped to collect a little girl going to school, and then a woman and two men. Seven of us were already squashed in the car when it slowed again:

Surely not! I thought.

There in front of us stood a man with a huge plastic bowl containing sixty fresh eggs. Everyone moved over and in he got, now we were eight plus luggage. I hoped we didn't have to do an emergency stop or we would have had scrambled eggs for breakfast!

By 8am we had arrived at the main road and swapped transport for a *matatu* headed towards Kampala. At one long stop, I watched a little boy having his fingernails cut by a man using a razor blade. I didn't take a photo in case he jumped when the flash went off and lost one! I stared in disbelief until it was done; the boy took his hand back, looked at his nails and smiled; I bet he was glad that was over.

We passed many houses that at one time would have looked awesome; they were huge and probably owned by people who had fled during Idi Amin's regime. Squatters were in them now and they had a sad, dilapidated appearance. By the time we reached Banana Village, it was just before noon, I felt much happier when I got my suitcase and was able to change into some clean clothes. That night we drove to Entebbe Airport to meet Sandra. Apparently it was snowing when she left England.

I lay in bed that night reflecting on the last few days. I saw how God had planned everything and kept us safe every step of the way.

After breakfast we packed our luggage, caught a *matatu*, and headed for Kampala to catch another one to Jinja. Under Maria's military instruction, people helped unload our nine pieces of luggage from one *matatu* to the next.

"Turn that awful noise off," Maria commanded as she boarded the Jinja bus.

She was referring to the radio blaring out some terrible music. The driver did as he was told.

It was a joy to reach Kamuli by mid-afternoon, and we unloaded outside Maria's house. (She had persuaded the driver to take us to her front door for extra money).

My first impression since my last visit was, 'Wow!'

The house was fantastic. Inside had all been painted blue, white, or cream; a shower had been installed and a proper toilet with a seat. There were matching curtains and flowers in pots all over the place. The kitchen was neat and tidy and had a warm lived-in feeling to it. You could see and feel Maria's homely touch everywhere. I could have cried with excitement at how God had answered our prayers and been so faithful, supplying the needs for this project.

I then took Sandra on a grand tour of the compound. As we arrived the children ran towards us with open arms. My goodness! How they had all grown! So many I remembered, although some I had never seen before. We walked around the compound and the children showed us places that I noticed had changed considerably. The goat house had survived; Maria's previous house in the compound was looking great with a new veranda outside and new decor within. I looked at the back extension, kitchen, spare bedroom, separate toilet, bathroom and a little store room which we desperately needed.

The whole compound was clean and tidy, little bricks had been neatly laid along the side of the path, the grass had been cut. Money had been donated to build a new little mushroom hut for the crèche, and erect a set of swings and slide; the children were so obviously happy here.

We visited the new dining room; in the corner stood an easel with Christian choruses and hymns written on a flip chart. On the wall was a board with Bible verses on for the children to learn each week. There was a huge kitchen at the back; Maria designed the brick sawdust cooking area with a powerful 'expel-air' that would take anyone's wig off once switched on.

People came from miles to see this new design and even measured the area with a view to copying it. I did notice the pit at the back needed filling in;

We would never know if we lost a child down there, I thought.

We walked around the various classrooms and saw the new wooden partitions between each class; Maria had copied the idea from the time she was interviewed at United Christian Broadcast in England.

We popped in on the boys' dormitory and then we were escorted to the new school hall. It looked brilliant; there were seats, and curtains hung both sides of the new stage, it was a great delight to see because the old stage had been so dangerous.

The office next door was now well-equipped with a desk, chair, typewriter, table and chairs for visitors, a large cupboard, and a kettle on a table in the corner. The bursar was in an office behind.

We came out of the office and walked to the 'round classroom'. Maria had this built the year before. It started life as a water tank but the builders didn't use the correct cement mixture and, on its first day of use, it burst with cement and bricks flying everywhere. Thank God no one was hurt.

Maria said it looked like a paddy field and the children and staff had to wade through it all. She decided to have electricity put in and it became a good study room for the students to do their homework in.

The girls' dormitory was across on the other side, opposite the main hall; we looked in and found all the beds neat and tidy. The children took such pride in what they had and really looked after their things; they showed us their blue tin boxes which contained all they possessed in the whole world.

After the evening meal, we all sat outside for a time of praise and worship. I stood up and praised God for the fantastic changes that had taken place. I thought back to how it had been the year before when Ann and Judith had visited; it was very different now. I wished they could see the improvements Maria had made. I relaxed that night reading 'The Macclesfield Express' that Sandra had brought with her.

We woke to the sound of Maria working the twin-tub. There was no other washing machine in the whole of the Busoga area, so people found it quite intriguing. When Maria had been in England in 1997, she had written an open letter to our local newspaper requesting a hi-fi system with microphones, tents, waterproof boots, a twin tub washing machine, and various other obscure things. I thought she would be very lucky to get just a few of these items.

God supplied everything.

Hearing the twin tub in operation reminded me of the sweet lady who donated it. She had bought a new washing machine but always felt one day someone would need her old one. How right she was. We struggled to load it into the church minibus but managed to get it home, and then all the way to Uganda. Another lady rang up whose husband had been an entertainer before he died; his hi-fi system, complete with microphones, was of no use to her, so that came to Uganda too.

We had our Bible study and then Sandra and Maria took some sick children with suspected malaria to the mission clinic. Later Sandra and I took a young man called John to the hospital for an X-ray; we thought he had TB and needed treatment. As we walked round a corner with John, a voice said:

"Morning, ladies, do you fancy a cup of tea?"

It was Gordon Birch. He had decided to stay in Uganda and had a four year work contract. He had moved from 'Maria's Care' and was now working at the hospital as a handyman. It was so good to see him again; we accepted his invitation and visited him in his cosy little house. We enjoyed a cup of tea and ate peanut butter sandwiches.

Once back at the compound, the builder arrived and gave us a quote to finish the house we had decided to call 'God's Miracle'. The biggest job to complete was the soakaway pit at the back for the bathroom, toilet and kitchen. This would cost nearly £500, but thankfully I was able to give them the go ahead as we had the money in the bank and the CRU committee had instructed me to get jobs finished and do any other necessary work.

We went back to the house and packed for our adventure with Maria to Jinja, Soroti and Tororo.

We arrived in Jinja at 3.45pm, and Maria shot off to arrange our accommodation, buy plumbing materials and electrical goods. Sandra and I had the best deal; we went to The Sailing Club and drank a pint of passion fruit whilst we went to the shore of lake Victoria and watched the fisherman casting their nets, and beautiful white birds, called Great Egrets, with long legs strut along the ground with their yellow beaks in the air. It was gorgeous just taking in the last of the sun.

We arrived back at the Busoga Guest House on *boda-bodas*, with not a soul in sight. We found a note that said:

'Dear Rhona, welcome. We have put you both in room two.'

Maria arrived back much later that night and proudly announced we were leaving the next morning at 6.30pm sharp. Oh boy! It was already 10pm; we shot off, packed and slept till 6am.

Up and out, we eventually arrived at Tororo nearly three hours later. We took in the sight of the huge Tororo Rock landmark and, after a break, piled back on the bus to our next place of interest, Soroti. I didn't see much scenery this time as I was sitting in the centre of the bus.

We all needed a drink when we arrived and found a little café that even charged us to use the toilet facilities such as they were. What a laugh! Maria disappeared on business on the back of a *boda-boda*, visiting one of her pupils that our charity supported at the local school in Soroti. She looked so lovely in her check dress and holding her umbrella up. I told her to stop and took a picture. Many people have seen this photo because I used it as a CRU poster in England.

Whilst Maria was away, Sandra and I explored the locality. To our utter amazement we saw a cinema called 'The Majestic.' In Macclesfield, 'The Majestic' cinema had been closed down, so I took a photo of Sandra outside it and had it published in the Macclesfield Express when we got home.

Once Maria had returned, we climbed back onboard our bus and travelled to Mbale where we waited over an hour for a *matatu* to take us to the top of Mt Elgon, the fourth largest mountain on the Uganda-Kenya border, being over four thousand feet high. Maria wanted us to see Sipi Falls at just over two thousand feet.

We left the taxi park at 4pm in a packed *matatu*, and made three stops before we got to the top, the last one being to check the tyres. What faith we needed to travel on these buses. I was squashed on the back seat with three others as we started the climb. We chatted and laughed at the crazy situation we were in. We passed little mud huts, some half-built or fallen down, others with grass roofs. Children collecting water at a bore hole shouted '*Bazungu, Bazungu!*' when they saw our white faces and waved as we passed them. We stopped twice to either give, or collect goods from stall holders halfway up the mountain. Eventually we got to Sipi Falls Rest House where we were staying.

It was truly magnificent. The view before us was breathtaking; we were on top of the world. We took one look at each other and laughed; we were covered from head to foot in red dust. We went to our basic little rooms and unpacked, showered, and dressed for tea. This shower was situated in a corrugated black room at the back of the building. There was a large black bag hanging in the corner with a bowl underneath and a red tube hung from the bag that we had to pull in and out to get the water from. Some shower!

We all went to bed at 10pm after an exhausting day. Needless to say, I slept like a log.

I had a rude awakening when the cock crowed right outside our window; I walked up a long path to the toilet and sat on the throne looking over the whole of Uganda. Talk about a room with a view! The sun was just rising over the mist covered mountains.

We ate a good hearty breakfast, and arranged to go with a guide on a two hour hike over to Sipi Falls. It wasn't too hot as we walked up hill and down dale, through back gardens surprising the folk who were bathing or eating their breakfast. We found children in a little mud classroom learning maths and I took a photo of one child hiding under the wooden table. After a long steep walk, we arrived at the entrance to a huge cave. Water poured over the entrance; we were under Musi Falls. We didn't get as far as Sipi Falls in the end as it would have been another long climb and we didn't have the right shoes on. We meandered down a small track following a stream and I took a photo from a little bridge of the clear fresh water. (I have since returned and it has all changed; there is a main road now and a charge to go to the cave, the pool has altered shape and the little bridge I stood on to take a photo has been replaced by a large concrete one).

We paid our guide Fred, £1.10 each and decided to stay a second night at the rest house. I was so glad Maria had taken us there to have this amazing experience.

The following morning we walked down the little track to catch a lift home. We waited and waited. At times like this Maria would calmly get her book out and read till something happened. Sandra and I wandered around looking at the little shops opening up to ply their trade.

A huge wagon came down the hill, the type you would see carrying sand, and Maria jumped up and waved to the driver who brought the wagon to a standstill. She chatted with him awhile and the next thing we knew she was up and over into the truck. Sandra and I, at nearly half her age, struggled to throw our bags in and had to get someone to help us into the vehicle. We sat on the dirty floor; Sandra wedged in a corner between the two sides of the wagon and me holding onto one side and a sack of maize in the middle. Maria was sitting on her rucksack, looking very happy and content.

We slowly meandered down the high mountain. I was just telling Sandra how I was thoroughly enjoying the view, the space and the trip, when we stopped to pick more passengers up. From then on we stopped at nearly every bend; some people had been shopping at the local market and bought vegetables to sell on their own stalls. We started counting: thirty, thirty-three, thirty-six people so far in the truck. A man handed a table to me and then jumped on with a kettle and his bicycle.

"Look out Sandra! A bike is coming over."

He couldn't get it on our side so started to walk around to the other side; by this time I couldn't see Maria but shouted to her:

"Watch out, there's a bike coming in your side."

We had to laugh. As the wagon began moving another man threw his bag on the truck, grabbed the side and was eventually hauled into the vehicle.

We passed spectacular sights, coloured flowers of vibrant gold, yellow, and white, children in rags, ladies in beautiful dresses and others with just material wrapped around them. The man with the bike was by now squeezed very tightly next to me, and asked how many children I had produced:

"Two daughters," I said

"Only two. Why no boys?" He obviously thought this was a great omission on my part.

"We produce ten children each here in Uganda," he said.

Good for you! I thought, *but I am not Ugandan.*

By the time we arrived in Mbale, he was very interested in meeting my two daughters and thought it would be a good idea if he came to England to visit them.

Not likely, I thought.

I asked him what he would give me if he married one of my daughters:

"A bike," he said.

"No, no, no. A motorbike," I argued.

"No, two cows!" he replied, and everyone laughed.

Eventually after over two hours and about thirty miles we got on the main road; it was heaven travelling on tarmac instead of the bumpy marum road. We arrived in Mbale with numb bottoms, jumped out into a small street and went into a café for a wash. I took off my sunglasses, and my whole face, except for where my glasses had been, was deep orange. I felt and looked pretty grim at that moment but it had been a fantastic experience that I wouldn't have wanted to miss.

We jumped on a *matatu* and arrived at Nakaloke crossroads, and then on to Salem Guest House. The whole site incorporated a hospital, orphanage, travel lodge, hostel, guest house, and craft shop.

We were given hostel rooms with a communal shower, basin and toilet. We felt so much better when we had washed and changed into clean clothes. We sat under a little mushroom hut drinking tea feeling a lot more human. We were all asleep by 9pm that night.

We went with a doctor the next day to visit the hospital; it was simple but well-equipped by Ugandan standards. We were shown a small room with an old wooden bed covered in worn out red plastic, complete with curtain and side table. It transpired that this was where injections took place.

We walked through the maternity unit and passed a room with its door open. I saw a woman desperately trying to breastfeed her tiny baby girl who was about five or six pounds in weight with a little scrawny neck, arms and body. As the others walked on, I went to see if I could assist her. Her nipple was so large and the baby's mouth so small. It was a precious moment when I was able to hold the baby's head, move the struggling arms out of the way, and direct the mouth to the nipple. With a gentle push, they made contact and the baby started suckling. A huge smile came over the mother's face. I had a lump in my throat; it was a very special moment. I caught the others up and couldn't speak for several minutes.

We viewed the kitchen area. Under a thatched roof stood a large tin box which they loaded up with firewood, on top of which two round metal car hubs acted as burners. A chimney came from the cooker up through the thatched roof. All very efficient!

Maria took us to the centre of Tororo and through the market where we met Mary's step-brother Timothy. Maria was very fond of Mary because she had nursed her when she was sick. Sadly, Mary died a few years later, and a guest house in Maria's Care compound was named after her called Mary's Memorial.

Timothy organised a private hire to go deep into the village where Mary lived. I felt sorry for the driver as we seemed to be going round in circles getting nowhere fast, and down tracks that only bikes usually travelled.

We did eventually find the village and met Robert, Mary's brother, then her grandmother, and some children. Robert showed us the granary; it was neatly constructed with woven straw and lined with dry cow dung. It was waterproof, rat proof, and stood on three legs.

We met Mary again who was not feeling well; she had malaria and a painful leg, Sandra examined her and said she had a bad sprain.

The family made us very welcome and pulled two large chairs and a settee out under the tree where we drank sodas and chatted; I took photos of Timothy and his grandmother. We drove to Mukuju Primary School to meet the other two children from Mary's family; there we met thirteen year old Oketcho Stephen who was a lovely, bright boy doing very well in primary year 7. He informed us that he liked Science, English and Maths, Social Studies, rice, beans, chickens, pineapple and bananas.

We had also come to visit Oketcho's sister Sylvia Nyachuo who was ten years old. When the teacher went to fetch Sylvia, she saw us from a distance and apparently someone told her the *bazungu* had come to take her away. She took one look at us and screamed and screamed for at least twenty minutes; a teacher tried pulling her towards us but we told them not to do that as she was frightened enough. Eventually, with a little coaxing she came and met us and we managed to take some lovely photos of her smiling. She liked netball, skipping, jumping, bananas and rice.

Mukuju's school motto was 'struggle for success' and they really had to out there in the wilderness. They had one-thousand-two hundred pupils and sixteen teachers, P4, Sylvia's class, had one hundred and thirty pupils and P7 had thirty pupils. We went into some of the classrooms, took photos and looked at the children's books.

We visited 11 year old Timothy Ocheing in P4 at Akadot Primary School. His mother had died and his father had gone off with many wives and children. Timothy was living with an old lady in the village of Lyokang near Tororo, where there are no shops or facilities. He was a very bright boy and wanted to be a doctor. With God all things are possible.

Mary's family were so grateful for all we had done for them that even though they had so little they wanted to show their appreciation and insisted on giving us a live duck to take home with us. It was hilarious; the duck was placed in a plastic bag with its legs tied up. Now, Sandra and I do not come from farming backgrounds and had no idea what we should do with it or how to treat it for the next few hours. We got a box and put the duck in it. Now we were three *bazungu* with a duck between our legs in the *matatu*. This made a change from the usual chicken.

We arrived in Jinja with stiff legs and numb bottoms, and prayed that the Busoga Guest House would be able to accommodate us. We jumped on *boda-bodas* and I carried the duck. Unfortunately, there was 'no room at the inn,' but the staff were super and moved furniture out of the office and placed three mattresses on the floor.

I asked what we should do with the duck because I thought it must be very thirsty by now after all the travelling.

The Call, the Cost, the Choice

"Is it a town duck or a country duck?" asked the lady running the guest house, as if that made all the difference.

I pulled a face and said, "Well, we were given it way out in the village so I think it's a country duck."

She told us it would be fine but if we wanted to give it some water we could, so that's what we did, poor thing.

The next day a friend of Maria's gave us a lift into Jinja with all our luggage which we left at the Busoga Office. Maria had a long list of things to do so Sandra and I left her to it and walked to the swimming pool. People were busy painting their shop fronts and offices because President Clinton was due in the area later that month.

We stayed at the pool for a couple of hours chatting, swimming, and just being lazy. On the way back we nipped into the supermarket and bought groceries, including sausages as a treat for Maria.

We made our way to Jinja Taxi Park with our luggage and the duck and journeyed safely back to Kamuli. We gave the duck to Aunt Rose who immediately set it free. We heard a few quacks of thanks as it fluttered its wings and waddled about in the compound.

We reflected on the way God had guided and protected us over the last few days. He had provided all our needs at the right time. We found ourselves saying:

"God is good all the time, all the time God is good."

Maria rested in the house the next day; she wasn't feeling very well with chest pains and coughing, but Sandra and I busied ourselves in the compound during the day and attended the praise and worship meeting that night. When we arrived, we were told that John had now been diagnosed with T.B. and a further infection and was in hospital. Two of our students, Becky and Topy, took it in turns to look after him. We knew that if anyone was ill in hospital they had to have attendants; no one could be admitted unless they had people to look after them. We were very grateful that Becky and Topy had been willing to go and help John.

Maria still wasn't well the following morning with a bad throat and chest so we made our own way to church without her company. The sermon was based on Matthew 7:13-14, "*Enter through the narrow gate. For wide is the gate and broad is the road that leads to destruction, and many enter through it. But small is the gate and narrow the road that leads to life, and only a few find it.*"

I reflected on the choices I had made in life. I had a choice to listen to God's call on my life or not, to go to church back in 1987 when I realised I knew nothing about God or the Bible. I felt foolish at the time but it was the best choice I ever made. I chose to follow Christ. At the time it seemed like the hardest step to take, but it cost me nothing. It cost Jesus his life.

In town afterwards we met John's sister, Helen, who had come from Kampala to visit him in hospital. It was extremely hot as we walked with her. We met Gordon and he informed us that Macclesfield, our home town football team, had just lost 5-1. I couldn't believe he had the results of the match so soon.

John was looking a lot better when we found him on the ward. He had been given injections every day, and the older girls from 'Maria's Care' had made a rota and visited him regularly with food, clothes, and clean sheets.

At home, Maria was feeling better too and ventured into town on her battery-operated scooter. We walked either side of her and felt like her entourage; me with an umbrella and Sandra with a torch. As I look back, I think this trip was all about supporting Maria and catching up with the children and events taking place in the compound. When she stopped and went in a little drug shop with Sandra, I took the opportunity of having a go on her scooter. I had never done this before and had no idea what to push when. I pressed a button thinking I would go back but to my surprise shot forward. I didn't have another chance because Maria came out of the shop.

With Maria on the road to recovery we decided to take a trip to Bukungu Village and prepared a picnic for the journey. Maria coughed and coughed as we sat in the *matatu*. She asked, so I thought, for a nasal spray, so off I went to the drug store to get her one. Whilst I waited in the queue I looked around at all the pills and potions. A large poster hung on the wall:

HOW TO KEEP YOUR FAMILY WORM FREE

It had detailed pictures of what happens when you take the de-worming mixture, how it travels through the digestive system, and works in the stomach to the end result of sitting over a pit latrine...hmm.

Eventually, I bought the nasal spray and took it back to Maria. She roared with laughter; she had wanted throat lozenges. We waited for over an hour for the *matatu* to leave but eventually the bus filled up and we left. It proved to be yet another eventful trip.

This time we discovered that two people were sitting on the roof of our *matatu*. The weather had been appalling; it had rained for weeks and the main road had disintegrated. We had been travelling for over an hour when the driver instructed us all to get out, though he made an exception for Maria. The *matatu* was stuck in the wet, muddy road so we all had to get out and push. Maria had quite an eventful time inside the bus as well as it swayed from one side to the other; she said it was like being on the dodgems!

As we all squeezed back on board, I felt something tickling my leg; I couldn't see what it was but my imagination was running overtime with thoughts of snakes or poisonous spiders. To this day, I have no idea what it was but I lived to tell the tale. We had only driven a few miles further when the bus broke down in the middle of nowhere but thankfully we had the shade of a tree to group under until the driver worked his magic and we got going again.

I watched a herd of twenty or more longhorn bulls pass by; they looked so dangerous. I thought how life was always full of surprises and there was never a dull moment. A man rode by taking a big fat black pig for a ride on the back of his bike; it was wrapped in banana leaves with its tail wagging like a dog.

After two hours, we arrived at Lake Kyogo in Bukungu. The water level had changed and was further in than last time I had visited. We sat under a beautiful tree full of blossom and ate our well-deserved picnic.

The same old man from before came out of the brick building near the lake and greeted Maria. We signed the visitors' book again and I found our signatures from 1996. It was a beautiful place; we enjoyed our food as we looked over the lake. Little boats bobbed up and down waiting for their owners to take them out on a fishing trip.

Maria, Sandra and Michelle, a young student we met, went in a boat on the lake; I chickened out after last year's performance which was enough to last me a lifetime. I walked around the village chatting to people who were mending fishing nets, playing with their babies, and doing the washing. I watched women counting hundreds of fish into some beautifully woven baskets; I was rather tempted to start counting aloud, 305-320-340 but resisted.

The vegetables had been displayed in amazing patterns on a wooden bench. Next door was the butchers; well, I think that's what it was! There was a whole cow cut up and displayed across a grassy table, including tripe, hooves, and the cows head. A large Ludo board was precariously balanced on a small stool and men sat around concentrating intently as they played the game. I wandered back to the lake past the now derelict Rwandan refugee mud huts. Some were incredibly small; about two - three feet across, with tin doors and huge padlocks on them. One big puff of wind and they would be over.

We all met and drank soda under a tree; the children were so friendly and shouted '*Jambo, Jambo*' and the women seated by their front doors greeted us.

Fortunately for me, I found a toilet. What relief, when you have to go you have to go! I opened the door to come out and a lady was standing there with water, soap and a hand towel. How thoughtful.

The bus driver called us over and said we had to leave in order to pick up a prisoner and take him to the police station. Can you imagine that happening in England?

The prisoner's hands were tied with a big rope behind his back and the policeman held onto the other end as they sat behind us. I wondered what he had done; stolen food, raped, beaten or killed someone, maybe he had been drunk and disorderly? We eventually arrived at the police station and he and the policeman disappeared inside.

We had a bumpy ride back to Kamuli, we couldn't shut the window due to a bike attached to the back of the bus and sticking through it so we ended up covered in dust. We saw some turkeys for sale and wondered as we were now experts at handling ducks, whether we should chance taking a turkey back with us; we thought better of it and didn't bother. We arrived safely in Kamuli after another great adventure and Maria felt much better after her enjoyable day out.

That evening I altered a white jacket for Maria because the rats had chewed through the top of the sleeve. I sewed a patch on each side so it didn't look odd. We don't encounter rats eating our clothes in England!

I woke in the small hours to the sound of heavy rain on the roof; once I had identified the sound I fell asleep again. The next sound I was aware of was Maria getting her scooter out of the tin garage; she was leaving to visit John in hospital; he had been sick in the night and she wanted to comfort him. One of our girls, Faith, wanted Maria to go with her to Namasagali High School to speak to the headmaster and ask if there was a place for her to study there so Maria had a full day ahead of her. (Faith was sponsored by the Stockport Soroptomist society, who helped to give her a good education. She is now a teacher, married to a pastor, and they now have two children).

Sandra and I spent the day at the school; we took photos of the little ones in the crèche, and watched students making crafts for sale, or sewing school uniforms. Maria had bought yards and yards of mattress cover material and the girls were busy measuring it out. Another class were learning bookkeeping skills.

In fact, we popped into all the classrooms to encourage the teachers. What a different atmosphere from last year; new teachers and, praise God, they didn't use a stick on the children. It was a common practice in Uganda for teachers to use a stick to hit or beat the children; we suspected it had been going on in our school and had advised the staff it was a sackable offence if it happened. Now there was a wonderful sense of peace, respect and contentment in the compound, I was so thankful.

In the primary school we met with Christopher, the bursar, and his secretary. A large amount of money had been used to finish 'God's Miracle.' Electrical equipment had been bought along with pipes for plumbing, the toilet and cistern, and bricks for the pits that took the waste away from the bathroom and kitchen.

We chatted to the staff and helpers in the sewing room. I set my favourite machine up and finished Maria's jacket whilst we talked about threads, scissors and paintings. Sandra decided to have a special cupboard made for the art and craft work so the materials wouldn't get eaten by the rats who loved to make a meal out of anything they could find.

We had lunch and then spent the next two hours with Beatrice in the office sorting out the details of all the sponsored children and checking I had taken photos of each one.

We then went to visit John in hospital; he had taken a turn for the worse and I felt so sorry for him; it was nearly ninety degrees inside and he looked terrible. Faith arrived to ask what food John wanted to eat; in Uganda the nurse only looks at the patient and says what is wrong with them, the patient has to have his own carer to wash, cook, feed, do toiletry duties, and administer pills, etc. That's why we had three other girls on a rota.

It was dusk and we slowly walked back to Maria's house; it had been a long day. I hadn't taken my torch because I hadn't intended being out so long so we had a tricky walk back with no overhead lights to guide our footsteps.

Maria organised a small pick-up truck the next day to take John and his sister to Jinja Hospital as he was getting worse. We collected him from Kamuli Hospital and put all his belongings in the truck. I hadn't appreciated that we had to take everything with us; we rolled his mattress up, two blankets and sheets, two pillows, a plastic bowl, wastepaper basket, water container, mat and plastic cup, soap, toilet paper, toothbrush and paste. Everything went into the open truck followed by me, Sandra and John's sister Faith. Maria, the driver and John sat inside the cab.

We put the mattress on top of the mat and settled down quickly with the two pillows behind us. I realise now how God protected us from catching TB ourselves.

This is the way to travel! I thought, as we sped along the road watching the exquisite scenery fly by each side of us. We drank it all in; the villages, plantations, tea bushes one side, sugar cane on the other. We seemed to swerve all over the road as the driver tried to avoid the pot-holes. Huge trees were stacked at the side of the road, waiting to be collected to be made into telegraph poles.

Again I thought how wonderful it would be to bring people from England to see all this, and started planning trips in my mind.

Eventually, we reached Jinja and St Frances Leprosy Clinic at Buluba. Maria went to the main office, while the rest of us were sent to outpatients. John was weighed, forms were completed and then he was taken across a field (yes, a field) to another ward. By this time he was looking dreadful and could hardly stand up, I was completely out of my depth and was very glad Sandra was with us. Maria spoke to a nurse about him being admitted but there were no beds free and they had to decide what they were going to do with him. Maria knew this decision could take hours so we left Sandra with John and went into Jinja.

Maria dashed off to retrieve Christmas boxes (although it was now March). She had met a man the week before who asked her how many children she was looking after. He had boxes left over from the consignment of Samaritans Purse Christmas Boxes. They had arrived late due to floods between Mombassa and Kampala in December; the bridges had collapsed preventing hundreds of vehicles from reaching their destination on time.

Maria was thrilled to be offered these boxes for her children, and she received about two hundred and fifty shoe boxes all neatly marked with BOY or GIRL and the appropriate age.

Maria was so excited: "God's timing is perfect, we have the truck with us," she laughed.

We popped in to see a Ugandan couple called Rose and James who had set up their own project looking after orphans in 1984. They were both doing this before they married and felt God was asking them to continue. We met Maria's friend, Andrew, in the office of the Busoga Trust Water; he bought us some juice and then drove us to the leprosy hospital to collect Sandra.

We found her and John by the canteen resting under a tree. She was pleased to see us and said we had to wait for John's sputum results but there were still no free beds. Maria made a suggestion that the hospital accepted; we put John's mattress and mat down in the middle of the ward, and he was to stay there until a bed became vacant. I felt so sad leaving him on that mattress, but knew he was in the best place. Maria paid £10 for a week's treatment in advance for John; nothing was free.

It was late by the time we arrived at the Busoga Guest House. I felt in desperate need of a shower; I put a plastic hook on the back of the door (it's a little quirk I have, I always carry plastic hooks with me because the Ugandans never think of putting them on the back of bathroom doors for *bazungu* to hang towels or night clothes up).

We took the opportunity, whilst in Jinja, to visit Busoga College Mwiri where we were given a warm welcome, and shown boxes of computers. Manchester Grammar School has had links with this college for years and had sent a consignment of computers to Uganda from their students. They would be pleased to know the boxes had been released from customs.

As we drove back down the hill, Maria asked the driver to stop because she wanted to visit the Good Shepherd Children's Home at Wairaka. Two students showed us around; we went upstairs into a room that had seven sets of triple-deck bunk beds; I had never seen so many beds before in such a small room. Apparently there were mattresses under the beds as well. At night the mattresses were put in the middle of the floor so other children could sleep on them. I was told that forty children slept in that room each night and the air was often stifling. I am not at all surprised, but at least these children were safe and loved.

Outside, women helped the children do their washing and there was food cooking in a huge cauldron over stones with naked flames. In the house there was a large dining room that was also used for praise and worship meetings. The man who ran the place sat in a wheelchair on the veranda giving simple instructions to various people; he had had both of his legs amputated.

I was able to give out balloons, pens, cards and stationery to try and make their lives a little easier. In the kitchen I gave them tea towels and cotton threads and needles to the man on the sewing machine. They were all thrilled with the little we had given them. Two helpers asked if they could come and visit our project in Kamuli so we exchanged addresses then drove on to the YWAM compound.

'Youth With A Mission' was a very different set-up. They showed us their goat project, kitchen (Maria liked the idea of how they had built the cooking area) bakery, orphanage, and school. We ate our picnic in the prayer garden, which was something else Maria found attractive.

Whilst I sat in the prayer garden, I wrote my diary and read 'Word for Today'.... *"And now, O Israel, what does the Lord your God ask of you but to fear the Lord your God, to walk in all his ways, to love him, to serve the Lord your God with all your heart and with all your soul..."* Deuteronomy 10:12.

I knew God was talking to me but had no idea what he wanted me to do; all I knew was I had to keep listening to his still small voice and be obedient.

We were met with frantic scenes as we headed back into Jinja town centre; President Clinton and his wife Hilary were due in two days time and all the shops on the main high street had to be painted. We were told that if shop owners didn't comply they had been threatened with closure or non-renewal of their trading licence. Some could hardly put food on the family table never mind paint the building. Everyone was out scraping paint off walls and repainting them in mainly blue and white colours.

The Call, the Cost, the Choice

The traffic system was almost at a standstill because workmen were using machines to break the 'sleeping policemen' up, and then resurface the road so the President's car wouldn't have to go over any bumps. The daft thing was that a few days later the President arrived and didn't go anywhere near that roundabout! This was such a waste of time and money.

It seemed so ridiculous that thousands of pounds had to be spent on all this work when the people themselves were suffering so much; President Clinton drove along the main street, waved to a few people and that was that. It's a crazy world! I felt he would miss all the everyday things that these people have to deal with.

We eventually reached Jinja Main Street. Top of Maria's to-do list was the cockroach problem; she wanted to get some moth balls to prevent them coming up the drains. Candles, matches, washing-up liquid, coffee and bread were also needed. All these things we could buy in Jinja but not Kamuli. (It has all changed in Kamuli now; we can get most things there, even salt bread).

Back in Kamuli, Maria went to the hospital to get John's records, and said she would meet us later after having a shower at Gordon's. Sandra and I went home, showered and met Michelle at the Country Club.

Michelle was a young lady we had met earlier in the week; we chatted till Maria and Gordon arrived. Gordon had invited a few of his medical friends from the hospital. We had a leaving party for a Dutch surgeon who just happened to have performed an appendectomy that day on one of our children, Peter.

Peter was ten years old when he lived in Gulu; he hid under his bed as men killed both his parents. He was totally traumatised as he silently lay there for many hours. He slowly crawled out and escaped from the little hut in the village, got a ride in the back of a truck from Gulu to Jinja where some people who owned a baker's shop took him in. He worked for them in the day and slept under the counter at night. In time he ran away to Kamuli and survived by begging for food and sleeping under shop buildings. Eventually a welfare officer caught up with him and suggested he went to live at 'Maria's Care'.

He was a quiet boy but street-wise and with Maria's help, he started to settle down. Maria had to be councillor, mother, provider and encourager to him but she trusted God for every situation she was placed in. Peter lived in the boys' dormitory with about twenty others; he went to school and really enjoyed drawing.

Whilst we were all out in Jinja, Peter had been taken to hospital by a visitor to the compound. This was amazing in itself because 'Maria's Care' rarely had anyone visit with a vehicle; people usually walked or got dropped off by *boda-bodas*.

The doctor had examined Peter, recognised the symptoms of appendicitis and operated straight away. He told us Peter was in a bad condition and had developed peritonitis. I thanked him and said we would visit the next day.

We managed to track Peter down at the hospital; he looked grim to say the least. He lay there, a skinny, limp body. He had a horrible black tube coming out of his side which was leaking yellow pus.

"He is going to die," said the nurse.

I couldn't believe my ears and with a knee jerk reaction I said:

"Oh no, he's not! God is a healer and we are going to pray for him."

The nurse agreed and called some of her friends; we stood round his bed and prayed for God to put his healing hand upon Peter. We bathed his head and left.

The next day Peter was asking the nurses for soda and boiled eggs and a few days after that he was sent home to recuperate. Praise the Lord!

Peter is now a healthy young man; he went to school in Jinja and regularly attended the local church. He passed his 'A' levels and went on to study human resource management, graduating from Kampala International University in November, 2011. I believe God has an amazing plan for Peter's life as he went to such great lengths to heal him.

I reflected later that evening on the last few days and saw the hand of God in each one directing us, protecting us, and making provision for all we had to do.

I dozed off, then suddenly opened my eyes. I couldn't believe it. I had been in Uganda three weeks, two days. Sandra would be going back to England in a week and I would be going in eleven days. Stop the world, it's moving too fast!

At 7.45am we were up, dressed, and making a picnic before Gordon arrived to take us to Bujagali Falls. We felt like royalty in his new red

The Call, the Cost, the Choice

Peugeot 405 limo, sheer luxury. The last time I went there it was free entry, this time we had to pay. Progress they call it!

Gordon then drove us over Owen Falls bridge to visit St Moses orphanage and school. A young man showed us around and we were all impressed with the set-up. Each house had a house-mother who looked after a dozen boys and girls. She did everything: washing, cooking, planting, and the children had a rota to help with all the activities. It was well organised but very western in its approach; the kitchen had a dual cooker of gas and electric just in case there was a power cut and I wondered how the children would cope once they were grown up and living back in villages where these luxuries didn't exist.

Outside each house there was a display of flowers growing and a small plot of land. The children helped to plant and harvest vegetables; everyone was out digging as the soil was nice and soft after the recent rain.

Next to the orphanage was a building where they made material. I was amazed to see six looms in action, producing a very good standard of weave. The students learnt how to make table mats, tea towels, curtains, cushion covers and throws to go over settees and chairs.

We had a cool drink of water while Maria told us about St Moses' Vocational Training School. Our students could go there to learn welding, electrical science, bricklaying, agriculture, cooking, childcare, arts and crafts, tailoring and textiles. It was a great opportunity for them.

On the way home, we stopped at the busy market in Kamuli. Sandra and I went off to buy groceries and a man asked us if we would like some brown bread. Would we ever! This was a new thing in Kamuli; he told us to order it and we would be able to pick it up on Monday. We were delighted.

I had an awful night's sleep; the house opposite was having a party and the music was blaring out till after dawn. I kept drifting off to sleep and then waking up again all through the night. I got up for breakfast just as an announcement came on the radio that the interviews were taking place for students who wanted to go to Namasagali College. Faith wanted to go there, so Maria went into action.

The first thing I did with Sandra that morning was to fill little bags with shampoo, soap, pens, needles and cotton threads. We put the teachers' names on ready to give them out in the evening as a parting gift. Sandra sorted out the medical supplies for different hospitals and clinics, and then sorted all the clothes and other gifts for the children.

We left Kamuli with Beatrice and went to visit the children we sponsored, after agreeing a price with the *boda-boda* men. They agreed to help us and we rode to many villages in remote parts of Kamuli; they were happy to wait whilst I took lots of photos of each child. Some lived miles out with grandmothers or a weak mother who couldn't manage to support her children.

We were taken a long way to the first child, way past the baptist church, down the hill faster than I had ever been before on the back of the *boda-boda*, then up the other side. We passed some buildings and turned right, (Beatrice informed us it was the local prison) then passed little mud huts around winding narrow paths and eventually came to a clearing and saw a little mud house and hut.

Beatrice introduced us to an elderly woman, the mother of Viola Mbwali and Matoma Smali. They lived in a place called Kiwolera Village; we could see children running from one mud hut through the bushes with the best little wooden seats for us to sit on. Viola's mum had five children and it looked as though she had another one on the way. She was so poor and had nothing but this little mud house and a few mats.

We left the village and headed back to Kamuli, as we approached the hill we got off the bikes and walked up, carrying on to Bulangaire Village where Ester Nangwe was living with her aunt as her grandmother was sick. When the aunt saw us she rushed off and got herself all neat and tidy; she displayed the lovely belt she was wearing, so it would look good in the picture.

Off we went again, up hill and down dale, a long way to Rubaga Village where we found Tibenda Eseza. She lived with her mother and brother Mpande Matege and other children including twins. They had no father. As we walked further into the bush, Sandra said:

"Rhona, what's that you have just stepped over?"

I looked down and picked up a long, strange,mangled thing; as we both examined the huge hard pod we realised it was a loofah. I was ecstatic as I had always thought a loofah came from the sea. We looked up and around and there high up on a vine wrapped around a tree was another loofah. A young girl called Lydia got a huge branch and I held it with her as it was so heavy; we knocked the loofah off the vine together and then her uncle got two more. This was going to be one of the highlights of my future talks in England. I just knew it!

Loofahs are called *ebwango* (plural) or *ekwango* (singular). They grow on a vine wrapped around a tree or a bush as parasites feeding off other plants and are soft and green like a cucumber. The sun dries them and they become brown and hard on the outside and then fall off the vine. The local people peel the outside off, take all the seeds out and cut them open forming something that resembles a fish; and we use them in the bath. Even after all these years, I can still get very excited about this amazing find.

I was a happy girl! What had we come to this village for? Oh yes, to meet the children and their families.

We chatted to the uncle who told us Lydia's grandmother had died and the grandfather was nearly eighty-five. I took a photo of Lydia for her sponsor.

We visited Barbara Bumpi in her home where she lived with a very sick grandmother and auntie, the uncle was well but between them they had a lot to manage. Barbara dashed into her home and put on a clean dress for the photo, I told her she was a lovely girl with very special sponsors who were good friends of mine; her smile reached from ear to ear.

We were invited into the mud hut to meet the two ladies. It was so dark in there that it took me a while for my eyes to adjust, then I saw a frail lady in a bed made from wood laid across a frame covered with straw; a few tatty blankets covered her. She held her hand out; I took it and held onto it for ages as I looked into her eyes. Without exchanging any words, I could read her pain. With tears in my eyes, I could hardly focus. Sandra followed and looked at the little bottles of tablets which had been prescribed; she said they were the right tablets and dosage for her condition. I shook the aunt's hand and smiled at her; we offered to pray for them both and, even though we didn't speak the same language, they knew we were praying for them. Our hearts were one.

Three seats suddenly appeared. We sat for about ten minutes and as I looked around, I could see light through the corrugated tin roof; which meant that when it rained water would come into the house. There were a few old, used plastic plates and cups and a baby lay fast asleep on a straw mat completely wrapped in a green sheet including over his head; this was to keep flies, mosquitoes and creepy things away from him. I took photos of Barbara with her uncle, who helped look after her and her brothers Twaha and Amusa; now called Andrew and Tom (because they had both become Christians and wanted new names). Andrew had suddenly appeared and quickly changed, I hadn't got the heart to leave him out as he had gone to so much trouble but I had already taken a photo of him a few days ago at school.

We travelled to Bukwege where Tades Jude lived with his mother who was quite ill; she was also looking after Regina's daughter. Regina was one of the first girls who Maria had taken under her wing. Some ladies went for soda and *mandazas* and brought Jude back with them. I was thrilled to see this lovely young man standing in front of me; he was eighteen years old and wanted to study to become an architect. We all sat in a little open mud hut drinking a soda. Sandra took a few photos of us sitting there just before the heavens opened and the rain came down.

When the rain had passed we went to Budumbula Village and took photos of Lydia Bakaira, a lovely young lady who lived with her sister and various aunties in an old, falling down brick house. Lydia was later able to study to become a midwife with the help of CRU sponsorship. We tried to chat to some of the family; I took a photo of a little girl in a blue tunic grinding wheat flour with a pestle and mortar. I took a close-up picture as I was standing just above her head.

We saw a lady cooking with a pot using banana leaves as the lid. We ran out of time with still so many people to visit. As we rode back we turned the corner onto the main road and saw a cow's hide being dried in the sun. It had been stretched out, pulled, and tied between three posts.

We continued along the road towards Kamuli roundabout. On the right behind the electricity pylons we walked around the land belonging to 'Maria's Care', where the children were growing vegetables, paw-paw and sweet potatoes; they tended the plot every Saturday and enjoyed eating the vegetables during the week. The *boda-boda* men took a picture of Sandra and me standing with Beatrice at the gate. I think these men were very grateful we had ended our journey as we had been out for nearly five hours. Once we returned to school, Beatrice took on her secretarial role and discussed how much the day's travelling had cost.

It really matters to have cool water after being out for the day; at home we take so much for granted but, without electricity or fridge, to sample cool water poured from a gourd is divine. We walked into 'God's Miracle' and we were given a glass of cool water which was very welcome, then ate a lovely meal consisting of rice, chapattis and green vegetables.

I know I mention food and drink so often, but it plays a large part in our lives. Some people have only one meal a day which could just be *posho*, a very thin type of porridge with very little taste; the consistency and colour look like wallpaper paste.

The children gathered at the gate with different-sized containers on their heads or in their hands and we walked down to a free-flowing stream where they bent down and collected the water. I looked up towards the grassy hill and could see children disappearing into the distance with jerry-cans on their heads; it looked very funny at times as all I could see were the bright yellow cans bobbing up and down just above the tall grass.

We walked back up the road in the dark, our footsteps guided by the moon, and we could see little candles glowing in mud huts, their flames flickering in the soft breeze. The electricity was off again. Our senses were heightened; we could hear fascinating and unidentifiable noises and discussed what we thought each one was. This was an experience I could never capture in a photograph.

Sandra made Maria breakfast as it was Mothering Sunday and Maria didn't feel like getting up. We walked to church and stopped at the crossroad because a huge crowd had gathered around a woman who was nearly naked. She was throwing herself all over the place lashing out at the crowd as they laughed and taunted her. One of our pupils said she was mad; I felt so sad seeing her in this state.

I shooed a few people away: "Leave her alone. Go on. move, and leave her alone."

The church slowly filled up as more people came in carrying benches from home with them; there were about sixty adults and twenty-four children.

I had a stirring in my spirit that I should go and do something for the 'mad' lady. I smiled at Sandra and said I would be back in a few minutes; I dashed back to the crossroad, and found she was still there. I felt in my heart I should try to clothe and feed her, so I bought a long colourful wrap and a bunch of bananas. As I approached her she was still lashing out.

I prayed aloud: "In the name of Jesus be healed, in the name of Jesus be still. Lord, please help me clothe this woman. Help me, Lord."

As the woman came closer to me, spitting and lashing out, I continued to use the name of Jesus and put the wrap around her; she quietened down when she realised I wasn't like the others and we sat together as I peeled a banana. Only then did I realise what a bad state she was in; she shoved the whole banana in her mouth and tried to chew it with hardly any teeth. She took the bunch from me and threw some bananas at the crowd that had gathered around us. She eventually got up, stumbled and walked away from them; I think and hope a little more content than before.

I returned to church and, after the service was over, we strolled in the heat to the Nile Hotel; rather a grand title for a little corrugated café with tables made of a plank of wood over a couple of beer crates. We sat on three-legged stools and ate our omelettes.

Back at the school we met the art and craft teacher who had arranged for us to go and see Patrick, the tree bark man. We climbed on the back of the *boda-bodas* and off we went. I must admit I do love doing this, down the huge hill at a rate of knots and up the other side. Suddenly, I gave a little 'yelp' as we went into a pot-hole and nearly lost our balance!

We arrived at Patrick's place; he and his wife didn't speak English but fortunately we had an interpreter. Patrick took us into a field and with a sharp axe demonstrated how to cut the tree down. As usual I was taking photos and hadn't estimated how swiftly the tree was going to fall; it missed me by about ten inches! I was startled and jumped out of the way as the whoosh of branches passed my ears. He used a sharp knife to score the whole tree trunk from top to bottom, and then with the axe he gently persuaded the bark off the branch in one piece; then held it up for me to take a photo.

He then shredded the rough bark off to expose the fresh new bark underneath. To begin with it was white but, just like an apple when you leave it for a few minutes, it started to go brown. I clicked away with my camera as he began to beat the bark with a homemade, wooden hammer. The bark expanded as Patrick hammered it from left to right, then called his son and they sat with their feet touching as they gently pulled the bark cloth (like we would when folding and straightening a sheet that had just come from the washing line.) Eventually when Patrick thought they couldn't pull it any longer in case it tore, he collected a few small rocks and placed them on top of the bark cloth stretched on the ground to dry. The stones helped keep the cloth in place and stopped it from shrinking.

The Call, the Cost, the Choice

We stood riveted, watching this fascinating demonstration.

Patrick's wife, Namukose Fidha, then demonstrated how she made the clay pots; she sat in the doorway of her little mud hut and pulled out clay from under some plastic and rolled it around on a smooth broken bit of what looked like coconut shell to make the base. Then she rolled the clay into long sausages and continually wrapped it round and round, dipping her fingers in water and fusing the joins together with a swift action of her thumbs, fingers and a flat seedpod. Then she trimmed the top and shaped the vessel. She dipped her finger into a terracotta-colour liquid and coated the new pot. We found out later this concoction was made with water and ant hill soil mixed together into a paste. For decoration she twisted a bit of plastic and rolled it around the pot to make an extraordinary pattern. I was enthralled, so simple yet so effective.

Patrick told us he would bring the bark cloth when it was dry and two little pots for us to take back to England. We told him that we would develop the photos in England and send them back, which we did.

We decided to take the opportunity to visit a boy we sponsored called Alone who had been out when we had visited before, to take a photo. He shot inside to change and came out of his little mud house looking so smart and grinning from ear to ear. His mother looked frail, sick, and fed up; she was about five months pregnant. We noticed that she had bark trees growing on her land; there are only certain trees that can be used to make cloth so they are very precious. We talked to her about selling them to Patrick; in that way it would give her a small income and keep Patrick in business.

We rode back and, just before we shot down a hill we stopped at a little nursery and bought five small trees for Adam's Prayer Garden. Friends of mine in England had given me money to commemorate the sad death of their first baby; they wanted a prayer garden made in 'Maria's Care.' I later bought lots of other small plants and some of the children helped me plant them. We made seats and a table out of a tree trunk that had been chopped down so people could sit in what became known as 'Adam's Prayer Garden', to be apart from the hustle and bustle of life, to read, and to pray. Later one of the teachers came with two little hand-made dolls to give as a thank you to my friends.

I had the pleasure of carrying the box of plants on my knees all the way down the hill and nearly up the other side. We reached the gates of 'Maria's Care' after a wonderful few hours.

Some of the children were watching the video I had made with staff and pupils from Hurdsfield Primary School. The Ugandan children were fascinated by the scenery and buildings around the school and by all the different activities the children were doing. They re-wound the video and watched it again several times after that.

Maria was up and out by 6.30am the next morning, Sandra and I weren't quite so eager! We spent time gathering together all the things we had in our cupboards for the children at school and the staff at the clinic.

In the afternoon, we met Maria at the taxi park and went with her to Jinja to visit Jackie Hodgkins at the Welcome Home Children's Centre. Jackie showed us around and introduced us to the work they did there. She had some incredible stories to tell; she rescued babies that were dying or left on the road; one baby girl had been strangled by her mother who couldn't afford to keep her but she was rescued and lived. Another baby was left on the side of the road in a black plastic bag; Jackie walked past the bag and saw it move; she looked in and there was the newborn baby. Another one was left outside her house with clothes and a note saying, 'Please look after my baby.'

We met Irene, a lovely well-spoken Ugandan lady in her forties. At one time she had been in politics and studied in England, now she was decorating a huge lounge for Jackie's fiftieth birthday party. We were invited to join in the celebration; Sandra declined as she felt she needed to meet with a nurse to discuss medical supplies but Maria and I were up for it.

With the party due to start at 6pm the usual cry from most women was heard from me:

"Whatever shall I wear?"

Irene took me by the hand and led me to her room, she offered me a shower which was very welcoming, and opened her wardrobe. Handing me an outfit, she said:

"Here you can wear this, I have chosen this for you, and it goes well together; here are the shoes."

I showered, dressed, and felt the bees' knees. I did look smart.

We ate spaghetti bolognaise, rice, salads, different meats, french sticks and real butter, followed by pineapple, birthday cake and another chocolate cake. What a feast! Then we watched Jackie open her presents; she was fasting at the time so gave us her chocolates to eat. We managed to force them down!

Eventually, the last three babies were fed and changed and by midnight we had all turned in and the house settled down. Maria and I were accommodated in comfortable beds and given T-shirts to sleep in and a toothbrush and towel each.

Maria and I prayed together at the start of every new day. Jackie came to us and said she had heard on the radio that a woman in a local village had given birth to sextuplets but that two had died. Jackie wanted to see this for herself and provide help if needed. We drove to one village asking different people about the woman who had given birth to sextuplets and received a variety of answers including the rumour that she had had five babies; one that talked, one that looked like a chicken, and the rest died at birth.

We decided to abandon this idea and drove to another village where a woman had died in childbirth nine months previous having had twins. One weighed 3.7 kilograms the other 4.5 kilograms; I recalled how my daughters were heavier than that at birth, never mind nine months later. The twins were severely malnourished; their father and grandmother had done what they could, but were only able to feed them on thin watered down milk.

The father agreed to Jackie's help and she explained to him that she could look after them till they were about two years old and strong, then she would bring them back to the village. If he didn't think he could manage them then, she would look after them till they were six and put them up for adoption in another village. We drove the father and twins, whom Jackie named Faith and Hope, to the probation officer and spent the morning there going through the legalities and form filling.

We took the babies for a medical examination at Jinja Hospital. I took photos of them being weighed; they looked so sad and pathetic. The twins had the TB, polio, and tetanus injection but needed to come back another time for the measles vaccination. I sat on a bench and watched all the comings and goings of porters, staff and relatives in the hospital. Next to me an urn started to boil, I hoped maybe we could be in for a coffee; no chance!

Each baby had a blood test; the haemoglobin count for one was 6.5, the other 7.7. Apparently the count should be between 12 and 14. Both girls had pneumonia; Faith also had malaria and Hope a fever with a temperature of 102 degrees. We collected their medicine and drove to the Welcome Home Children's Centre. The father returned to the village and said he would keep in touch with Jackie. Irene was delighted to see the twins and got a bottle and medicine ready to feed them. I held the babies one in each arm and had a photo taken under a tree outside the home.

I needed to get back to Kamuli and was dropped off at the taxi park. Clutching my bottle of water I boarded the *matatu*. As we left I could see the newly-painted High Street; flags decorated many shop fronts and hung limply on the flag poles as there was no breeze.

There was a lot of excitement going on as President Clinton and Hilary were due to visit. Flowers suddenly popped up in the middle of Jinja High Street; they had been planted the night before. New road signs and advertising boards with travel, lager, bedding, etc, on them had also gone up overnight. The whole place was a buzz of activity; men filled in holes in the road, while others were painting, gardening and setting out stalls.

I reached Kamuli mid-afternoon and dashed around the compound taking photos of children I had missed previously. We were going to celebrate Maria's seventy-second birthday that afternoon and I had so much to do before the party started. I walked past the kitchen and popped my head in to check on Maria's cake, it looked scrumptious. Next on my list was the office to discuss the sponsors' thank you letters with Beatrice and to make sure I had the right code on the photo of each child so I could match them with the proper sponsor.

Sandra had organised the decorating of the dining room which looked so colourful with all the new Christmas decorations up. She had ordered soda for everyone and Aunt Rose had prepared a feast. I was ushered to my seat next to Maria on the top table.

As the food appeared from the kitchen Maria asked what happened to the duck.

"They killed it this afternoon," a little boy shouted.

Whoops, I think Maria was sorry she asked; now we were eating 'Daffy' our duck. I must admit it was delicious, with rice, greens and Irish potatoes.

After the party, the little children shot off to bed and we read them a bedtime story in their dormitory. We distributed gifts to the children and staff so that everyone received something; bras, toiletries, pens, diaries, sweets and posters. It was like Christmas all over again.

Sandra and I only had one torch between us so decided to make tracks whilst it was still dusk. We strolled along watching the beautiful bright-red fire-flies dancing around.

Maria joined us and we all sat on the veranda enjoying our last drink and chat together in Kamuli. Maria had decided it would be nice for Sandra to have a few days rest before returning to England and, as there was so much to do in Kampala; it wasn't worth Maria or I coming back to Kamuli as I would be leaving the following week anyway.

In the middle of the night the heavens opened and I remembered my loofah drying on the roof outside. I grabbed the key, opened the back door and nearly stood on a huge toad on the doorstep; it gave me such a fright. Thankfully I saw it in time and stepped over it. I retrieved the loofah and locked up leaving the toad to enjoy the much needed rain.

I set off on my own that last morning in Kamuli to visit Richard the dentist. He told me he had written to many people in England and had received no replies; he wondered if the letters had got through. He had asked people to send any old equipment as he was desperate for anything: posters, gloves, models of teeth to do demonstrations with...

It was an incredibly hot day. I said my goodbyes to him and then crossed the road to get some photocopying done. Suddenly my flip-flop broke and I stood there not quite knowing what I was going to do. I put my foot on the tarmac; it was red hot. I stood like a stork on one foot and looked around to see if I could see a shop. No, nothing.

Now what? I thought.

Just then a little girl shot over from the other side of the roundabout; she had seen my dilemma and come to my rescue. She took her oversized flip flop off her foot and chucked it down for me. With tears in my eyes, I put it on and praised God. I told her she was an angel sent from heaven but she couldn't understand me; she kept smiling as we walked hand-in-hand to the nearest shop. I bought a new pair of flip-flops and handed hers back, along with my old pair that I knew she would find a use for. She was happy and so was I. What a God incidence that child was in the right place at the right time and had a good heart.

I popped into the Nile Hotel and gave them two Guinness towel bar mats; the man was over the moon and asked me how much I wanted for them.

"Nothing," I said, "they are a gift." He was very pleased with that.

I walked back to school and paid for the crafts they had made for me to take back to England. I was moving fast as I had so much to do in a very short time. My next visit was to the class for the deaf. Maria had wanted to help a shy, deaf girl called Harriet grow in confidence so she encouraged her to help with the little children and eventually set up a special area for the hard of hearing. That was the beginning of Maria's vision for the deaf children coming to fruition.

The teachers were marvellous with the children as they were doing a specialised job. There were lots of pictures on the wall and on the table were objects to feel, count, and look at. This room was the most colourful of all in the compound as the deaf children needed to have visual aids around them; I took some photos so people in England could see how we had progressed.

I arrived at 'Maria's Care' just in time to eat, put my clean clothes in the suitcase, and lock up Maria's house. I looked at it and knew I would be back, I was certain God had a purpose for me in Uganda. With all the experiences he had taught me so much.

We piled on the *boda-bodas* with our luggage and arrived at Kamuli Taxi Park just as a bus was waiting to leave. I didn't think for one moment that he would fit us and our entire luggage in, but thankfully we did. Suddenly I remembered I needed a new film for my camera and asked the driver to please wait. If I didn't get a film I would have withdrawal symptoms. I eventually found a film and got back to the bus. Sandra was sitting in the front seat so I jumped in beside her just as a young man appeared at my open window:

"Where's my money, you pay me?"

I looked at him and wondered what on earth was he was talking about. Then it dawned on me that with all the running around I had done, I hadn't paid for the *boda-boda* ride. Silly me!

During the bus journey, I reflected on some of the things we had done and seen over the last few weeks: the children, the village visits, Peter and John in hospital, now both improving. I remembered the children in the school and others who had been sick, the fun during meal times, and the duck. So many memories made me smile.

The Call, the Cost, the Choice

I spoke to Sandra about the time she was standing in my lounge talking about coming to Uganda; it didn't seem five minutes ago and now she was going back to England after three weeks here.

We arrived in Jinja, unloaded our luggage and watched the world go by. You could come to Jinja and sit on a *matatu* and have everything you wanted to buy come to the window: newspapers, plates, cups, watches, cutlery, earrings, jewellery, clothes, soda, water, bread and biscuits, body lotions, creams, shampoo, safety pins, toothpaste and soap.

Maria appeared all of a flurry through a gap in the wall, beckoned us and off we went like two obedient little puppies following their master. We jumped on a well-upholstered *matatu* for once, and sat together on the back seat with the luggage underneath and behind us.

The journey from Jinja to Kampala was interesting as usual; we passed a man with a single bed strapped to the back of his bike, another had a plank of wood and what looked like rags of bark cloth tied onto it; we found out later it was a dead body that needed to be transported back to the village they hailed from. Ivy met us at the main railway station, and we returned with her to her house. We loved staying with her and her husband Dick because it was nice and cosy and Ivy always told us to make ourselves at home; we had a shower, read, and relaxed.

That night there were several guests for the evening meal. Ivy made a wonderful buffet of rice, matooke, peanut sauce, meat and vegetables. We all had to sit next to someone we didn't know and it was good chatting and finding out why others were in Uganda.

Dick kindly invited Maria and I to stay at their house after Sandra had left for England and we gratefully accepted. After homemade waffles for breakfast, Ivy drove us to Kampala Taxi Park and we boarded a *matatu* to Entebbe. Because of Bill Clinton's visit, there were flags flying everywhere in Kampala; buildings had been painted or renovated and streets cleaned, the place was 100% better than I had ever seen it look before, but at what cost?

We decided to visit the botanic gardens in Entebbe and walked through some stunning scenery with Lake Victoria as the backdrop. Words cannot describe the sheer beauty; the sun shone through the trees and glistened on the water, it was warm and peaceful, we could hear the birds singing, monkeys chatting to one another, and we smelt the aroma of mixed bark, grass, and a pile of leaves smouldering on a bonfire in a corner of the garden.

We continued up the slight incline and came to the back of the Imperial Hotel. The man with the key had gone (to quote a phrase!) and it took us fifteen minutes to walk all the way round to the front entrance where we saw a huge sign stretched across the top of the gate:

WELCOME TO PRESIDENT CLINTON AND ALL THE HONOURABLE GUESTS

That's us! I thought.

The day before there had been an official party in the hotel and we passed at least ten plush American cars and jeeps with the presidential flag on. One of the American security men held the keys to a car in front of our noses and asked if we would like to test drive one, Sandra went to take them and he quickly retracted them from her saying he was only joking. He did let us look through the windows of the President's car though. There were monkeys jumping on and off the vehicles; it was amusing to watch as the security men tried to shoo them away.

As we walked through the hotel foyer and banqueting room with its beautiful drapes and red leather upholstered chairs, I wished I had been a fly on the wall and witnessed the party in all its splendour. It was such a big occasion for the Ugandan people to host an American President on an official visit; Ugandans will talk about it for years to come and they will pass it on to their grandchildren and great-grandchildren.

From there we walked into Entebbe town where we sat and had a soda after which we got in a *matatu* and arrived in Garuga at Banana Village in time for a meal. The electricity had been on the whole time President Clinton had been in Entebbe but now he had gone it was off again so we had to eat by hurricane lamp.

After breakfast we caught a *matatu* to Lake Victoria Hotel and spent the day there. I caught up on writing to my daughters so Sandra could post the letters at home for me, Maria wrote a report to go in the next newsletter and we chatted and reflected on the things we had done together and our visions and dreams for the future, including fund raising possibilities.

All too soon we bid farewell to Sandra and went to spend the night at Banana Village. The power was off so we ate by candlelight and turned in early. I had a restless night; probably all the excitement of the day.

The minute I woke I thought of Sandra, who would be nearly home.

I wondered what the weather was like in England and who would greet her.

It was a beautiful day; the birds were singing, the sun shining. I looked at my Bible reading: *"He who delights in the Lord is like a tree planted by streams of water, which yields its fruit in season and whose leaf does not wither. Whatever he does prospers."* Psalm 1:3. I thought about this idea of bearing fruit, putting roots down to be nourished and fed. As we put our hand to the work of the Lord so he will prosper us. This is what Maria had been doing since she first came to Uganda. God was blessing her.

I spent time myself writing ideas for the newsletter and my report to the CRU committee. So much good to thank God for had taken place this year: sponsorship, future plans, food and water, volunteers, pupils' great achievements, scholarships and the cost of education, the children's welfare, their physical, spiritual and intellectual growth, the teachers, staff, compound, new constructions, progress, acknowledgments of money donated, new projects, visiting the villages. The list was endless.

Four little weaver birds flew in and out of my room as I tried to write up my daily journal; it took me over four hours and was still nowhere near complete. I always find condensing my stories a hard task!

We set off for Dick and Ivy's and managed to get there despite taking the wrong bus and ending up somewhere we didn't plan to be; Ivy had to rescue us and it was so nice to be in a place that felt like home.

I climbed into bed that night just as the neighbours started their all-night party; the one good thing about it was I was able to sing along to most of the 60's and 70's music they were playing. I rooted around in my suitcase and found my earplugs, shut the window and fell asleep to Lulu blaring out 'I want to shout, shout, shout.' Thankfully they did turn it down in the end.

A cat meowing outside my window woke me at 7am; I prayed it away and slept another hour.

We went with Dick and Ivy to their little church called Logogo Baptist Church. The church consisted of about eighty people including many children who sang to us with all the actions that they had practised earlier. Nelson and Jessica from the Gideons were at the church with four of their children; we had a lovely service.

We relaxed over the next few days and celebrated Maria's birthday... again! Amongst her presents were two tickets to go to the theatre the following night. I was thrilled because one of the tickets was for me.

Ivy tempted me with a new dish to try; *nsenene* (fried grasshoppers)! I couldn't imagine eating them but after bracing myself I did and they weren't too bad, not that I would rush out and buy more. Ivy took a photo as proof. Can you believe it? I pretended I was eating fried green peppers and once I had eaten one I ate the others in the bowl.

The night at the theatre was a charming way to round off my visit. We watched a performance of 'Joseph And His Amazing Technicolor Dream Coat' performed by students who went to Lincoln International School where Ivy worked. We had probably the best seats in the house; in the middle of the circle. The students performed well and we thoroughly enjoyed ourselves.

After a supper of soup and toast, I reluctantly put my light out on my last night in Uganda.

God had been consistently gracious to me in Uganda. I had seen and experienced so much and was sure that he would not let it all go to waste but wondered how he could use it all. I knew that as I trusted him step by step, he would reveal his plan to me. I was certainly excited about the future as I had many new photos and slides that would make my presentations so much more interesting.

After breakfast we loaded the van, gave Dick and Ivy a big hug and said a grateful 'thank you' as they had accommodated our needs in so many different ways whilst we had been staying with them.

Ivy drove us to Kampala Taxi Park in the middle of the city where we switched *matatus* for Entebbe and the Lake Victoria Hotel. Maria and I visited the local market and then camped out for the day by the hotel pool. We spent our last moments together in comfortable friendship before I escorted her to the main gates and watched her walk away. I thought of the way she jumped on and off buses, taxis, *piki-pikis* or *boda-bodas*. There isn't one single person she reminds me of; she is unique. Mind you she doesn't think she is seventy-two and that's probably the key to it all.

That evening Maria set off back to Kamuli, and I for England via Nairobi and Brussels.

We eventually arrived in Brussels and it took ages to get everyone off the plane and passports checked. In the ladies' room at the airport it was so refreshing to have a wash after not having hot water for such a long time. I emerged with clean clothes on ready to face the rest of my journey; I still couldn't believe I was on my way home. By the time I came out of the washroom, everyone had disappeared, I looked up and down the corridors, not one person in sight, the end of the world could have happened whilst I was in the toilets! I went through transfer department and passport control and took the lift up to the Sabina business lounge. Over the next hour, I drank three hot chocolates and ate lots of chocolate biscuits. It was good to relax and read a newspaper as this was something I hadn't done for five weeks, and had no idea what had been going on in the world!

As I boarded my last plane home at 9am the following morning I wondered if and when I would be back in Uganda. I had no idea what God had planned for me!

Chapter 7

Freely you have received, freely give

My next Ugandan adventure started on Wednesday, November, 4th, 1998, at 4.32am when I woke ahead of my three alarm clocks. I had breakfast and prayed God would oversee all my suitcases. A strange emotional feeling overwhelmed me; I was excited at the thought of seeing Maria and the children and the fact that God was sending me to Uganda twice in one year.

My daughter Sarah picked me up an hour later. It was cold and frosty and the roads had been gritted.

We drove to Manchester Airport and I checked in at the Sabina desk. As usual they were efficient and helpful and I felt a huge sense of relief when they allowed me an extra 20kg. It wasn't long before I was in the air again heading to Uganda, this time via Brussels. My plane from Brussels to Entebbe was delayed three hours so it would be at least 1pm before we left. I was given a lunch voucher to use; I wasn't very hungry but was thirsty and longed for a coffee.

I thought of what I had read in 'Every Day with Jesus.' It spoke about life being a huge story. I thought how each one of us could write a book as God had already written our individual life from beginning to end.

Yes, life is like a rich tapestry. I thought, *with every colour in it including the black times and the orange sunny times and all colours in between.*

I decided to sit and listen to the soothing music playing in Brussels Airport, read my little Bible, and then go to eat when my tummy rumbled.

The Call, the Cost, the Choice

I looked at the well-dressed men and women in their beautifully tailored suits, leather suitcases and shoes, manicured nails, and posh hairdo's.

Everyone here is a millionaire compared to where I'm going. I thought. The contrast was striking.

A while before noon I strolled over to the restaurant. I found it quite tricky trying to balance my tray in one hand, keep my shoulder at the right height to keep my bag on it, and pull my hand luggage along. A cartoonist would have had a field day, watching and sketching characters like me.

Shortly before my 1pm flight, I decided to visit the bathroom and make myself comfortable. As I made my way to the 'ladies', I glanced up at the monitor with the flight details on. My heart sank when I read that my flight was now five hours late, and wouldn't be leaving before 3pm.

Great!

I walked over to the boarding area and cat-napped until it was announced that we could board our plane. We were on our way at last. The doors to the plane were shut and we rolled along the runway leaving Brussels Airport behind. I knew it was going to be in the early hours when I reached Nairobi and then Entebbe after all the delays. I thanked God that at least I had been safe, warm and fed, unlike some who are starving with no shelter, or in floods, fires, or even killed in huge avalanches.

I fell asleep and woke to the sound of "Turkey or fish, Madam?" The stewardess was standing there holding a tin foil tray in front of me waiting for an answer.

"Turkey please," I said. I thought how marvellous it was that whilst I and others were fast asleep so many things were going on behind the scenes to make our journey pleasant.

By 5pm, I was tucking into turkey with a lovely sauce poured over the rice, a fresh bread roll, followed by strawberry mousse. The steward came around and asked if anyone would like another roll and butter:

"Yes, please," I said, thinking to myself that if we got delayed again at Nairobi Airport then I certainly didn't want to be hungry. I put it in my paper napkin and into my bag. (Maria had taught me to make the most of every opportunity, I knew she would approve).

I fell asleep warm, comfortable, and full of food. I woke a couple of hours later and found myself thinking of Maria, the children and friends in Kampala. I wondered if Maria knew I had been delayed as I had no way of contacting her.

"Freely you have received, freely give"

It was after midnight when we arrived in Nairobi where many passengers disembarked. The plane was quickly cleaned and we took off again, finally arriving at Entebbe Airport before dawn. I put my luggage on a trolley and walked through the main doors where a sea of faces greeted me. I didn't know a soul. I wasn't expecting anyone to meet me; neither did I know how I was going to get to Kampala. I prayed, asking God to guide my footsteps.

"Do not be anxious about anything, but in everything, by prayer and petition, with thanksgiving, present your requests to God. And the peace of God, which transcends all understanding, will guard your hearts and minds in Christ Jesus." Philippians 4:6.

It was remarkable how God gave me his peace. I didn't realise at this point how many times I was going to rely on the truth of that verse.

I checked the exchange rate and to my surprise it was the highest I had ever known: 2,000/- to the £1. I changed £100 and went out of the airport to look for transport. I prayed God would supply all my needs and he didn't let me down.

In front of me was the Sheraton Hotel bus, which was ready to go to Kampala. It was still pitch black outside; the only bit of light was at the front of the bus in the doorway. I climbed on board and within minutes we were off. As we approached Kampala, it suddenly became light at exactly 6.15am. It was incredible how fast it happened; now I could see the man next to me; before it had been so dark I could hardly make him out.

When we arrived at the Sheraton Hotel, I left my luggage in a corner and bought a phone card to ring Dick and Ivy, but their phone was engaged. I decided to try the coffee which was delicious. I rang again at 7am; still engaged. The coffee was good. I felt like a princess in the grandest hotel in Kampala with a king as my father who wanted the best for me.

By 8am, I had rung Dick and Ivy's phone many times to no avail. Most of the porters and the receptionists had tried too! I decided to look at a map to see if I could recognise the area where they lived but I only had a P.O. box number. I spotted the American Embassy and decided to phone them as I knew Dick and Ivy's daughter, Nancy, worked there. I got through and left a message for her. The porters were happy about this, and told me to sit still and wait as now there was hope. Once again

The Call, the Cost, the Choice

I thought about the verse I had read earlier ..."Do not be anxious about anything"... I had to apply it now.

I sat opposite the main entrance in a comfortable seat feeling tired. I could have done with a snooze and breakfast. I closed my eyes and began to pray and praise the Lord. I thanked him for his goodness to me and the provision of such a magnificent hotel. There was a hustle and bustle about as new passengers arrived and people met friends and loved ones. Businessmen and women arrived for different conferences.

"Excuse me, Madam," a voice said.

I opened my eyes and saw one of the porters standing there. There was a phone call for me at the reception desk. I took the call; it was the American Embassy to say that Nancy's mum was on her way. Praise the Lord, it was only 8.10am. Ivy arrived fifteen minutes later; it was so good to see her and I felt as though I had never been away. We packed all my luggage into her car and drove to her home.

Maria and I were thrilled to see each other again but I was so tired and just wanted to sleep. I sat in bed and ate the cheese and biscuits that I had saved from the plane, then put my head on the pillow and slept for three hours. When I got up, Nancy had arrived from the Embassy for lunch.

Maria, Ivy, Nancy, and I all enjoyed catching up and discussing the last few months. JayJay Madhvani then arrived to take us to Speak Hotel to meet her mother who had given Maria the three old warehouses in Kamuli, now transformed into 'Maria's Care'. Mrs Madhvani had travelled from Calcutta to see her family and do some business. She was a remarkable lady, similar in age to Maria, and they got on like a house on fire. I took photos of them sitting together as they discussed the land in Kamuli including the extra plot by the main road. The deeds were all in the hands of Maria's solicitor, Peter Nyombi; we needed to make sure the street children in Kamuli would always be provided for. After that meeting we drove back to Dick and Ivy's home, where we rested, sat on the veranda and enjoyed a good cup of tea.

Dick and Ivy were missionaries in Uganda. They held Bible studies in their home where many local couples came to discuss how the Bible approached sex and marriage. They were good teachers and when they spoke everything made sense. Usually Dick studied with the men and Ivy with the women, although sometimes it was a joint session.

"Freely you have received, freely give"

After a decent night's sleep and then breakfast of waffles and jam, Dick drove us to Kampala Taxi Park. Now that is something else! It was always a challenge to cross from one side to the other with suitcases and not get squashed.

"Nothing is impossible with God!" Maria would say this about many things, including the taxi park. 'We can't do it' is not in her vocabulary. So with three suitcases, our own bags, a guitar, and a box of Bibles we made our way to the Jinja *matatu*. Thankfully, Maria asked a man with a wooden wheelbarrow to load everything into it. He walked steadily weaving in and out of the *matatus*, steering the wheelbarrow with great accuracy managing not to get crushed; an accomplishment indeed considering the buses were parked tightly together about two feet apart.

We had great fun negotiating a price for the entire luggage. Maria said one price, the conductor another, then the inspector joined in. There were lots of raised voices and arms waving in the air; Maria and I found it hilarious. Eventually a miracle happened; the luggage was put on the *matatu* and to this day I have no idea who won the price war.

We left just before noon and the journey was the usual breathtaking white-knuckle ride. I could see the progress that had been made in the last seven months: roads rebuilt, houses finished and people living in them, seven feet high crops in fields, and new buildings on what had been empty plots of land.

Maria and I sat at the front of the *matatu* from Kampala to Jinja and enjoyed the trip. We chatted and laughed all the way as we overtook vehicles going up and down hills.

We arrived in Jinja at 1pm. I jumped out before we reached the taxi park and dashed over to the Busoga Trust Office. I contacted Mwiri High School and arranged for a driver to pick me up the following Tuesday; I needed to take photos of the college computer class, to show the staff and students at Manchester Grammar who had donated the technical equipment.

I made the most of this opportunity and borrowed the toilet key from the office to spend a penny. Those who live in Uganda or have travelled there know how you really appreciate people who allow you to use their toilets.

Maria and I jumped aboard the Kamuli *matatu* which was filling up quickly. I had bought a cool soda to drink and had to finish it fast as the bus was nearly ready to go and I needed to hand the bottle back before we left.

We left Jinja and drove through horrendous weather. It was raining hard and deep puddles spread across the road. The driver had to swerve on many occasions to miss the flooded pot holes; sometimes he couldn't avoid them and hit them with such a bump it didn't do the passengers or the vehicle any good at all.

When we reached Kamuli, Maria paid an extra 50p (1,000/-) for the *matatu* to take us to 'Maria's Care'. We worked out that the whole four hour journey cost us about £6 each.

After unloading all the goods with the help of children and staff, Maria was shattered and went for a sleep. I walked over to the orphanage and school where I received a wonderful welcome, and was introduced to new staff. I was then escorted around the compound, the changes were extraordinary.

"Wow! Look at that, isn't that great?' I said, pointing to the boys' washing area with a shower and two new urinals. The boys were excited, too; they had never before had such luxury. The whole area had been painted and at one end there was a place to wash and hang clothes.

Everyone dashed about getting ready for the party they had prepared for my return. (Any excuse!)

Stephen the new resident carpenter in 'Maria's Care,' showed me his new store cupboard. He was so proud of his workplace and kept it immaculate. He had begun teaching woodwork to the children and some of their efforts were displayed on a shelf.

We walked past the primary school and into the TSOLS. To my surprise there was a class of about twenty students learning to type. I thought they would have gone home by now but to my delight they had all wanted to stay and show me their skills.

We continued on the guided tour into the girls' dormitories, and viewed all the neatly-made beds in rows, and the mosquito nets which had, thankfully, survived the mice, rats, and cockroaches that were prone to chew them to shreds. The girls laughed as they rushed up and hugged me and shook my hand. I walked through the dormitory into a bathing area similar to the boys'. I noticed the wall was in desperate need of repair; it bowed and I thought it wouldn't be long before the whole thing fell down.

"Freely you have received, freely give"

We walked over to the gate where Mr George, the new welfare man, was waiting with his bike to transport me to the party at Maria's house. I sat side-saddle on the cushion on the back, and having always been an adventurous type of person, I loved flying down the hill as we passed startled people open mouthed looking at this crazy *muzungu* travelling past them at great speed.

We flew past the dilapidated dairy, past the road where David, the carpenter, lived, and the 'Grain Mill'; a little snack area with wooden walls, a table and bench. We continued along the road and saw some men making a bed frame, and others drinking through very long straws from a huge pot. We passed a large piece of wasteland, where a young man was holding a radio on his shoulder as he directed the cows back to their field.

I smiled and thought, *All over the world people are tending their animals and it's no different here.*

We passed the bore hole near the police barracks, where many people had placed their jerry-cans in long lines going out from the tap in different directions waiting for the town water to come on. We turned left and shot down a hill, passing Mulago Hospital, then turned right along a small road to Maria's house.

The garden looked lovely; full of tables and chairs. Aunt Rose welcomed me as she carried food over in two huge containers. The accountant had sent three crates of sodas, Maria had the music blaring out, and there was a lot of fun and laughter. It was good to be back.

I went inside and changed into clean clothes and then I clicked away with my camera taking pictures of the party. Maria and I saw the funny side of sitting in a hot climate surrounded by Ugandans listening to Julie Andrews singing, and joining in the best they could:

The hills are alive with the sound of music. It was hilarious.

We ate the food with our fingers, greens beans, *posho* and chicken. The staff stood up and told everyone who they were and what they taught. I gave a speech and cried because I couldn't believe God would send me twice in one year to Uganda again and the fantastic way everything had come together.

Later we packed everything up that had been transferred from 'Maria's Care' for the party, and just before people departed I gave them all lollies. They thoroughly enjoyed this treat as it wasn't something they would normally eat. I had bought them with donated money from two gentlemen who did car body repairs in Macclesfield.

Maria and I discussed the future of our children as we walked back into the house from the veranda. I put all my belongings in their place and thought how it felt like a second home to me especially as I had made the curtains, cushion covers, and bedspread for the 'blue room'. I looked around and could see how Maria had added her distinctive touch. We prayed, and eventually went to bed.

I had a restless night and talked to God about what I should be doing whilst I was in Uganda this time. I asked for guidance and help. Eventually I fell asleep in the early hours. I could hear a baby crying, music in the background, and people shuffling past the house on the dark, dusty road. The moon was very thin and didn't shine on the land much, so quite how these people could see to walk along a dark road or ride a bike I can't imagine.

When I first woke it was still dark but I heard Maria getting her scooter out of the garage. The door kept sticking as she pulled it open making an awful scraping noise. I turned over and went back to dreaming. When I did get up there was a lot of activity outside; Godfrey was doing his washing whilst Alex cut the grass with a very sharp, long, curved knife called a slasher. Robert and Alex are twins and Godfrey is their older brother. Maria had accommodated them in the boys' quarters behind her house. Their father, Christopher, had been the bursar in our school, Kamuli Parents' Primary School. Many of his older brothers and sisters had died leaving him with two dozen children to look after. Maria recognised he couldn't possibly manage to look after them all so had offered to help three of them. They cared for themselves and even though they were only primary school age, they cooked, washed their clothes, made their beds, and cleaned their room without any supervision from Maria.

Two young girls, Scovia and Bertha, bent down and brushed our rooms with a very small hand brush and then wiped the whole floor with a damp cloth. Maria helped them with their education, and in return they helped her with domestic duties.

As I ate the breakfast that was prepared for me, I wondered what sort of day God had planned for us all. I read the passage in 'Word for Today': *"Then because so many people were coming and going that they did not even have a chance to eat, he said to them, 'Come with me to a quiet place and get some rest.'"* Mark 6:31.

"Freely you have received, freely give"

I must take heed, I thought.

The prayer in 'Every Day with Jesus' read: *'Father, I open my heart to accept everything you want me to know. Give me a new understanding of sin and grace. Help me to hate the one and love the other, in Jesus' name. Amen.'* I have an overwhelming love for the Ugandan people and their situation, I need to release this love to encourage them and build them up. I decided to write a list of all the things I wanted to achieve whilst I was here this time.

I collected a ream of paper and pencils for the children to write to their sponsors. On the way I stopped at the little hospital and met Richard, the local dentist, his wife, and assistant. He was delighted with the new instruments I brought with me and insisted on taking the few old instruments out of the sterilised tin and putting the new ones in. As I left him and walked towards 'Maria's Care,' three children ran up to me:

"Jambo muzungu, Jambo muzungu," they shouted. They wanted a photo taken as they walked along balancing sacks on their heads. Every walk I took was always interesting.

I continued and met David Kasolo, the carpenter. We stood, surrounded by sawdust, chatting about how wonderful it was that his business had expanded over the last six years. His wife Kasolo Janet Nabirye couldn't speak any English then, but she waved and gave me a beautiful smile when I saw her with their little family. Janet now speaks fluent English and was Deputy Mayor in Kamuli until she retired from Kamuli Town Council and is in her final year of a three year degree course in Social Work and social Administration at Busoga universuty, Kamuli Branch. She hopes to graduate in June/July 2012.

I carried on walking in the warm breeze that was gently blowing, passing the cows tethered by one leg to a thick branch or trunk of a tree in the ground. Children stood at the water pump with bright-coloured jerry-cans waiting their turn to collect water. I walked past the disused dairy and noticed a few cows in the field by the abattoir. I could see 'Maria's Care' from here and thought how Maria had transformed the huge warehouses; making them a home for sixty-eight children, and a Primary School with over three hundred and fifty children attending. She was also employing many people in the compound, enabling them to support their own families in the surrounding villages.

At the age of sixty-five, Maria had been obedient to God's call on her life. Now her vision was coming to fruition because she made that choice and hundreds of people, including myself, had benefited.

I arrived at the gate of 'Maria's Care' armed with pencils and paper. Peter, the lad who had had appendicitis, came to greet me. He took my bag and carried it the whole time I was taking photos of the children. We had such fun and laughed as they chased the chickens into the bushes and caught them so that they could be photographed holding one. I distributed the pens and paper to the children sitting at the tables in the wooden dining room with the leaking roof. Those who could write to their sponsors did so, and the little ones who couldn't write drew pictures.

There was a great deal of activity in the kitchen and I could see smoke billowing out from the cooking area. This was quite normal because they cooked on sawdust given to them by David. Each day after school, the children visited his workshop with plastic basins and any other big containers they found and he allowed them to take sawdust free of charge, which they then tipped into a home-made concrete container near the kitchen in the compound.

By 2pm the children had eaten, washed up, and some had already walked over to Maria's house to watch a video; this was the big Saturday afternoon treat for them.

Overhead, the sky was rumbling; I looked up and reckoned it might rain. I thought what a privilege it was that God had called me here again and the children had accepted my crazy lifestyle of going to and fro between Uganda and England. At least there was some consistency and I was building relationships each time.

Later that afternoon, Maria had a visitor called Stella who was housing and teaching eight deaf children in her home. I sat to find out more about Stella's work with these children. Parents often abandoned deaf children because they couldn't communicate with them and Stella rescued any she knew of in this situation. I was beginning to understand more about the vision Maria had shared with me why she had wanted a hostel and school for deaf children.

I wandered back along the road as various people passed me by: a heavily pregnant lady carrying a suitcase on her head, another woman with a baby on her back, shopping on her head and a child by her side. An older lady had a heavy jerry-can balanced on her head, whilst another carried huge logs about six feet long, probably to be used for cooking.

"Freely you have received, freely give"

I passed two oxen walking together sharing a wooden yoke, and thought about the scripture in Matthew 11:28. *"Then Jesus said, 'Come to me, all of you who are weary and carry heavy burdens, and I will give you rest. Take my yoke upon you. Let me teach you, because I am humble and gentle, and you will find rest for your souls. For my yoke fits perfectly and the burden I give you is light.'"* I watched the oxen walk by and thought how Jesus helps to carry our load if we let him.

I noticed many half-built houses. This often puzzled me until I discovered that people started building properties until they ran out of money, often returning years later to complete them or pass them on to other family members.

I returned to Maria's house to discover that she had been next door to the Malabu Centre and found out that President Museveni (the Ugandan President) was visiting in two days time. She was told that guards were going to be posted all around the building, including in our garden as it backed onto the site. There was great excitement and news of the President's visit spread like wildfire. What a privilege! The President coming to visit Kamuli, and right next door to us as well!

Maria and I went back to the compound to take part in the praise and worship meeting which was regularly held on Saturday night. This was a treat not to be missed; the children sang with such love and praise in their hearts for Jesus.

Maria had taught them to bring God into everything; she was wonderful with the children and staff and led early morning Bible study each day. The children learnt quickly to find scriptures; young twelve year old students would open the Bible and preach on the word of God in such a mature way. As they don't have other things to distract them during the day, they would often read their Bibles, and I could see it made a tremendous difference to their understanding of the scriptures. After the meeting, we made our way back home, Maria on her scooter and I walking by her side.

The following morning we went to church. There was only one bench at the front of the church building and we sat on it. As the service progressed more people arrived and put benches in front of us; they had brought them from their homes, carrying them on their heads or their bikes.

After the service, Maria told me about the young girls she had first looked after in Kamuli: Grace, Regina, Florence, and Lydia were just a few. Maria had taught them under the 'Freedom Tree' how to use a cheque book, be self-sufficient, and understand their responsibilities in life.

We arrived back at Maria's house to find Joan, the Malabu Centre manager, checking security. She stationed an armed guard in our garden that night. We were quite excited about this as were the three boys, Godfrey, Alex, and Robert.

I went next door into the grounds of the Malabu Centre; it was a hive of activity and ladies were busy peeling and cutting a huge pile of *matooke* with great pride. Joan showed me around the centre and I took a few photos of the busy ladies and offered to be the official photographer, but Joan politely declined. We chatted about the programme, and she told me President Museveni was coming to speak at a conference the next day. They hadn't been given an official time for his arrival so everyone was on red alert.

Later that afternoon, at Maria's house, there was no electricity so we had to light candles. As we sat on the veranda looking at the light coming from the moon, suddenly the lights came on again. We realised that as the President was due the next day, Kamuli was given extra power.

The guard on duty at the bottom of the garden was a lovely young man. Godfrey, Alex, Robert and I chatted to him as he watched the boys cook their only meal of the day which they ate around 9pm each night. I took a photo of them cooking sweet potato and grasshoppers - *nsenene*. We felt very safe that night as we put our heads down to sleep, with our own guard in the garden.

Unfortunately though, we didn't sleep well for all the noise as people shifted tables and chairs around ready for the conference, with the radio blaring out all night to keep them company, and us awake.

The next day Maria wanted photos taken of the craft room and compound. It was such a shame that we didn't have the money to paint the three warehouses. More doors and windows had been added since my last visit, and I could see the new grey cement around them. As we had no disposable income and only enough money for the basic needs of food and education for the children, any extras would have to wait.

As we walked back to her house for lunch, we saw more armed guards lining the roads. Maria rested after lunch while I went next door to the

"Freely you have received, freely give"

Malabu Centre. Many people had gathered waiting for the President, and police were everywhere. I was told to put my camera away or they would take it from me.

I returned home to do some paperwork, and later on walked to 'Maria's Care'. This time I passed masses of people sitting under trees in small groups along the roadside waiting for the President. As I approached the crossroads a few men stood up and looked expectantly along the street. I turned around to see a vehicle approach with armed guards, followed by the Presidential car with the Ugandan flag waving on the bonnet.

As the car drew alongside, President Museveni smiled as he looked at me. I waved. He waved. And that was that. I was walking on my own along this little stretch of road; no camera, no one to share the experience with, just me and him. To think that earlier on I had been waiting at the gate with hundreds of others, some of whom had been there four or five hours for a three second glance and wave. I continued to walk; it all felt quite surreal.

The evening meal at the Country Club was fun. Gordon had brought colleagues from Kamuli Mission Hospital Lubaga and we all had a great time eating omelette and chips and sharing stories. What cuisine!

Early next morning, Maria and I set off for Jinja. The sun was hot, a warm breeze was blowing, and children were walking to school in gaily coloured uniforms: bright pink, yellow, green, purple, and red.

Everyone was shouting, *"Jambo!"* "Hello, how are you?"

"I am fine thank you," I replied.

I just loved this interaction; people were so friendly. (I miss this in England where people have their heads down and don't make eye contact as they walk along the street).

As we travelled along, we saw the sights I had come to know and love in Uganda: children running around huge fields in the intense heat, little children carrying their tiny baby brother or sister on their back, wrapped in cloth and tied on, whilst older babies instinctively clung onto their siblings for dear life. We passed small wooden huts that had seen better days (the shed at the bottom of my garden in England was in better condition than some of these). They each had a sign: 'Bettie's Beauty Parlour', 'Butchers', 'Sam's Saloon', and clothes shops with a few articles on small stalls outside.

I shall never forget seeing one lady pick up a goat, put it around her

160

neck like a scarf, and then lead another one on a small rope down the road. There is nearly always a scary moment when an animal decides to dash across a road and drivers have to brake suddenly and swerve to avoid an accident. I praise God every time we manage to arrive safely at our destination.

Groups of people stood at the side of the road waiting for an empty *matatu,* they just put their hand out and hope there is space. Many times the vehicle would ignore them; I would glance at the speedometer and then quickly look away again. My imagination worked overtime as I thought of all the things that could happen to us as we were going so fast.

As we approached Owen Falls in Jinja, the conductor who had squashed himself into the bus along with the other twenty-two people, live hens, and luggage, suddenly looked behind at us. He put his hand out and without saying a word collected everyone's fare.

Maria went to the Busoga Water Offices on Main Street, and I went to the Forex Bureaux and changed some money, then I sent a fax to my prayer partner, Val, from the main post office to say I was fine. I bought some new film to go in my camera, approximately £3.70 for 3 x 24 exposure films; I really hoped they would be o.k. at that price. I didn't have a digital camera back then.

I was very impressed that the head of Mwiri High School arrived on time to pick up Maria and me. We drove up a steep hill and looked down to see the spectacular view. We had a marvellous time as the head teacher escorted us in and out of classrooms. We met the teachers and watched different classes in progress. I was asked to speak in the main staff room; something I was not used to doing at that time.

As we drove back down the hill, I asked if we could stop at the YWAM camp as I had a letter to hand-deliver from Christine, my lodger in England, to a young man called Richard who was originally from Preston. Richard was delighted to see someone from England, especially carrying a letter from home. He enjoyed showing us around the 'prayer garden' in particular. He also showed us the animal projects in operation and said how happy he was there.

I realise now as I look back at that moment how God was inspiring my head and my heart to begin our own 'animal project' at 'Maria's Care.'

On our way back to Kamuli, we could see high in the sky rain coming from huge black clouds in lines across our path about a mile ahead. We drove straight into a dreadful storm and the bus stopped. I assumed we had run out of petrol but Maria and I were asked to move from our front seats as the driver needed to get to the engine underneath. We both had to climb over the back of our seats in a most un-ladylike fashion, and we couldn't stop laughing. The bus was packed and everyone had to re-shuffle.

The driver lifted the bonnet, did something underneath it, and the bus started.

Then stopped again.

Everyone groaned. He tried again and eventually the engine roared into life. We were asked to get back in our seats but Maria who was seventy-two by then refused, and some men climbed into the front instead. The rain was torrential by now but we managed to arrive safely in Kamuli after two police checks, and several more stops.

I left Maria cooking a lovely meal, and went next door to buy some sodas. We had just sat down with a well-earned drink in our hands and said how lovely everything was, when the lights went out. After a quick scrabble round, we found some candles and a match and attempted to dish up the meal in near darkness. We wobbled slowly to the table trying to make sure everything stayed on the tray, and ate the meal by candle-light on the veranda, followed by Angel Delight mousse. (I brought a packet from home as a treat).

We reflected on the day, amused at our shenanigans in the *matatu*. I wondered who else could have handled it the way Maria had. She has always been such a great sport, laughing in these situations and dealing with them as best she could.

We didn't get much sleep due to the noisy cats that kept wailing and crying all night.

In the morning, Maria went to the primary school, whilst I stayed and read 'Every Day with Jesus'. It was good to have time to read, pray and reflect. This was something I hadn't had much time to do... *"for I have learned to be content whatever the circumstances."* Philippians 4:11.

With God's strength, I would try to learn this secret. Here I was in Uganda surrounded by so many appalling situations; 'content' wasn't a word I was using.

As my readings continued, I thought about the people in England who were faithfully praying for us and how we needed to be obedient and follow God's plans. Maria had certainly been obedient even when many people had thought she was crazy taking on such a task at her age. I praise God she heard the call, weighed up the cost and made the choice. Maria recognised his voice encouraging her to step out in faith and do this work for him.

Like Joseph in the Bible, Maria had no idea what was going to take place and why God allowed difficult situations to happen. They both had to live by faith, trusting God. For Maria that meant trusting him for all her needs and the needs of the children he had asked her to look after. Her faith had been stretched so many times already and had frequently driven her to seek respite in Glenda's small hut at the bottom of the garden to pray and rest.

It was the middle of the morning before I finished reading and praying.

A friend arrived and handed me an invitation to speak at the International Women's Organisation in Kampala at 10am on Wednesday, 18th, November. I was due to fly back to England later that day. *What perfect timing,* I thought. I felt very privileged to share with others the work Maria was doing; she needed a higher profile and more support from local people.

I sat with Maria one day writing down every detail of each child she was looking after, including name, age, and family background. We discussed how precious it was for a child to receive a letter from their sponsor; it gave the child a sense of belonging and that was important. We had already seen how children who had letters had blossomed and performed well at school.

If an adult came to Maria and said they had a 'problem', it usually meant that a family member had died leaving children behind. Often Maria would take them in and look after them. A few months later, however, she might discover that the child did have family but they had been placed with her because the relatives knew the child would have a better chance of education and survival with Maria. Eventually she decided to do everything through the probation officer; this was a much better idea. He would know if the case was a genuine one or not, and she would have papers stamped with the correct local council designation.

My remit from the committee was to tell Maria that the amount of money coming in would only fund the children she had at present, and that we couldn't take on any more children or buildings! I always knew when Maria was listening or deciding to take no notice. She would give me a sideways glance as if to say: *Yeah, right!*

She gave me that look now as I explained she was running ahead of what we had in the bank. Her experience was that God always supplied her needs, even if she did have to go begging around the town for food for the children.

I spent a few hours taking a photo of every child we were sponsoring. We had a lot of fun doing this as I believe that if a child is happy where he or she is standing; they smile at the camera with more confidence. This was certainly the case with our children at 'Maria's Care'. Consequently, we moved all around the compound. They loved standing by flowers or resting one foot on a tree stump; I think they thought they looked cool! They smiled; I snapped, and hoped for the best. It was an expensive business as the films and developing them cost a lot of money. Unfortunately, if a child had blinked or pulled a funny face I had no way of knowing till the photo was developed.

At last it was time for our evening meal. Maria was great at throwing what food she had into a pan and working a miracle; this was one of those days and it was delicious. After that Maria went to bed and, as usual, I carried on doing paperwork and writing my diary. So much happened in a day that I felt if I didn't write it down I would forget.

I wrote as I listened to the rain outside; it was a lovely sound. I knew the local people were praying for rain so their crops would grow, but then I thought of the people who lived in mud huts with leaky straw roofs; I was nice and warm and cosy inside my bedroom.

I was up early the next day but Maria had already gone. I read the little note she left:

'Sorry – Crisis – gone to school early'.

I never found out what the crisis was, except it was something to do with food for the weekend.

I had another busy day sorting out all the letters the children had written for their sponsors.

One of the secretaries, Eunice, had taken a jigger (little worm) out of Maria's foot. Thank goodness I didn't see it as I am sure I would have passed out. We never knew what each day would bring. One of our staff had a seriously sick child and had to go to hospital with her. A few hours later we received the sad news that the child had died. People wonder why Africans have so many children, and this is precisely why. Often the children die young from illnesses they don't have the money to treat, or lack education and knowledge of what to do. Some parents take their children to the local healer (witch doctor/shaman) and this can often do more damage than good.

Maria had prepared a meal for me that night before retiring to bed exhausted. I ate by candlelight and then visited the three boys at the bottom of the garden. They had made me a football out of a blown up balloon with rags tied round and round it. I was delighted; it showed me how innovative these children were and made me think of how in England we throw so much away because we expect footballs and toys to be bought for us from the toy shop. These children had never even seen a toy shop in Kamuli so had to make what they could. Before I went to bed I put the ball in my suitcase, ready to show people when I got back to England. Believe it or not, the balloon did not deflate for years and I trailed round English schools with it in my artefacts box!

Up once again bright and early, we were on a mission! Maria had decided to take the crafts her students had made to sell at the Christmas bazaar in Lincoln School, Kampala. We packed two very large plastic laundry bags ready to take after breakfast. Maria was not feeling well and had to make a choice; should she travel with these cumbersome bags of crafts to Kampala or not. She decided to take up the challenge and off we set.

We discussed how we would spend various donations from England, and made a list: a new hedge and paint for the wall in the prayer garden, a goat for the children at Christmas (this was the only time the children had meat) transport for some children going on Teen Mission. The exchange rate was 2,000/- £1. We had 100,000 Ugandan shillings to spend.

Maria loved to get out when she could and it was a good excuse to go visiting. I'm just grateful we went to so many places and met people that I am still in touch with years later. After drinking tea and chatting with James and Jemima, we headed for a little coffee shop for lunch. I didn't know then that Jemima who now owns Banana Village in Entebbe was going to become such a good friend. Maria first met her when she owned a café on the Main Street in Jinja.

After lunch we carried the two large bags to the taxi park and journeyed to Kampala. Once again Maria confidently handed over the luggage to the conductor who pushed it into the back of the bus, and, lo and behold, at the end of the journey after many stops and people taking their luggage, hers would still be there; a miracle every time!

The *matatu* reached Kampala after a few hairy moments where vehicles, animals, or people shot out in front of us. We had our own bags and the two large craft bags to carry. Maria decided we were going to save money and not have transport across town, so we walked and walked, nearly breaking our backs and necks. Eventually we left the bags with the security men in a huge block of offices where Maria's solicitor worked.

Maria was hoping her friends, Dick and Ivy, would still be in Jinja, and not off on one of their many missionary journeys, so we took a private taxi to the other side of town to a place called Kololo. Maria was praying that we would both have a bed for the night. To her surprise and delight Dick and Ivy were at home. (You might be thinking, *Why is this so significant?* It's because we had to trust God that they would be there; we didn't have mobile phones and we had used money for a private taxi that we could ill afford to waste).

They greeted us with open arms, escorted us to our bedrooms and pointed to the shower. Wonderful! We really enjoyed that hot shower (anyone reading this that has lived in the remote Ugandan villages can relate to this delightful extravagance). We ate our meal and fell into our neatly-made beds. I must say the bed and pillow I had was the very best I had ever slept in while in Uganda. So much so I slept for nine hours and woke ready to face another day that the Lord had given me.

I was thrilled for Maria that she had this wonderful haven; Dick and Ivy had been her friends for many years and they had also been wise advisors to her and us as a charity. Their wisdom and years of experience had been a great blessing to hundreds of people.

It was early when Maria and I woke up. We prayed and read our Bibles together and committed the day to the Lord. Ivy drove us to Lincoln School, after picking up the two bags of crafts from where we had left them the previous day, and we set up stall at the Christmas bazaar. Aunt Rose travelled from Kamuli and joined us for the day and I had a wonderful time walking around chatting to English and American women who also had stalls there. Some of them were disappointed that they were going home sooner than anticipated; the project their husbands had come to do at the Owens Fall Dam in Jinja had finished earlier than expected.

I took some photos of Aunt Rose holding a bark-cloth angel which could be hung on a Christmas tree. I knew the students in the TSOLS could easily make them. There were many diverse stalls with hand-made crafts: beautiful needlework goods, home-made jam and pickles, woven baskets, hand-made paper, jewellery, Christmas cards, and hundreds of bunches of different coloured fresh roses. It was all so colourful.

Maria was pleased that we had made the effort with the stall, and, even though we didn't take much money, we had promoted 'Maria's Care' in Kamuli and people were getting to know about the work she was doing there. Aunt Rose took the remaining crafts back to Kamuli and Maria and I continued our journey to Entebbe.

We arrived late afternoon and each jumped onto a *piki-piki*. Maria directed them to Everet's house. She had known Everet and his wife Terry quite a while and they both made us welcome. I walked and chatted with Terry as she watered her plants in the garden. The trees were in blossom and the flowers in bloom. I admired the magnificent view from her garden; we could see as far as the airport and over to Lake Victoria. Unfortunately, the mosquitoes started to bite and we had to go in. It went dark quickly at 7pm and by 7.30pm it was pitch black.

After our lovely fondue meal, we retired to our rooms, when I heard Terry suddenly let out a shriek; she had found ants all around her kitchen, even in the fridge. It was a typical hazard of living in Uganda. I drifted to sleep as my thoughts turned to home; I was leaving in a few days time and knew I had a lot to do when I got back, especially with Christmas only five weeks away.

Terry cooked a scrumptious breakfast for us of pancakes, boiled eggs, sausage, and toast (no ants) and Everet made sweet syrup for the pancakes. We then drove to their church for morning service which was lovely. The singing was beautiful with such harmonious voices, a baby was being christened, and a visiting choir from Kampala Miracle Centre sang. The pastor spoke for an hour and a half on being set free by Jesus and then a man from the International Gideons spoke. After that we crept out by which time it was nearly 2pm.

We collected our bags, boarded a *matatu* in Entebbe Village to Kampala, Jinja, and eventually arrived in Kamuli. We decided to finish the long day off with a meal at the Country Club. (Sounds so up-market

"Freely you have received, freely give"

but those who have been there will enjoy the joke).

The next morning I read Matthew 10:8, *"Freely you have received, freely give."*

I could relate to this; so many people have encouraged and believed in me that it has changed my whole outlook on life. It has also changed inward feelings; the negative thoughts have been replaced by positive ones. God has completely changed my life and made a huge difference to the way I trust him, he meets my daily needs in the most extraordinary ways, not just the finance but also my cars. Sadly my old K registered car had failed its MOT, had been fixed many times, but this time it had to be scrapped as too much needed to be done.

I was at home in England when God spoke to someone about my need of a car. It was late one Friday afternoon when this person (I still have no idea who) pushed an envelope through my front door containing money and a little red plastic car.

A note attached read: "How about one of these?"

I sat on the stairs in a state of shock and called my daughter to count the money. There was £1,200 in the envelope. I cried and thanked God for the obedience of whomever it was who had seen my need

I went with a friend to look at cars but I didn't feel I should rush this so I put the money in the bank over the weekend. My daughters and I prayed about it, and I said to God that the only sort of car I was used to driving was a Cavalier and if I could have one in pillar box red (the colour of the plastic car) that would be great. I realised afterwards that as long as it had four tyres and a steering wheel I would be happy.

The following day I went to the Christian Mission in Macclesfield to tell my friend, Annie, what had happened. As I passed a notice board on the wall my eyes caught sight of a card:

FOR SALE. PILLAR BOX RED CAVALIER SUN ROOF £1,195 please contact... Congleton.

I froze as I re-read the little card with the details. I took the notice off the board and sat down on the stairs, my eyes filling up with tears. Just then Annie arrived and found me weeping:

"Rhona!" She said. "Whatever is the matter?"

I told her my story and we both ended up in tears, thanking God for his goodness to me and the testimony we could both pass on to others.

The Call, the Cost, the Choice

Needless to say, I bought the car which lasted me a few years until God decided to upgrade me with another one. This time a businessman and his wife in Bristol were about to sell their company car. They had decided that my car was on its last legs, so they offered me their british racing green Rover.

By 2004, my left knee was crippled with arthritis and a damaged cartilage and I struggled to get in and out of the Rover. God knew all about this and prompted a man to offer me a wonderful Daewoo hatchback.

I praise God for the obedience of those people who gave me their cars. I hope they have all been blessed. I had received so much in my life through God, I was thrilled that I could also freely give and bless others too.

That morning in Uganda I was taken by Mr Abwa to Nawaikoke College. I bought a cushion after the last uncomfortable experience I had on the back of a bike. We travelled for over two hours up and down, in and out of pot-holes. The road was incredibly bad and there was only one foot rest on the bike so my right foot was aching; I tried some of the time to hold the back of my sandal so I could take the strain off my leg. We passed beautiful trees in flower, people walking with goats tethered on the end of a bit of rope, and hundreds of bright yellow weaver birds flying in and out of their nests. People waved as we passed and children ran out shouting '*Jambo.*' There was a light warm breeze blowing; it was a beautiful day for this sort of trip.

At the college I took hundreds of photos for various people who supported this particular project. It was very quiet that day as exams were taking place.

On our way home we stopped at the trading centre where we ate bananas and drank soda. We rode for miles and in the end we got off the bike because we both had numb bottoms. We walked for a while up a hill and a man stopped to offer us a lift thinking we had run out of petrol. As we later rode down a hill we struck a pot-hole, I nearly came off and as I went in the air Mr Abwa saved me. Thankfully, he was able to slow down. It was so funny, it all happened in seconds; by now it was tea-time and we were nearly home.

We passed two people walking with their motorbike; they had run out of petrol. The only container I had was a water bottle so I drank the remaining water and we transferred some petrol from our bike to theirs.

"Freely you have received, freely give"

After performing our 'good samaritan' deed we all managed to get going. I realised how much God is with us in all circumstances, I didn't come off the bike, we were able to help two others, and we had done the job we had set out to do.

I remember years ago listening to the car radio; A man said we had to be flexible, if we went with the flow life would be much easier; if we were rigid we would break or snap easily. My experiences in Uganda taught me he was probably right.

Back at 'Maria's Care' we drank tea and then I changed my clothes in readiness for my leaving party. The food was delicious: beans, my favourite peanut sauce, chapattis, and soda. There was no electricity so it was all by candlelight which made it look like a beautiful fairy grotto.

I was taken back to the house on the back of the bike. Sadly for me, there was no cushion and my bottom was sore after travelling for hours. I had to suffer in silence as we careered through the dark streets.

Back home Maria and I drank coffee and ate chocolate cake at the end of another busy day.

Next morning once again I felt I would run out of time to do all the things I had planned. I dashed up to the school just in time to share the morning praise and worship with the students. It was only when I sat down that I realised how bruised my bottom really was, and my back ached terribly, but I soon forgot the pain as I got caught up in taking last-minute pictures of children I had previously missed and dashed around saying goodbye to everyone.

We quickly ate lunch, and I packed all my belongings into one suitcase; I had come to Uganda with three but they had been full of gifts for the school. By 1.15pm I was ready to go; I said goodbye to the staff in Maria's house and walked to the taxi park, Maria beside me on her four-wheel scooter. She had some of my hand luggage piled on her lap, which made a change from the little children who often used to sit on her knee as she drove up the road.

We climbed into the *matatu* from Kamuli to Jinja for the last time. One of the students, Corrie, rushed up and gave me the little straw pot that she had made; it was beautiful, so intricate with a perfectly-fitting woven lid. We said our goodbyes and the bus slowly moved out into the bustling traffic.

I began to think about what the weather would be like when I arrived home, probably cold, wet and damp; after all it was winter. Everyone would be rushing around in a pre-Christmas frenzy. It would all be 'go, go, go!'

We drove down the street away from Kamuli; I had no idea if and when I would be back again. We rushed past the familiar scenes: children carrying books, boxes, jerry-cans, stools, chairs, tables, whatever they could, on their heads. We passed men riding bikes carrying charcoal, twigs, a bed, a window frame, pineapples, even a lady with a baby on her back and two toddlers on the cross bar. One man had about thirty three-legged stools tied on his bike. I found the whole journey fascinating. A motorbike shot past with three grown men squashed on, followed by a bicycle with the frame of a settee and two chairs fitted into it tied with black rubber on the back.

The scaffolding around the buildings as we approached Jinja was a sight to behold. How anyone ran up and down with a wheelbarrow full of cement or bricks without falling off, or the scaffolding breaking, was a mystery to me.

I wish I had been quick enough with my camera when in the middle of nowhere we passed a row of little shops. Above one of them in clear writing was the fax number of the business. I could imagine someone faxing these people assuming the communication was going to some prestigious office block!

We successfully made it through chaotic traffic and on to the next part of our journey. The bus stopped and a lady climbed on board with a couple of live chickens tied together. Another passenger helped her as she put the chickens on her knee and they stared out the window. Later a man got on with a chicken in a bag, he put it under my seat and for the rest of the journey its feathers tickled my feet.

The bus itself was a concern to me; the front windscreen had seen better days, there was a chip in the middle of the glass with many cracks fanning out from it, the out-of-date paperwork was stuck at an angle and the inside mirror was broken in half and hanging on by a thread. A group of men had pushed the bus to begin with as the driver put a couple of wires together to start the vehicle. There were wires dangling everywhere. I hadn't looked at the tyres, which was probably a good thing.

The people all looked very serious; usually they were full of fun and chatting but today it was different. The lady sitting next to me had a baby on her knee and a small child standing crushed next to her; he kept falling asleep so I ended up with the baby on my knee and the child seated on his mother's. The baby was gorgeous and I took the opportunity to pray silently for this little bundle.

We eventually arrived at Dick and Ivy's at 4.30pm. Ivy explained that Dick had had some time on his hands and had taken a sledge hammer to the wall in the room I usually slept in.

This changes the meaning of air conditioning. I thought to myself.

I was given another room to sleep in. It was a pleasure a few years later to host Dick and Ivy in England, and let them experience life in a tent at Benllech in Anglesey.

We always had wonderful fellowship with this couple and their extended family. Ivy played the piano and we all sang; we shared testimonies of what God had been doing in Kamuli and Kampala and the various districts Dick had been working in. I was shattered by the time we all retired to bed and it wasn't even 9pm.

I slept well and woke early on Wednesday, 18th. This was going to be a busy day. I was feeling rather apprehensive about the International Women's Organisation meeting I had been asked to speak at. I knew there would be many rich people there who didn't believe in God and I wasn't sure how to start or end the talk I was giving. I really prayed that God would direct me and anoint my words and mind.

J.J. Madhvani arrived and took us to Laltu's home. Laltu was a diplomat's wife living in a fantastic house in an exclusive area in Kampala. We were offered tea or coffee and little home-made cakes, and escorted into the exquisite, manicured gardens. Whilst Maria chatted to various people, I dreamily sat down and placed my cup and saucer on the white lattice-work table and looked at a garden bed of the most beautiful flowers and shrubs in rich soil. I observed the ladies chatting in small groups until reality suddenly hit. *Gosh! I am going to be talking to these ladies in a few moments; I had better get the visual aids ready and my brain in gear.*

There were about thirty ladies present from all over the world: Bombay, South Africa, England, America, Canada, Pakistan and Uganda. After a short introduction, I was asked to share the work Maria was doing in Kamuli. As this was my best subject I was soon in full flow talking with passion about her work. I spoke about her calling to Uganda, the library, the orphaned children and teenagers, the choices Maria had made over the last few years, and how she managed on her pension and a little money people sent her from Holland, Australia and England.

At the end people went up to Maria and asked her what the most urgent needs were at the moment in Kamuli, how they could help, and directions to get there if they wanted to go and visit. Many of them bought the laminated posters I had made and brought with me from England. I felt God had clearly been in all that was said and done. Maria looked extremely pleased and the lady who had invited us to attend was delighted that Maria had at last got a higher profile.

It was a strange feeling sitting in that beautiful garden in Uganda with temperatures in the eighties, knowing that soon I would be back in England—and cold.

We were given a lift to Kampala Taxi Park where I had to manoeuvre my hand-luggage and suitcase amongst people who were hot and bothered, pushing past us to catch their own *matatus*. I did notice men with huge wooden wheelbarrows waiting for business; they are the equivalent of porters with trolleys, but I soldiered on without their assistance.

On our bus a man tried on part of a soft green three-piece suit; it looked good on him so he bargained for a while till he got the price he wanted to pay and then bought it. Another man ate soup followed by a hot dinner on a plate on his knee whilst he waited for the *matatu* to fill up. We bought two bottles of water after checking the seal on the bottle wasn't broken. I had recently heard about the new trick some people did with plastic water bottles; they made a hole in the bottom of an old one, filled it with water (which probably didn't come from a good supply) melted the bottom of the bottle to seal it and then sold it at the recommended price of a new one. We had to learn to keep one step ahead.

Eventually we arrived in Entebbe and walked into Lake Victoria Hotel; Maria loved this place. We headed for the pool, sorted out our sunbeds, and both fell asleep. Later we swam in the warm water and when we climbed out the hot sun dried us. This is my idea of heaven because I hate getting out of a pool with a cold breeze blowing and having to wrap up to keep warm. Yuk.

Everet joined us for our evening meal, and Maria joked about how I hadn't eaten any carrots. Apparently, if you eat carrots, you will return to Uganda, so she gave me her portion too, just to make sure I would come back (so much for trusting God!)

I collected my luggage, gave Maria and Everet a big hug, got on the hotel bus and headed to Entebbe Airport. I felt happy and content; I put my luggage on a trolley and went up in the lift to the lounge as I knew there was going to be a long wait.

Just as I sat down with a cool drink, there was an announcement that the gates for my flight had opened; I decided to check-in then, and have my drink later. Thank the Lord I did. Just as I approached the desk, I met JayJay who was looking for me. She had forgotten to give me the address of a doctor who used to live in Kamuli but now lived in London, whom she wanted me to contact. He has since become a good friend and regular supporter of CRU.

After a long flight to Brussels, I watched the sunrise through the mist which I hoped would clear and not delay my flight to Manchester. I thought about the successful trip that I had been sent on and how God had directed my actions and reactions and all my step; the protection we had as we travelled on dubious public transport back and forth from Kampala to Jinja and Kamuli, the people we had met, and the new contacts, the fun we had eating meals with students, staff and people from the hospital. I realised with God all things really are possible. I know this is the motto at 'Maria's Care' but saying it and believing it are two different things.

By 9.25am I was flying home. When I left Uganda the temperature was around eighty degrees, now the captain was welcoming us to Manchester saying it wasn't raining but it was three degrees. What a difference!

We landed safely. I had so many things in my head that needed to be done before Christmas. Why is it that I have twelve months to get ready, yet I am nearly always late and everything is done at the last minute?

Chapter 8

'Lives Changed'

After travelling to Uganda for over seventeen years I have had the pleasure of watching hundreds of young people grow up. Many of the pupils who were at 'Maria's Care' from 1994 have kept in touch with me, and below are some of their personal stories.

Kasenke Godfrey

I was thirteen years old when I joined 'Maria's Care', and had just completed my primary five school year at Kaliro Church of Uganda Primary School, in my home district. My late father (Christopher Kasenke) brought me to the orphanage as he knew there was a school attached and he wanted me to study there. He was the bursar at this school and was renting small premises where we stayed with my twin brothers Robert and Alex; they were ten years old and were also studying from this very school – Kamuli Parents Primary school. So that is how I came to know 'Maria's Care'. I had polio when I was eleven and could only drag myself around the compound; everyone was very kind to me and helped me wherever possible.

There was some staff restructuring at 'Maria's Care' and father had to leave work. I can't tell what exactly happened because I was too young to understand. So when he left we were brought into the orphanage and stayed there. I thought we were just finishing up the term and then would have to leave, but to my surprise Maria told us that we were now her children and that she would help us in our further studies. I was overjoyed and thanked Maria together with the other sponsors whom I didn't know personally.

I studied my primary six in Kamuli Parents Primary School; I was the second in class after my close friend Moses Katagwa leading the whole class. I was so happy and thanked the Lord for the love and wisdom he had given me. I was thrilled at being number two after coming from a village school! I think this thrilled Maria and other fellow whites like you, 'mum Rhona', and they brought for me two wheelchairs, believe it or not; I was so excited because I had never seen such beautiful wheels. I thanked Maria and Rhona for the love they had for me to see to it that I had easy mobility to move around when I studied.

I kept my position of being second in the class up to primary seven and managed to get fifteen aggregates (the lower the better). This gave me the opportunity to go to secondary school at Kamuli Progressive College for my senior one and two school years. Whilst I was there it was time for Maria to leave Uganda and go and rest in her home country. So she left and others came in to replace her.

I had no idea that when Maria was leaving she was planning to give her four-wheel scooter to me. When we stayed with her in the boys quarters at the back of her house next to the Malamu Conference Centre, she never explained how the scooter worked. I could never imagine that one day I would sit on such a machine – it would be a miracle having such an electronic machine at that time. So at first I just heard rumours that I was going to be given the scooter; inside I thought they were meaning another Godfrey. So finally I was called in by Ian and Pat who were now running 'Maria's Care', and handed me the key to the scooter! Oh my God! I thought I was dreaming but it was finally real. I was very happy that day. I spent sleepless nights thinking I was not the one to whom the wheelchair had been given. I started using this scooter to go to school; the other manual wheelchair couldn't continue helping me because the road was rough and full of stones that couldn't sustain it. So I used that one at home and used the scooter for going to school.

Eventually after some time, the scooter's tyres and wheels had problems. Ian and Pat bought me a hand operated tri-cycle because I had to go to school and we couldn't wait for spare parts from abroad. Once again this bike was like a miracle to me because I had never shared with them my need for this kind of three-wheeler bike, which are locally made in Uganda. I was called in by them one day when I had just come back from school; Ian took pictures of me in the old wheelchair and then he opened the boot of the car and immediately I glanced at the bike.

"What is that in the car?" he asked me. I replied it was a tri-cycle. So he then told me that the bike now belonged to me! I was amazed; I could hardly speak and I couldn't believe it. I started using this bike when the scooter had problems. This was another joy for me in my life.

I was transferred from Kamuli Progressive College because the management could see my potential and wanted me to study at St. James Senior School in Jinja for my senior three year. I was there with my twin brothers Robert and Alex and my friends Malingu Peter and Abdul Salem. When I joined St. James' I had to leave my scooter, so I went along with the tri-cycle and another wheelchair that I could use in Jinja Boys Hostel where I stayed. I was there for just one year. I have no idea why it was decided that I should go back to Kamuli and study from there. There were rumours that we boys were not studying and were spending most of the times enjoying the beautiful scenery of Jinja, going to the source of the Nile, watching films and not attending classes, which was totally not true.

So it was in the morning while on school holiday in my village that I received a letter informing me to look for a school in the village, that's if my sponsors could continue helping me! I cried after reading this letter, but afterwards I had to discuss it with my father and finally opted to look for a school to finish my 'O' levels. By then I had passed my senior three exams at St. James'. My father looked around; he never gave up and finally we went to Kaliro High School where I was admitted into the senior four year. I sat my 'O' levels there and though there were a lot of challenges, I managed to endure and indeed did well by getting second grade in the final Uganda National Examination Board exams. Rhona visited me at this school; I was so happy and pleased. Fellow students were amazed of seeing white bazungu visiting a mere Godfrey! You really encouraged me so much. Later Maria came with other staff; she could not believe this had happened to me and she encouraged me and I promised her my performance would be good. She didn't tell me if she would come back or even help me further in my studies, and then she left again because she had only come to Uganda to celebrate her seventieth birthday.

I was told that I should look for any technical school around because I was not going to be taken for further studies at Kaliro. During my holidays whilst waiting for my exam results I would sometimes cry to God and ask him for help to do further studies. For sure God hears when we cry for his help; it was around 4pm and I didn't even know that Maria was back in Uganda when she came to visit me at home in my village:

"I have come for you, do you hope to perform well in your exams?" she asked.

"I hope so," I replied. Maria finally told me that even if I didn't do well she would sponsor me for further studies and even up to university level. I thought she was joking, I responded by telling her that any school of her choice was good for me. I was so confused and tried to take in this miraculous moment! Surely I could not believe it, I was going for further studies! So immediately she suggested any school my answer would remain – "where you take me is where I will go". So I packed my luggage and left the village for further studies.

Maria took me to Lords Meade Vocational College in Jinja, and indeed the students were very welcoming; I think they had been told about me because at first sight I was known as we moved around the school premises. Finally I told Maria that I appreciated the school and would like to study there. My proposal was accepted and I joined the school for my senior five and six years. Now it was here again that I received an electronic wheelchair from mum Rhona! Oh my God, what a blessing from people! I was so happy and I loved this wheelchair so much. I used it for some time but eventually due to the topography of the school my wheels got worn out; they were spoiled and friends had to go to my village and bring back the scooter that had spent some good years without working, but that one had battery problems so the students just pushed me around. I think this is favour from God because I was loved by every student irrespective of their class or status. They would sometimes make timetable changes in favour of pushing me wherever I wanted to go around the school compound, and sometimes outside the school too if there was a sports gala, like football or tennis happening.

So when I finished my 'A' levels I thought of how I was going to join the university campus. I heard rumours that Maria's no longer had enough money to sponsor me as there were other children she was helping. During my senior six school year at Lords Meade I asked God to help me do well and at least allow me to have a government sponsorship. As I have already said, God answers prayers; he heard me though I didn't realize it then. This is because when the results came out I was one of those who had to go to Makerere University and fill in the forms for a government sponsorship! I was amazed and thanked God for answered prayer.

I managed to fill in the forms and wrote application letters. My first choice I applied for was information technology, second was industrial art & fine art, and third was law. Amidst all of what was going on, before I could even take my senior six results to show my father what his son had done, he became seriously ill. He could neither talk nor see and finally passed away without even hearing my voice.

Things got delayed; I didn't have any communication from the campus apart from Helen who was Okanya Robert's sister, who lived near. She really struggled to help me because I was late applying due to everything that had happened and the university had already closed the chapter of admission. It was a gift from God to me when finally I was admitted into this university to do my first choice, IT. I was so happy to be able to do this course because it taught me so much for life today. As it got nearer to graduation there was a paper that was misplaced and I had to repeat it; this meant I had to pay tuition fees myself. Imagine, I had no-one who could now help me and this was the last paper. I decided the only thing I could do was sell off my computer so that I could pay the examination fees, tuition fees, graduation and gown etc.

I decided to give my computer to my brother Robert to go and sell because I had totally failed to get money for my paper. I didn't know that mum Rhona and some colleagues were already in Uganda. I really don't know how Robert got in touch with her and explained to her my problems but I received a call from her asking me how much I would need for my paper. The following day I was able to get the money the group sent and I paid for the paper and certificate and all that was remaining. This was another blessing; I really saw how God was on my side because he had once again done things that I could never have imagined or even begun to believe would happen at that moment.

I asked mum Rhona to try and bring me a wheelchair or to repair my scooter; miraculously she brought an electric one. I want to thank you and the group for always thinking about me and supporting me wherever there is need. You and others have been so instrumental in my success, I am what I am now because of this and God will bless you abundantly for the love and care that you have given me.

I graduated in 2011 and am looking for a paid job; I believe God will show me at the right time. At the moment I have a small scale business and am training people how to use a computer. I just want to say I am glad and happy for the help you people gave me and others in general not forgetting Linda Price who has been a special vessel in my life for the whole of last year. I am happy for her support and may God really bless her.

I would like to conclude by thanking you, I really thank you so much and may the Almighty be a blessing to you all.

Medie Musoke Mohammed

From Mukono in MBuiba Village comes a poor little orphan boy who joins a care home in Kamuli and finds himself happiness after a good samaritan called Maria Maw found pity for the miserable thing (boy). The little boy had never seen his father, not even a photo; he heard from his mum that his father was murdered in 1984 during the war. So he lived with his single mother Joweria who later died of AIDS, two years after him joining 'Maria's Care', when he was twelve years old.

Maria loved him, giving him all the attention he needed just to let him forget the misery of his parents. She nicknamed him 'Sergeant' because of his strictness, smartness, and brilliant ideas. A friend of Maria's called Frances, visited the home and the little boy opened the gate for her to come in and go out.

Born a lucky one, she (Frances) promised to find someone to help him. The once orphan boy got a family to belong to (Bakr family) with a caring and loving mum and daddy, plus a sister and brother.

He left the care home when he became a young adult and luck was on his side, so that after his senior four school year he decided to join a teaching course from 2003 to 2005 at Kibuli Muslim Teachers College. He got good grades and found himself a small school, taught for one-and-a-half years and finally got himself a government school placement by Allah's (God's) grace.

The misery is gone. He is now referred to as Master Medie, not the 'poor boy' any more.

He uses the little salary from the government to rent a single room, for food, and tuition fees at the Islamic University in Uganda at the Kampala campus, doing a diploma in primary education. He also has a grand-mum to care for in the village. To him the sky is the limit but studying is part of him so he tried his best to at least get a degree. This he did and graduated in February 2010.

His appreciation goes to: Maria Maw, Mummy and Daddy (RIP), Frances David, The Bakr family, and all friends.

Katagwa Moses

I joined 'Maria's Care' on becoming an orphan around 1996 and I was too young to take care of myself. Thus life wasn't easy for me at a very young age but I thank God that he cared about me and has never forsaken me to date, and I thank CRU for the care and support.

Life was new in 'Maria's Care', I met children of my kind and people who cared about us all. 'Maria's Care' is a Christian based NGO thus I learnt a lot more about God, to work hard, and stay with people of different characters, tribe and colour. It was all fun at the orphanage. I am proud that 'Maria's Care' laid a good foundation for all of us there. I have now graduated and have a bachelor's degree in biomedical technology, which was just a dream to me years ago.

Thanks go to God the Almighty, CRU, Maria Maw, Rhona Marshall, Robin and Ali and Jamie among others, who helped me become what I am now.

Bravo!!   Many blessings.

Muwangala David.

I lost my father in 1994, and after I became half-orphaned living with my peasant mother and eight other siblings, going back to school had become a nightmare. Rebecca, my cousin was already involved with 'Maria's Care', and because I had finished my 'O' levels at senior school I was asked to go into 'Maria's Care' and start teaching in the primary school, while Maria looked for a sponsor for me to go back to school to do 'A' levels. While I was there I also helped in the reconstruction of the old strong buildings that were given to us by Indians. These were warehouses so we had to break parts of the walls to make windows. I would also help in rehabilitating children who were from the street through counselling sessions and prayer.

One day, Maria Maw went to Banana Village in Entebbe to rest. While there, she found other bazungu from the USA and they exchanged pleasantries and talked about their projects. When she heard that they had established a secondary school for bright but financially disadvantaged boys, she told them she had a bright boy called David who needed to go for 'A' levels. She later forgot about the whole issue.

One year later, I was invited by those good samaritans to go for interviews that would later give me entry into that school. After passing the interview stage they admitted me into Cornerstone Leadership Academy where I excelled, and then went on to the state university with the help of a government grant. To have a government grant one had to be among the best two thousand students out of over three hundred thousand students who sat 'A' level exams in the whole of Uganda. In 1998 I was admitted to Makerere University to do management and political science, and in 2001 I graduated with a bachelors degree. I also started a master's degree and in 2005 qualified in international relations and diplomatic studies.

Since 2003 I have worked in different positions and organisations as a lecturer, manager, public relations officer, and research consultant. Currently I have no job, but I feel it is time to go back to school and do another masters degree or PhD. I was accepted at Robert Gordon University in Aberdeen, for a masters leading to PhD in oil and gas law. The course began in January 2012, but I did not get a scholarship to help do this course so I was unable to start. One day God will pave the way for a sponsor to help undertake this course I dream of. After this course, I will be helpful to the new found oil and gas industry in Uganda. I also nurture ambitions to go into parliament one day as a politician.

I want to thank CRU for all the support and care given to me and others who struggle and have no one to call family.

Okanya Robert

Before I went into 'Maria's Care' I was staying in the village with my grandmother in the Soroti district. My elder sister Helen and brother Michael and my late elder brother John, were already in 'Maria's Care'. In the village life was hard; we used to have one meal a day and I was not studying because grandma could not afford school fees.

One day we got a surprise visit when Maria came to our village together with my late elder brother John. She met me and my young brother Simon and asked us whether we were schooling and we told her 'no'. Maria realized that we needed help and the following week she

The Call, the Cost, the Choice

requested we should all be taken into 'Maria's Care.' We went there in April, 1993, when I was seven years old and I am glad to be amongst the first people who went there, and grateful for all the benefits and things I learnt. Whilst there I accepted Christ as my personal saviour and therefore lived a Christian life. This has enabled me to overcome all the obstacles and challenges that would hinder me in life. Besides that I was also hard working both at home and at school; I used to fetch sawdust, sweep the compound and wash utensils.

At school I made sure I was always the best in class which made Maria very proud of me. I also made many friends at the orphanage who always encouraged me and kept me moving on.

After completing my 'A' levels with the support of 'Maria's Care' I was accepted at Makerere University for a course in animal production technology & management, at the faculty of Veterinary Medicine. But before joining the university my sister planned for me to do a diploma course instead because she couldn't afford the university fees; I prayed hard against that because I preferred studying a degree course. God blessed her with someone who voluntarily lent her some money for my first year tuition fees. I was so grateful for that. I studied my first year while praying and searching for a sponsor. Miraculously God blessed me with the Madhavani group who agreed to pay my fees for the next two years (but not food or accommodation) on condition that I didn't fail any exam paper. I was so grateful; I studied hard and passed all my papers. I scored grade 3.87; a second class honours degree which is a good result for me. I graduated on the 16th January, 2012.

I want to express my gratitude and thanks to Christian Relief Uganda. May God bless all of you abundantly; if it hadn't been for CRU and all the care and support my sponsors have given me over the years I would not be where I am today. I am very grateful, thank you very much. (In case you need more information in any of the above subsections please inform me. I declare that the above information is correct).

Thanks and God bless you.

Kaudha Rebecca

I was with Maria from 1993; I was one of the first girls Maria had in the little house before she moved to the lodge. Then we moved to the warehouses in 'Maria's Care', and I learnt how to do secretarial work in the Training School Of Life Skills from 1995 to 1998, when I qualified with a Uganda National Education Board Certificate. I went to work as a secretary in the Mokono district, and then with a company called BIKA. Later I was transferred to Busembatia. I started off renting a small stationery and computer shop, and lived behind it in one room with five young girls I took in who were all destitute and needed help. Their names are Saida, Vicky, Prossy, Azedha and Robina. They started to grow up and I supported them through high school raising the money through shop sales. I met Richard and married him and we now have two beautiful daughters called Happy Joy and Mercy, and also a son we have called Prince Morris.

I love them very much. We worship at Kingdom Life Centre in Busembatia and are very happy.

It is because of the love Maria and all you people showed us that we are the way we are today. I want to thank CRU for the vision and being obedient, it has made such a difference to all of our lives; you are great role models.

Thank you very much, may God bless all of you.

Kawuta Richard

We are really very grateful and happy for the wonderful work CRU is doing for the orphans to live a better life. I joined 'Maria's Care' and lived there from 1995 and registered as an orphan and a protestant by the name of Kawuta Richard, then God touched my heart and changed me, I became a born again Christian.

I joined when I was eight years old and started primary school under the control of Maria Maw, Rhona Marshall and Frances David who helped us to be the people we are now. After primary school I went to secondary level where I performed very well.

Rhona gave me several pieces of advice about my future and counselled me on which courses I should take. Then after, like a child who listens to his mum, I decided to do a hotel management course at the Hotel and Tourism Training Institute at Crested Crane in Jinja. I completed a year's study there and managed to get a place to do further training at one of the leading hotels in the world called Serena Hotel in Kampala.

CRU is supporting me with sponsors who help me with all of my training. I really want to thank all of you for making a better future for me.

Yours faithfully

Ngobi Tom

I lived in a small house along the Jinja road with my grandmother, brother Andrew and sister Barbara Bumpi. Our uncle was Maria Maw's neighbour, and one day whilst I was digging in the garden with my brother my uncle suggested we accepted sponsorship for school, we were about seven or eight years old.

My name then was Amuza and my brother was Twaha as we were Muslims, our auntie took us to meet Maria and she was very happy to meet us. Maria told us she would like to help pay school fees for us; she asked what religion we were and we said we were Muslims. We were given tea, fruit, and books to read.

Later in the afternoon we saw our sick grandmother and told her about Maria. Maria was very kind; she gave us clothes, uncooked food, and medical supplies for our grandmother. We didn't sleep at the orphanage though, we went home every night.

Maria asked me what I did after school; I really didn't understand the question because my English was very poor. Eventually, after speaking to a friend who translated I understood what Maria wanted to know. I told her I didn't do anything because we didn't have electricity at home and very little land. Maria wanted to help our family and gave us a chicken project to look after. The day came when a poultry house was erected in a small garden next to our grandmother's house and a hundred chickens were put in there. Maria told us we could raise the chickens and she helped us open a bank account in Kamuli, and encouraged us to bank the money from the sale of the eggs we sold, then we could use this money to pay for scholastic materials for school.

When I look back I remember that many books Maria gave us to read were Bible stories. I read stories about Moses, about Noah and the ark; how all the animals went in there. We would talk to her about this and we saw lots of pictures in the books. A special one was Jesus with his arms and hands open and the verse 'Suffer little children to come unto me'. When we were digging we thought we were the little children. Maria would often say "With God all things are possible," and this later became our motto. This really made us think. We used to sing with Maria and the other children. One song I remember was this:

Baby Jesus, baby Jesus I love you,

I love you, you are my saviour,

You are my saviour, every day, every day.

Each day we would listen and were part of morning prayers at 'Maria's Care'. After some time friends of ours, Simon and Robert, encouraged Twaha and me to become Christians but we wanted to observe more before making this big decision; as Muslims we were scared to change our religion. Maria encouraged us to go to church as we were part of her family and we saw lots of people being baptised by Pastor Herbert. Maria would give us some money every Sunday to go in the collection. One Sunday Pastor Herbert was talking about Jesus and said:

"If you haven't given your life to Jesus Christ and you want to, come to the front." Maria glanced at me and Twaha. He said to me: "shall we go?"

At first I was scared but then agreed to, and my friend Robert tapped me on the elbow to encourage me. We went to the front and lots of people clapped. We were asked to face the congregation and say our names and the pastor asked if we wanted to change them, but we didn't for the moment. He prayed for us with his hands on our heads. We were both given a Bible and told to read it every day, to go to prayers and pray for others and ourselves. He said if there were any problems we had to go to him. We were encouraged to say a prayer about wanting to live a new life and we repeated it after him.

After reading the Bible things began to trouble me; the people we were with all day were Christians but then we were going home at night and they were all Muslims. One day we went to Maria and told her we would like to change our names, I don't think she thought we were serious. She gave us names but when we saw Rhona we asked her to make a list of all the boys' names in the Bible. I looked at them and chose Tom and my brother became Andrew. We visited Pastor Herbert and asked if we could be baptised, he agreed and said we had made good name choices. There was a group of us who were baptised together; I had seen others do this so I had spare shorts and a T-shirt ready to put on afterwards.

I was a bright boy and came first for three terms in my primary one and primary two school years, I had good results in primary three and four too. In primary five the school system changed and universal primary education was introduced. I had a good friend called Richard who I was always with at Kamuli Parents Primary School and we played and studied together, and lived in the orphanage at 'Maria's Care'. At first I did very well but by primary six I was with a group of friends and didn't study seriously; I only got an aggregate of twenty-one and I was encouraged to do better. After sitting my primary leaving examination I got an aggregate of fifteen. I was taken for careers guidance; these were a group of experts who asked me what I would like to do in the future.

As I lived in Kamuli Village I didn't really have any ideas. I thought I could be a builder, mechanic, driver or shopkeeper. I studied for two years at St James in Jinja and a year in a catholic school.

Eventually Madam Rhona and the CRU chairman Steve suggested Richard and I went to the Crested Crane Hotel to do a hotel management course. They came to visit us and told us we looked very smart. We enjoyed it there and passed the short course. The following year we took the certificate of hotel operations and passed again. We had to find a hotel to do our practical studies and miraculously we both got a place at the new Serena Hotel in Kampala. We both graduated after spending a year working there. This was a wonderful experience and we would never have believed we would work in such a hotel when we came from a very humble mud house in Kamuli.

Life has not been easy but I can't write all of the stories down because there are so many.

In Uganda at least a third of males are put in prison each year, the innocent along with the guilty. Then you can be there for many months before a trial in court. I had heard about this but never believed in such words; also you must have solid cash if proved 'innocent' to get out of prison.

The year 2009, I call it a dead year because so many strange things happened to me and my brother Andrew. Both of us were in prison but lucky enough I only slept one night there but my brother spent three months in prison, which I call dark and cursed days in our lives. Without God's mercy Andrew would still be in prison!! He is my big brother and narrated the true story to me in tears; he said he was beaten, had one meal a day, and bitten by fleas and bed bugs. God's power carried Rhona (who we call our God given mum) and other members of CRU to come and rescue Andrew. It was a miracle the way God helped us get Andrew out of prison, a long story in itself.

Two days after Andrew had been let out of jail, I was also put in prison with three fellow students. I had been given money to go and have my decayed tooth removed, this I had done. I was sleeping downstairs after the extraction and was so surprised when I saw three gentlemen dressed in police uniforms looking for me and my other friends; they said a laptop was missing and we were the first suspects. The laptop had been upstairs and we didn't even know it was there.

This is the reason I was taken to prison, we were put in the vehicle and taken to the police station near the bridge. This marked the first time I had ever appeared in a police station as a thief. We registered all our property at the counter, and even switched off our phones which we could have used to call other friends for help. This station was an interrogation station where all kinds of thieves were punished seriously. As they were opening the cell room where I was going to stay I said to God.

"Help me and get me out of this place because whatever case they are putting on me I don't know anything, please help me!"

The first room was full, dirty, smelling, with so many terrified faces! With the gap in my gum bleeding seriously I wanted to use a wash room, but I was charged 5,000/-, yet this area was in a terrible condition due to many years without being attended to. After that I was taken to another cell which was a bit cleaner because I was bleeding and needed some clean water. As it approached noon we were brought a plate of posho with beans to share with thirteen other prisoners per room. This confirmed to me that I was going to die of hunger and bleeding from my mouth. The following morning we were lined up to parade and told to report to the CID office to give some statements about the laptop of which I had never looked at with my naked eyes!

Before entering the office I said a short prayer to God for help and remembered 'Maria's Care' motto, 'With God all things are possible,' which was always emphasised by mum Rhona. This marked the first night of sleeping in prison; I was so scared. After giving my information I begged a policeman to lend me his mobile phone and immediately I called Rhona who was at 'Maria's Care', and she responded positively. She asked people in the office how she could help me get out of prison, and told me to "keep calm, help was coming".

First and foremost I thank God and CRU because in every sort of problem they have always been around for us. I was taken back to the prison cell with a big smile on my face; this showed my cell mates that there was good news. In the morning we still had to attend to the general cleaning and ate breakfast from outside the cell. Then a prison officer said:

"You and your school mates are to leave just after lunch on a bond of 50,000/- (£16-60)".

I thanked God for what he had done for me and promised to tell my testimony before the church and to my friends and family. Never lean on yourself but put your trust in God. He is the only way out of traps even when we are not guilty. I thank my mum Rhona, Madam Sue and people at 'Maria's Care' who were sent to my rescue. Finally I thank CRU for the great work they are doing for us. I also want to thank my sponsors who have been very faithful helping me and Richard over so many years.

I continued at Crested Crane doing the hotel management course and was doing very well. I was taking some exams and had finished my papers when a student behind me asked for help. As I wrote some of his papers the teacher sent me out of the classroom; four others were also sent out because they had information with them relating to the exam subject. Sadly it ended up that all of us were expelled. This was very painful because I was just trying to help a friend.

I am very sorry for not completing my course because I know a lot of money has been invested in me over many years. The consequence of doing something I knew was wrong has left me with no certificate and I have to support myself and find work. As a committed Christian I have asked for forgiveness and friends have told me not to give up, there is always hope. I am trusting God for the next stage of my life and hope he will direct me to a job very soon.

May God bless you all.

(The latest news from Tom is that he flew to Dubai in June 2012 to start work there!)

Oketcho Steven

I am Steven Oketcho, twenty-four years of age, born to the family of the late Mr. Obbo William and the late Awor Jane Flora. We were three children by the time our parents passed away and we can't establish their actual cause of death because we were still very young. I am the elder son, followed by my brother Timothy who is twenty-one, and our sister Sylvia who is nineteen. We were raised by our grandmother who had also lost her husband early before we were born. Our grandee worked hard to provide food and clothing for us, however it was not easy because sometimes we could only have one meal. We never had clothes but she bought for us the ones we could use for going to church.

Our school life was not easy at all because every time we went we were sent home for fees. I resorted to digging as a job to get fees and also sold soya beans to get money for salt, soap and paraffin for the family. In 1998 I met a white lady called Maria Maw who took me and my siblings to an orphanage she had established with her other friends from England. At this time I was in primary seven school year and I had always dreamed of being a doctor in the future. At some point we left the orphanage because we became grown-ups and Maria put some money in the bank for us to continue our studies.

However, the money was not enough for us all, so my siblings had to drop out of school to allow me to finish my senior six school year and have further education. This money was not enough to support me to do medicine at university, so I decided to do nursing instead. I have completed my studies and graduate in September 2012. My siblings are at home with no education because there is no money for them. But I still have faith and trust in God that one day I will be a doctor so that I can treat and heal God's people, and also hope that my siblings can at least have some vocational training so that they are able to support their family financially.

For this reason I dearly thank God for Maria and her family; the CRU co-ordinator Rhona Marshall; for the great support to my family and me in particular towards my education, and in knowing more about God. May God bless you always.

The Call, the Cost, the Choice

Mugono Nevi

I was born in 1989, with four sisters and three brothers in my family. Around 1992 'Maria's Care' was started in our neighbourhood and I got to know about it from my two sisters who were already part of Maria's family. Sometimes after their visits home, I would follow them right to the compound where there was a tree with juicy mangoes. I sometimes sat under the tree or on the veranda near the dining room. There I would salivate for the food; it really had a good smell! I was excited when Maria invited me into the tidy dining room to have lunch on the table, moreover with a fork and spoon, and with the rest of the children. This was the day Maria got to know that I was related to two of the girls there.

In 1994 Maria talked to my mum and I was invited to start nursery at the crèche. Life was fabulous there with a lot of games and toys, not forgetting the food. There were games I'd never dreamt of; toy cars and bicycles made the days of my childhood very bright. No other school had anything like this then. I was doing so well that a year later my dad proposed that I should start primary one, so I was sent to Kamuli Township Primary School where life was kind of miserable. During my second year at school Maria requested that I join the orphanage and give a child called Paul some company; he was a young boy my age that lacked a playmate.

I came to stay at 'Maria's Care' on a Saturday evening and I was welcomed with great music!

Then I realised this music wasn't meant for me, it was meant for God; this was the Bible study time and praise and worship was going on. It was fun! That same night I was surprised when I was led into a beautiful room by Auntie Rebecca. This was like a heaven; I was shown a bed with beautiful bed sheets, and given a towel and blanket among other things. I'd never seen a room as beautiful as that because our home was a mud house. So school continued there with Nevi as a completely new boy in class with a very nice uniform, shoes, socks and superior stationery. My life had been transformed.

In 'Maria's Care' I was shown love; I could never imagine myself on the laps of a muzungu, eating sweets in all kinds of flavours, colours and shapes; I would look to these ladies as mothers. Oh, life was like a dream I could not afford to wake up from.

Around 1996 Maria acquired new buildings and garden as a donation from the Madhvani family. Many big boys from 'Maria's Care' worked so hard in preparing that place. Paul and I helped clearing light rubbish and piling stones to mention but a few jobs. When the whole place was ready it gave me pride since I'd been part of it. I acquired skills like art and craftwork and simple cooking (there was a cooking rota) though it took me time to learn about washing my clothes because the bigger girls would wash for us, then later a washing machine appeared. Life went on.

In 2000 when I was in primary six I made a mistake that made me shed tears many times after. I picked maize from a neighbour's garden and that qualified me to be expelled. But by God's favour, I was allowed to complete my primary schooling, and I walked home each night which wasn't very far from school. This was just the beginning of my tears. At 'Maria's Care' my friends felt pity for me but back home I was blamed and my very own parents were bitter with me. Children who knew what happened made fun of me and called me 'omwiibi wa dhuuma' meaning 'thief'. It was misery at home with no money and dad was almost abandoning home as he'd gotten younger wives.

At the end of my primary schooling in January 2002 the primary leaving examinations results where released and I emerged the best 'Maria's Care' pupil, but this did not give me any joy as I didn't know what would happen next. It was then that I learnt to pray and Rhona replied to a letter in which I was seeking forgiveness. In her reply she comforted me and assured me of forgiveness with scriptures. It relieved my guilt and this letter gave me a lot of hope.

I then joined a secondary school after much waiting. Many bad things had happened to me before joining this school but they made me stronger. Life in this school was not so good for me as it was expensive but God comforted me and I also consoled myself many times. I excelled here and qualified for partial scholarships. This meant that I could spend weeks at home and missed some schooling as I had not cleared my school fees.

Dad could afford the fees maybe but he'd got a load of expense himself with the wives and of course more children. This made me bitter since one of the wives mistreated us maybe because she saw us as threats. I saw myself surrounded by witchcraft and almost got into it. These four years in secondary school were not easy ones but the Lord kept me excelling. During school holidays my faith got stronger, and I fasted and prayed endlessly so I would never experience such situations again. The Lord answered all my prayers perfectly!! I went in senior five year at the best school of my dreams (one of the best in the country) and it had Christian principles. Each term here I qualified for bursaries and after that I qualified for government sponsorship at university; at the time I'd almost lost hope since the list I was on was published late.

I have now completed a bachelor's degree in microfinance at Kyambogo University and graduate in September 2012. The Lord keeps providing my needs. The Lord is so true to us all if we trust him and welcome him into our lives; he won't impose himself on us. Some of my favourite verses are; Jeremiah 29:11-14, 1 John 4:4, 5:14-15 and 1Timothy 3:16-17.

I am so thankful to all who've been praying for CRU and given all kinds of support. One of the best things I got out of 'Maria's Care' was to know God because my brothers who never went there aren't doing well and never reached where I am.

God bless you all.

Atingu Beatrice Stella.

Well, my brief testimony is that in December 1992, Maria Maw kindly invited me and my other siblings to her home in Kamuli for Christmas which we gladly accepted; I had just completed my primary education and had to join secondary school the following year. I had done very well in my primary leaving examinations and had gained admission to my first school choice but had no one to pay my school fees;

Maria took pity on me and paid fees for me in that school.

Maria had set up the Training School of Life Skills by then and cared for needy children whom she took in and catered for. As the number of children increased she reached out to people back in England for sponsorships and her daughters were among the first sponsors that she got. After some time CRU was formed and their general sponsorship enabled me to complete my 'A' level education, and I did very well.

I had the opportunity to enter university to do a law degree but since I had no specific sponsor like some others did, I somehow lost hope; Maria had no money personally to pay my fees. Then guess what! A miracle happened! A couple came for their first time to Uganda and to 'Maria's Care', called Geoff & Linda Oliver; they were so friendly, kind and inquisitive. When they discovered my situation they gladly assured me that they would sponsor me for a bachelor's degree in Law at Makerere University. This they did along with several other people as the fees were very expensive; this sponsorship continued through the bar course and indeed they kept their promise till I completed. I graduated with a law degree and am now a barrister in Kampala.

So basically that is how I can put it. However, I also have to note that my success was also as a result of the difficult situations that I have gone through and the hard work learned through those circumstances.

Those circumstances made me believe that all I had was God and nobody else, and I kept on telling God that if he changed my plans then I wouldn't mind if it brought him joy and happiness.

The whole situation at the orphanage was a blessing to me. I learnt a lot about God and understood almost every situation and want to admit that my stay there moulded my character; though I am sure those who have never discovered this privilege will not understand.

Thank you.

Kaima Sula

Hi mum Rhona, hope everything is fine! I received your message saying to write a short note about my past. I will be precise because my sweet baby is crying at my back.

My father grew up by himself on the street; he eventually succeeded and gradually got some money. He had six wives and produced over forty kids. I remember he told us his mother had run away from her family because she was pregnant. Unfortunately my father lost his mother when he was little; he never knew about his mother's background so he was on his own. Eventually a good samaritan raised him but he didn't go to school. He become a very hard working man and was a strong Muslim.

I was told he was betrayed by his fellow businessmen; he had a gun and was caught and put in jail for years; he eventually sold his assets in order to bribe his way out, He was only released in president Museveni's regime; he had been tortured and his legs were broken. He died eventually and my mother followed a year after. My late father left us an old unfinished house where we used to sleep after our parents death. Unfortunately my step-mother's sons, who are older than me, sold the iron sheets and poles that held the house up, claiming the pieces belonged to them since my mother was my father's fifth and youngest wife. Eventually the house fell down and we started meandering round town. I remember one day I fell over when we were being chased from the street; I was caught and seriously beaten.

I started selling sodas and clothes in the market just for food; my life was so miserable with no hope. I was seven years old when I was sent to a district called Jinja, to assist my aunt who was very sick with AIDS, but I was not sent to school. I was mistreated and had to run to an uncle who offered me a job washing cups in the kitchen. I used to sleep with fellow workers in triple decked bunk-beds; I worked till late at night then was up early to start again.

When I was about ten years old I thought of going to school with some money I had saved; I asked my uncle for some extra money; he agreed and I started schooling. I jumped the lower classes to primary three because I thought I was too big for the class and felt shy. Still working and schooling, I was clever and got seventeen aggregates.

I started senior one school year in Jinja but it was difficult; I failed to balance work and school because I had to walk miles each day there and back. At the hostel I used to go to sleep at 7pm and wake up at 2am to study by candle-light till it was time to walk to school. Electric power in Uganda is not stable so I used candles or electricity depending. I thought this way I could catch up with the other pupils who got proper studies when they were young. This life wasn't so bad compared to the one I passed through when I was younger..

That is when I met God's ambassador, Rhona Marshall. I said to her: "How can I be saved?" I wanted to be born again.

She was so excited to hear this from a young gentleman. She met me after work one day and we read a small book together called 'Bridge to Life.' There was a prayer I read as Madam Rhona asked me if I wanted to pray the prayer from my heart. I did this on October 16th. 2005. Whenever she came to where I was working we talked a lot about Jesus. She would take me with her to the nearest church. The first day I stepped in the church the pastor asked if there were any visitors. I didn't know what to do but after watching the other visitors I stood up and said:

"My name is Sula, I was once a Muslim but I am now a Christian."

Everyone went wild, clapping and praising the Lord. A few minutes later I saw the power of God; I witnessed a terrible storm, heavy rain with wind. Doors and windows flew open, the mosquito nets fell off the windows onto the floor, and I was terrified. I felt a battle for my life had just taken place.

A few weeks later I was asked if I wanted to be baptised, Madam Rhona was in England and I didn't think she was going to be in Uganda, so I was very surprised when she walked in on the day I was being baptised. It was such a lovely day; I was given a certificate of baptism and this meant a lot to me as it signified a real relationship with God.

Days and years passed, and each time Rhona brought visitors to Uganda she would meet me unexpectedly. One day she bought me a bike to ease my journey to school. Things got difficult for me when my boss heard I had become a Christian; he called me in and ordered me to sell the bike and at once stopped the little money he used to top up my school fees. Days after, he ordered me to leave his hotel claiming there was nothing remaining for me; I had seen the truth, reforming myself and taken Jesus as my only saviour. Lots of things happened during this time after being sacked; I used to sneak about looking for food

Briefly, when I was sick and fed up of hiding and sneaking for food I thought of going back to my village but wasn't sure how I could as it was a long way from Jinja; I had left there when I was seven and was feeling very miserable. I called mum Rhona to say goodbye, and she was touched and felt the Holy Spirit in her heart, and great sympathy for me. She immediately told me to stay and said that God would take care of me. It was a miracle; everything changed from then on. She took me back to school and I finished my 'O' levels, then branched to an institution where I achieved a certificate in hotel operations. I was the first person from my village to graduate. Then I upgraded for a diploma in hotel management at the Crested Crane in Jinja.

Everything is working out. I have another year to study then I hope I will get a good job to be able to support my baby boy Jordan and Rachael, my wife-to-be. I am very proud of my baby, but I don't want him to face the challenges that I had years ago. I always tell Rachael not to worry because God will provide, I am not sure how but I am positive. we are due to marry on September 15th, 2012. I want to thank everyone who has encouraged and supported me over the years.

May God bless you.

The Call, the Cost, the Choice
Nakalma Angellah

When I was very small I lived with my mother, brother Paul and sister Fiona, and my cousins Tom, Andrew, Med, Sophie & Barbara Bumpi came to stay when their grandmother died. We only had two rooms, it was a tight squeeze and we had to push the mattresses together so all the girls slept in one room and the boys in the other.

When I was eight years old I was studying in my primary two school year at Mountain View Primary School when people at 'Maria's Care' were told about our situation. Many of us were taken into the Orphans Destitute Abode for Children and we were very happy there. I was in primary three up to seven; I did very well in primary three and was amongst the top three children. In primary six I became ill and missed a lot of school as I had malaria. In primary seven I got an aggregate of twenty-six and went to St Noa's, in Mawagali, Jinja. I did very well but when I was in senior four I was very sick again and didn't do well in the exams. It was suggested I trained to be a tailor and I asked if I could repeat the year because I knew I could do better. Sadly this request was refused and I went back to my village. In 2010 I was sitting at home when an auntie called me to help her in the house, she realised I was a bright girl and offered to pay school fees for me. I repeated my senior three year and didn't do very well at the beginning but by the second term I performed better and my health improved. I was given a choice to go into senior four or do a catering course for two years.

I chose the catering course which finishes in November 2012. I have accommodation in a local convent; I get up around 5am, I bathe, dress, wash clothes, and prepare my breakfast. I clean my room before leaving at 7.30am to walk to the classroom which I have to be in by 8am. This can be very tricky when it has rained and the roads and lanes are muddy. We are in class from 8am learning to prepare food which we can eat for lunch. At 2pm we are back in the classroom for lessons until 5pm, when I walk back to the convent and prepare supper, do revision, and bathe before prayers at 8pm.

I would like to thank CRU for exposing me to new people. As I lived in the village this helped me talk to big people, to be able to stand on my own and to socialise with others. I was also taught how to live a Christian life and became a Christian when I was about nine. I learnt to speak English very well and my mum encouraged all of us to do this in our village home.

When I was little I liked playing with the deaf children at 'Maria's Care' and learnt how to communicate with them. I play netball and love music and drama. I am learning how to cook mainly Dutch, Italian and French food at the moment and would like to continue further in catering studies, then one day work in a good hotel.

Thank you very much.

Mufumba Sharon

I was born into a family with a Muslim background but my mum never married our dad. They just one time loved each other and so I was conceived and produced. Since they were not married I grew up with my mum alone. When I approached nine years of age, in 1996, my mum converted to Christianity and so did I, but she died when I was fifteen and so I had to go and stay with my dad who was a Muslim. The moment he discovered that I was a born again Christian he made all possible ways to stop me from continuing in my faith. I loved Christ so much that I could not accept leaving Him. One day, after being caned seriously, my father told me that if I could not accept his command and leave Christianity, I had to leave his home. He sent me away and I went to stay with ono of my church elders.

What I remember though before I left my father's home was that he made me sit down and spoke to me these words: "I am no longer your father, my children are never your brothers and sisters and my wife is no longer your step-mother. You will have to suffer for the rest of your life."

He followed this with an act of putting off his shirt to show that he had put off any kind of responsibility he would have rendered to me as his child. Even though he spoke these words to threaten me and make me submit to his command, I had already made up my mind to follow Christ.

Life wasn't easy in my new home but I had to bear up. By this time I had just started at 'Maria's Care' doing my secretarial training and I therefore struggled with life to see that I could make my education successful, because my dad had promised not to support me financially. But I very much thank God because when I was so much troubled and wondering what to do, I came across a caring woman of God called Rhona, with whom I sat and explained my problems. With a lot of love she encouraged me and gave me wonderful presents which became part of my success. I always remember the wonderful yellow paper which had writings about the four reasons why I had to smile (truly, whenever I read this paper I got peace in my heart and found myself smiling) and the small doll which whenever I held it and put it to my chest, I felt like Christ was always with me, caring and feeling my pain.

I continued to live in the church elder's home until it was suggested I should go back to live with my father; this would mean submission to his orders and having to turn my back on my salvation, which I did not want to do. I was asked to leave the home I was in and I felt a lot of pain and life became very hard for me. I regretted that my mum had died but I very much thanked God because he never abandoned me. Eventually I went to live with my uncle who was also a staunch Muslim.

After living with him for three weeks, my uncle told me my father wanted me back at home and the door was open to me, but only if I gave up Christianity. After a huge amount of pressure and mistreatment I agreed that I would leave Christianity and go back home. But immediately after I had spoken such a word, I had three consecutive thoughts in my head. *"Whoever denies me before people, I will do the same before my father in heaven."*

"Fear him who has the power to destroy both the spirit and the body but not the body alone. Many gave up because they feared men's approval and being chased away from their company but missed eternal life."

"When a person wants to build a house, he has to first sit down and calculate whether he has enough materials for full construction, but if he builds up to the middle and runs out of resources, passers-by laugh at his defeat."

After these voices, uncontrollable tears began to flow out of my eyes. I realized that the Lord was talking to me. I immediately changed my mind and said: "Come what may, I will never leave salvation"

The Lord remained faithful to me and did not abandon me, his word sounded true in my ears. I continued to live with my uncle and carried on going to school at 'Maria's Care'. I was so upset about my home situation that I thought I might as well end my education and go and live on the streets like other street children. But God is good at all times because when I went home that night, I found my uncle eagerly waiting for me, telling me my dad had told him that he wanted to see and talk to his daughter. I went to my dad's home and we sat and talked. If I am to clearly remember my dad's words this time, they were:

"My daughter, I have seen how much you love your Jesus, I now leave you to serve your God the way you want because it is the Lord who enabled me also to produce you and take care of you up to this age. Please come back home any day you feel like it, and meet your brothers and sisters. How much money do they need for your school fees?"

I told him the amount and he gave me not just half but the whole amount to take to school.

Though he had allowed me to go back home, I didn't rush back but frequently visited instead. I remember that with every visit my father prepared for me only special things a person can prepare for a special visitor. I therefore continued with my studies at 'Maria's Care' Training School of Life Skills and achieved a certificate in secretarial studies. I thank God that over the last few years I have held a good job as a secretary in Uganda. I now have dreams of setting up my own stationery shop in the near future if God allows and provides.

I greatly thank the power of the Lord because it was not by power or by might that I managed to overcome, but by the grace of the Lord my God. The glory belongs to him forever and ever, Amen. I also thank my friend Rhona and my friend Sarah, (the young girl) who stood with me, for their encouragement and prayers.

May God bless you so much.

Kasenke Robert

My name is Robert, brother to Kasenke Godfrey and twin brother to Alex. I joined 'Maria's Care' in 1997 when I was 10 years old, my late dad worked at the orphanage and when he died we remained there. It was a challenge! Talking to you people was not easy and we had to have a translator. The other challenge was waking early!

I went to a technical college rather than a secondary school and the orphanage sponsored me till I got a certificate in motor vehicle mechanics and driving. I left 'Maria's Care' to look for a job but sadly failed because my academic qualifications were low compared to people with university degrees. I prayed to God all the time and eventually someone decided to sponsor me and this enabled me to study advanced motor vehicle mechanics at Lugogo Vocational College in Kampala; I knew this would help me to compete with other people for jobs.

Presently I am working in Kampala in a garage exercising my skills and I hope to establish my own workshop. I know it's not easy but I believe I will succeed, and I just request your prayers as it is one of the most important things for me as far as life is concerned. I also plan to open up a Travel & Tour Company. It sounds a big thing talking about a company but from small things big things can grow. So now mum Rhona, the qualifications and skills I have can help me do things for myself and also help others.

I am really very happy for my life right now. Though we meet many challenges in life there is a solution for everything as long as we think and do things right and put our trust in God. God never fails to reply to all our cries.

I still think about you and Maria; thanks also go to all the sponsors and staff at 'Maria's Care' who were there when we were kids; they did a great job putting us right and teaching us how to work. We have now grown up and try to be good citizens and better fathers and mothers of tomorrow to our nation.

I am sorry for when you saw I was doing things wrong; I always welcomed your advice and ideas because I knew they could help me in the future. Thanks for being so good to us and all your support. Even though we have left 'Maria's Care', you still look out for us and find out how we are progressing in life; this alone shows the heart you have for us and how much you do think about 'Maria's Care' children.

Abdu Salem Peter

Rhona writes: I told Peter's story in chapter six; I recently met up with him again in May 2012. He said to me:

"Can you imagine I have a degree?" He told me that he had done very well and in November 2011 qualified with a degree in human resource management after studying at Kampala International University.

He was thrilled and so was I because Peter had found life very difficult. He was just collecting a couple of references to take to Sudan in a few weeks time where he hopes to fulfil a position of work. We talked about his life and how God had saved him when the nurse had told me: 'this boy is going to die.' As I recalled the story he gave me one of his beautiful smiles.

"You see what God has done?" he said. Peter seemed relaxed and at peace with his life now; he had great hopes and was trusting in God. It is always interesting for me to watch and see what the Lord is going to do with these young men and women.

Kasolo David

I came to Kamuli with very little in 1989 and set up a small wooden hut where I slept and worked from. In 1992 I met Maria; she needed some furniture made but didn't have any money. We both trusted God; I made the furniture and she eventually gave me the money for it. That's how it was at the beginning. We were very good friends and she encouraged me to keep going. I would lie in bed and dream up how I was going to make the machinery to cut the wood and make shapes for legs of chairs and tables. Eventually I made a lot of my own machinery.

Rhona writes: I saw a lot of machinery David had designed in his newly constructed workshop in 1995; we both laughed at how unsafe a lot of it was, but it worked! David worked long hours and was very pleased with what he made. With the profit he sent his wife and children to study. He and his wife Janet have five children; they both worked hard and sacrificed a lot of their own comforts to put their children through education and it has paid off: Paul has a degree in business administration and is now an auditor, Mark has followed in David's footsteps and is a carpenter and joiner; he is preparing for his diploma eventually in civil engineering, Anthony studied from primary one to senior four and is doing a three year veterinary course in Lowero district, consisting of a two year certificate course, and one year to do a diploma course; he hopes to have completed in 2015, Esther is now in her senior four school year; she would like to study to work in medical personnel or general nursing.

When I first met David's wife, Kasolo Janet Nabirye, she was very quiet and didn't speak any English and therefore had little confidence. When I met her in 2012 she was able to converse with me and she told me her incredible story:

"I only went to primary school, I never went to senior school until I was much older. At fourteen I did a short typing and accounts course, I learnt fast and when I was fifteen I was asked if I would go and work for Father Grimms at Namasagali College. I started to produce my children when

I was eighteen. I was thirty-two when I went back to school and started in senior one. I had my first-born in senior two. I was at the Modern Christian School at Pastor Herbert's church in Kamuli and I studied up to senior four.

In 1998 I started to work in Kamuli Town Council and in 2000 became a councillor; I was invited to go to Niarobi on a two week study tour because I was involved with PWD (people with disabilities); we were involved in workshops to do with farming and home projects.

I was deputy mayor for four years and retired from the Council in 2011 when I was forty-one years old in order to study a degree in social work and social administration at Busoga University in Kamuli."

I understood every word as Janet spoke and excitedly gave me her story. What a lady; to bring up five children and put them first, then think about herself and her future.

These next stories are just a few highlights from *bazungu* who have been on a 'Ugandan experience' over the years:

Sheila Jamieson

There are so many happy, sad and humorous memories to choose from, here are a few:

Arriving at 'Maria's Care' was very moving as the big blue gates opened and there was a sea of little faces, all smiling. What a welcome we got! Never to be forgotten. Then there was the time I was invited to have breakfast with Tappy, a young girl who helped clean at 'Maria's Care'; we walked into the kitchen and there on the table were rows of red and blue plastic cups with hot steaming something in them, on asking what it was I was told it was Porac (porridge). I'm a Scot, I'll stick to Quakers, thank you!

Listening to the wonderful singing of the students with their perfect natural harmony; working with the deaf and dumb children, they sign with one hand and I needed to use two so you can imagine their lovely big smiles when I made a mistake; making and flying paper airplanes, teaching simple decoupage of animals; helping Godfrey make a sponge cake and pastry with these ingredients:

1 egg
1 tin runny margarine
Flour, take your pick, self-raising or plain.
1 bag of grey sugar
1lb. of prayers (that the electricity would not go off)
1 x 24inch square cake tin.

Getting lost in Jinja with Mark, Ruth and Neil, and standing in the middle of the road on an island praying we would be rescued and returned to the rest of the party, we were rescued when four young men arrived on bicycles looking for 'Sheila Jimmy!" That was fun! Going to church on Sunday and seeing all the children dressed in their Sunday best clothes. A notice on the church door said:

'At the end of your rope? Try Jesus.'

All wonderful times in Uganda.

Sue Pratt

Apart from the miracle of three healthy babies delivered safely I remember an incident Rhona and I both shared at the end of the trip. It was while we were up at Murchison Falls staying at The Red Chilli Camp Site. We had all got up early to go out on safari and were sitting in the land rover when Rhona said to me:

"What is on your wish list for this morning's safari?"

Without any hesitation I replied: "leopard."

In spite of several previous safaris whilst living in South Africa I had never seen one. Off we went and had not journeyed far when it was fairly obvious our ranger sensed we were near to one of the big cats, and yes! There we were a few hundred yards away from a lone leopard! Amazing! I was so excited. We sat and watched from close quarters for some time and we were all able to take photos of this magnificent creature. Rhona just looked at me and smiled; her face seemed to say: 'another of God's miracles.' Thank you for the moment. I will never forget that little cameo from Uganda.

The Call, the Cost, the Choice

Susan Clayton

On the face of it my journey to Uganda began on 19th December 2003, when I was asked if I'd like to go with friends (Gavin, Fiona and Anthea) on a visit to Uganda in March 2004 to see the work being done by Christian Relief Uganda. It was a surprise to be asked. I had just retired early from teaching after nearly a year out with ill health, so I had no problems with getting time off. I had my doubts as to whether I would have the energy to go for the two weeks but I thought why not, and duly said: 'Yes I'd love to come'. Several injections later and a few visits with Barbara going round local schools and groups talking about Uganda and the work being done out there, and I was ready to go.

The United Church in Rhyl sent the four of us off with their prayers. It was while prayers were being said that I remembered something that had happened to me when I was about nine or ten years old; whilst I was reading the story of Gladys Aylward on the back page in a comic a thought came into my mind: You could do that, and my immediate reaction was: No I can't, I'm too young. That was the last I heard of that thought, though I must admit there was something nagging me in my later teens but I ignored it and carried on with becoming a teacher. I suppose looking back with hindsight, it could be said that that was the beginning of my journey to Uganda.

Sue Field

I was blown away by a talk I heard by Rhona Marshall about her experiences in Uganda but due to family commitments it was to be another five years before I joined her and others on a trip to Africa.

During my fiftieth year I realised I wanted to get to the end of my life and say I had done something different, and I knew when I was at 'Maria's Care' I would be back; how I didn't know, but God did.

Over the next five years I was to return to Uganda another five times in my role as child sponsorship secretary. The experiences I have had there have had a profound effect on my life as God revealed himself to me in a way I could never have imagined, even to the point of actually saving my life.

Words cannot express the privilege it has been to serve him in Uganda even in this short time.

Barbara Koffman

Picture the scene: July 1995, Christian Camp in Anglesey. Rhona and I were sitting in the sunshine on the fields in Benllech; she was reading her favourite newspaper and there was an advert for sensible sandals, the kind she would need next time she went to Uganda. As we talked Rhona simply asked me if I would like to go to Uganda with her.

After speaking with friends and family it was decided that 'yes', I would go. A friend offered to pay my airfare and my parents offered to look after my girls who were teenagers at the time. Everything was arranged and we planned to go out in February, 1996. We have always tried to take as much as we can out with us in the way of donations, but in 1996 the rules on luggage were quite restricted; we ended up with a builder's jig-saw in the hand luggage, and Rho asked me to wear two of everything so that we maximised our weight allowance.

Little did I know that becoming part of the vision would change the direction in my life. Rho and I shared many scary and enjoyable moments; we prayed a lot and saw God move in the most amazing ways.

We have had the pleasure of seeing many children come to faith in the Lord, and some adults too. Over the years I have matured and grown spiritually; God has directed my path, been by my side and helped me in all situations.

With qualifications as a dental hygienist my passion was to help the indigenous population of Uganda improve their oral health. This started in a very simple way by giving presentations and talking to groups of people in the local villages. The project has been transformed over the years and there has been a natural progression for me to join with the charity Dentaid, which I did in 2012, to enhance and further this work.

Barbara Heal

I live in Bradford now but resided in Macclesfield for eighteen years prior to the family's move to Yorkshire in 1991. I had got to know Rhona through a couple of catering jobs she did for me, then more intimately when she started attending Tytherington Family Worship Church. We kept in touch when I moved and Rhona's enthusiasm always grabbed my attention when I received the newsletters about CRU or attended fund raising events, but can't say I was 'drawn' to get involved.

In 2002, my husband Derek died suddenly, I moved house and took early retirement from the NHS but continued to work on a locum basis as a nurse. This meant that my time, both working and social was my own. Everybody said:

"Oh Barbara; you are making too many changes at once. You have lost your husband. Be gentle with yourself and take longer over such decisions". I know they were being kind but there was a certainty within me that God was in charge.

This was confirmed when the day I told my boss I would be retiring in the summer, Rhona rang quite out of the blue and asked if I would consider going to Uganda with her. My immediate response was:

"Well, I can because today I've just given my retirement notice!" Definitely God in charge.

My first trip was in April 2004 for a month. What an eye opener! When I recall my experiences now, they flood back in such clarity: there was the lady with the infected foot who we helped with treatment and transport to a clinic; the clothes we distributed to the scantily clad; the children we sang 'round and round the garden' with and the schools with over a hundred students in one class; the most basic and poorest of living conditions coupled with the warmest of welcomes and hospitality. I remember the heat, food, and discomforts; the blue skies; the prolific vegetation and best of sunsets. What a place of opposites but what a work to be involved in. Just one month but so much achieved for the good.

On my return, I started to give talks about CRU to various groups and undertook to sell the crafts brought back, which always fascinate and appeal.

In 2005, Rhona asked me to join a trip with her and David Young, a children's evangelist from Australia. This proved a tougher time due to a smaller team, overwhelming numbers of children and a tummy bug that left me feeling ill for the latter part of the trip. I lost a stone in weight and arrived home to a horrified son who asked me what on earth I had been doing to get to look the way I did! I include this bit because sometimes the trip isn't all fascination and a wonderful experience; we are human and prone to these problems, but how do you know what's going to happen unless you go in the first place?.

I remarried in 2006 and became a grandma, so you could say there are new areas in my life to enjoy and Mike, my new husband, has an interest in Africa too, so it may be that we will return to Uganda together. This is how God works in CRU; he brings the right folk at the right time for the needs to be met. He may then draw them away for a time or, as in Rhona and Barbara's case, present them with a full time project. It doesn't matter in CRU, God's in charge and as long as that is recognised it will continue to thrive.

Mike Kendrick

The day I want to comment on was in October, 2006; we held the first 'Maranatha' meeting in the 'Taste and See Cafe' in Jinja, Uganda. This was a very special day. The group travelled from Kamuli and we arrived in Jinja late morning; we received a great welcome and shortly afterwards the meeting started. The numbers grew and the cafe was soon very full. It was a surprise when at lunchtime Godfrey served bacon sandwiches! This was a fantastic experience; sadly the overheads of the café were too expensive but they still hold a monthly meeting in a local parishioner's home in Jinja on the last Monday of each month.

Kathleen and Brian Wood

When Kathleen and I retired from teaching we thought that a spell of VSO (voluntary services overseas) would be the right way to use our talents. We had been to Africa for family reasons and so this was the area we decided to concentrate on but God said 'no'. He had other plans for us to do and we have spent the last ten years as part of a chaplaincy team in a big Birmingham hospital. God has a sense of humour though and when our son decided to marry a Ugandan our paths crossed with Rhona and Barbara.

We arrived at 'Maria's Care' during a hot spell in July 2006, with a suitcase full of bits and bobs and the chance to give it a go in Africa.

For the short spell we were with the children we were able to experience so much of their situation first hand, and we were blessed to be able to bring more colour into their lives; we will never forget our time there. We always pass on our experiences in Africa and 'Maria's Care' to anyone who is prepared to listen. We are often given contributions which we pass on to CRU for their projects in Uganda

The Call, the Cost, the Choice

Jim Tryon

It's not often that you're invited to visit an orphanage in the middle of Africa, and travel into bush villages to find grannies looking after a group of orphaned grandchildren in a dilapidated hut; certainly not when you're seventy-nine years old. Well, that happened to me!

My wife died in 2002, after we'd been happily married for fifty-five years, and the following year I was persuaded by God to help at a Christian youth camp in Anglesey; run for one hundred-and-sixty children with about forty Christian helpers. At the end of the camp I was invited by Rhona to join a group that was travelling to Uganda in Spring, 2004. I thought I was too old for that sort of thing, but God thought otherwise.

You see, although I was part of a Christian family and was baptised when I was fourteen; I had become a lazy Christian, not bothering about church and rarely reading the Bible or praying. From Psalm 139:16, we know that God has plans for us before we were born, and in his infinite patience and perseverance he'd waited until at last the message had got through.

So, having been told by my doctor to 'go for it' when I told her about my intended first visit, I joined a group from CRU, led by Rhona and Barbara, and went out to Kamuli in 2004. I knew then I was 'hooked' on Uganda, so I went again in the autumn, and almost every year since. I've recently booked my air ticket for my eleventh visit.

Uganda really is a lovely green and pleasant country but there is so much that needs to be done; there are still far too many orphans and poor people in the bush country, let alone the towns. I have always felt welcome there. So I continually thank God for his patience and I'm certain that instead of growing older, I'm just beginning to grow up... well, just a bit!

Lesley Twigg

I have been to Uganda three times to date and have met many people whose lives have been changed by 'Maria's Care', either in the school or the projects they are involved in; without 'Maria's Care' they would not have had such wonderful opportunities. Each visit I have taken I have learnt a lot about how amazing God is and how much he loves me and how that will never change. I have learnt to trust and be obedient to what he calls me to do. I have been on an amazing journey over the past few years; have met some inspirational people and look forward to seeing what God has in store for my future. It's such a privilege to be involved with the charity CRU.

Lynette Marshall

When Rhona first asked me to write a paragraph on my Ugandan experience, I thought no problem, but how wrong was I? I now think it would have been easier to write a full novel! Where do I begin? What was especially significant? How would I describe these beautiful Ugandan people? What difference has 'Maria's Care' made to the pupils both past and present? What would I put in? What would I leave out? How do I even begin to describe the miracles I have witnessed on my trips? Maybe I should tell of the time God 'shrunk' our luggage and fitted ten huge suitcases, five large pieces of hand-luggage, a full-size electric wheelchair, and seven people into two saloon cars! Or when our little group shared communion at the top of Mount Elgon overlooking the breathtaking scenery beneath us, whilst singing 'How Great Thou Art'; the memory still brings me out in goose bumps. Or should I say more about the awesome work of CRU and 'Maria's Care' whose love and dedication have changed so many lives? Or the privilege of being blessed with sharing the recent stories of love, encouragement and faith from those with first-hand experience of living in the compound? Should I say something about how these trips have changed my life and given me a new respect, love and compassion for the Ugandan people, who are so poor in wealth but have riches beyond my understanding? No, I think I should say: "Go see for yourself!" – I promise you will never be the same again!

Chapter 9

'Your labour in the Lord is not in vain'

Throughout this book you have read my thoughts about encouraging people to go on a 'Ugandan experience'.

In 1997, after talking to people in my home church I found there was a lot of interest. Ted and Janet Hughes, a church elder and his wife, invited me to their home for a meal. I had spoken to them on numerous occasions about my ideas of taking people to Uganda and wondered if they thought it was viable or me just being crazy. They sat me next to a close friend of theirs called Helen who had many years experience taking small groups abroad, and encouraged me to write ideas down and pray about my heart's desire. After listening to Helen's experiences I felt excited and believed I could do something similar in Uganda. Janet would later play a part in proof reading this book. Thank you, Janet.

Later that year I took the first group with me to Africa. Maria thoroughly enjoyed us visiting 'Maria's Care'; although it was hard work for her we were able to get a lot done.

The trip in 1999 was a lot of fun because my daughters Sarah and Emma came to see what I was doing, and Barbara Koffman came on her second visit. Barbara really loved going to Uganda but at this stage neither of us knew why the Lord was encouraging her to go yet again. I was thrilled my daughters were with me because it meant when I spoke about a place in future they knew where I was referring to. Maria made us very welcome as she always did and enjoyed having young people playing with the children, especially after school hours.

I remember one occasion when Sarah and Emma brought a few desks outside so they could get a sun-tan whilst cutting small strips of white paper into false eyelashes; the Ugandan teachers thought my girls were mad because Africans always sit in the shade. The children were given two strips of lashes; they spat on them and stuck them on their eyelids. It was hilarious as they all held their heads back, trying to blink and peer out from under these white lashes; apparently my daughters had seen Dawn French do something like this on TV. The teaching staff could hardly keep a straight face and some joined in; we had a lot of fun with such a simple idea.

Over the years I have had the pleasure of travelling all over Uganda with Maria. Whenever I arrived she would say that she needed to visit Steven in Tororo, or Joyce in Masaka. Maria loved company, especially when she had been busy doing so much on her own in Kamuli, and in the early days she had to talk very slowly to the local Ugandans because their English was poor. We visited Mount Elgon and Sipi Falls; friends in Jinja and Entebbe. I loved these little adventures.

In my wildest dreams I never thought I would go on safari but over the years many visitors wanted to go to either Murchison Falls and the safari park there or Queen Elisabeth Safari Park. It has always been a joy to facilitate these trips; each has been unique and always exciting.

On one of our trips we saw many wild animals and had an unforgettable experience when one of the guides decided to throw rocks into the lions den so they would come out for us. Another time a herd of elephants with babies in tow walked across our path; the matriarch female didn't want us to come between her family and her body rose up and she made a loud trumpet call that sent our driver into a panic. Our guide put his hand to his gun and said:

"Rev up!"

The driver thought he said 'reverse', which apparently is the worst thing you can do; as we started to go backwards the guide shouted:

"No, no! Rev up!"

Eventually the herd crossed safely, and for good measure the matriarch elephant trumpeted again raising her head up and down and stamping one foot on the ground. I must admit it frightened the living daylights out of most of us.

On one trip Barbara and I were asked if we would like to speak to a group of ladies deep in a remote village; Barbara would speak about why and how to clean teeth and I would speak about Jesus. We were given a huge blackboard that we carried all the way to this little village in the middle of nowhere. I stepped forward to speak and as I did I realised I was covered in huge black ants, they were all over me; the more Barbara and I tried to brush them off the more they clung on. I was jumping up and down shrieking and I soon discovered I was standing on an ants nest. I had to pull them off one by one. The group of ladies who were sitting down kept repeating; 'sorry madam, sorry madam'.

All who come on a 'Ugandan experience' are volunteers who pay for themselves and are encouraged to raise funds which can be used at 'Maria's Care' on one of the needy projects. On their return to England many decide to support the projects financially or sponsor a child; this is wonderful for CRU and a great gift to the Ugandan people. You will have read in chapter eight the testimonies of many of 'Maria's Care' students. If they hadn't had that support they might still be in the villages, uneducated and with less opportunity to broaden their horizons.

Another benefit for the pupils has been to talk with the visitors and improve their English. One of our students told me he wasn't able to hold a conversation in English and was frightened of talking to older people; the visitors encouraged him to chat, play games and have a bedtime story read to him; he said he loved this and he felt very special and cared for.

Maria was frequently told by high school teachers that her children always stood out; they had good manners, were well behaved, spoke good English and they shone in the classroom. I was thrilled when she told me this.

At one point Maria became ill and was flown back to the UK thoroughly exhausted. It was suggested that Maria should rest and was placed in a home called The Rowans in Macclesfield. I visited her on many occasions and during one such time as we sat chatting, I looked around at all the old people and remembered the TV programme 'Waiting for God'; this was certainly the case here. Suddenly Maria asked me for a pen and paper and started to make a list of all thirty-eight children in 'Maria's Care'. She wrote down which school they should attend and what they needed: socks, shoes, white shirts, green skirts, black skirts or trousers, toothpaste and brush, TP (it took me ages to remember toilet paper was always TP) soap, pens, protractor set, 12 exercise books. The list was endless. Boarding children had to take their own mattress, blanket, sheets, towel and a blue tin with a padlock to hold all of their precious belongings (invariable they lost the key); they also took pangas to cut the school grass.

I remember thinking what an incredible lady Maria was, surrounded by all these people; she wasn't in good health and yet she was interested in the needs of the little ones in her care even though she was hundreds of miles away. The next day I was able to fax the list to Kamuli; a miracle since the electricity was on!

In 2002 Maria was awarded the MBE for her services in Uganda; she already held a Paul Harris Fellow Award, which is given for exceptional service, from Macclesfield Castle Rotary Club. In 2008 I followed in Maria's footsteps and was also honoured with the MBE. My two daughters and Barbara Koffman attended the magnificent occasion with me. I am very grateful to all the people who put my name forward and supported the application. An award like this can only be acquired by hard work and support from people who believe in the work being done. It is a team effort and that is what the Christian Relief Uganda committee is all about; individuals with different gifts and talents all working together and focused on the same cause.

It isn't often I am stuck for words but recently, after giving a Ugandan presentation to the Macclesfield Castle Rotary Club, I too was presented with the Paul Harris Fellow Award. I was speechless; it certainly is a real honour to be given this award, especially when I am doing something I love and am passionate about.

Many people ask me how Maria is; now in her middle eighty's she has been in a lot of pain recently, and the lovely staff at the nursing home in Ingleton have been trying to keep her pain management under control. The legacy Maria has left behind in Uganda is I am sure, far greater than she could ever have imagined. She would often say:

"I am just doing what God has asked me to do, he does it you know."

Maria is a lady of great faith, a pioneering spirit, a trail blazer and wonderful role model, a great encourager who empowers people. We both learnt in Uganda that 'nothing is impossible with God.' This is still the motto today at 'Maria's Care', Kamuli, Uganda. As time goes on I am able to watch 'Maria's Care' original children grow up, graduate, get jobs, mature, and have children of their own; what a privilege for me.

Over many years I have had the pleasure of facilitating 'Ugandan experience' trips; these are some of the people who have been with me, several on more than one occasion, and some who have had a specific role to play:

Erik Ahlbom, Sarah Alford, Judith Anderson (Rowe), Pauline

The Call, the Cost, the Choice

Anderson, Christopher Ankers, Stewart Ashworth, Natasha Azzopardi, Christine Blakeley, Nick and Katrina Beirne, Gordon Birch, David and Audrey Bomford, Angela Booth, Alex Browning, Neil and Ruth Bridle, Claudia Brown, John Burn, the late MP Patsy Calton & Clive Calton, Barbara Heal (Charnley), Jo Clare, Steve Clare, Helen Clark, Susan Clayton, Siobhan Clowes, Mike and Chris Collett, Steve and Jo Collett, Michael Connolly, Katrina Connolly, Nikkie Connors, Simone Cowan, Gavin and Fiona Craigen, Peter and Heather Ellis, Gareth Davies, Anthea Davies, Donna Dodd, Jane Dawkins, Georgina De Caux, Sarah Dilloway, Ian and Pat Dixon, Maureen Douglas, Thelma Edwards, Liz Evans, Heather Fielding, Roy and Sue Field, Chris Fitzsimmons, Ursula Freestone, Denise Greaves, Ross Owen Greaves, Michael Halsey, Sara Hambridge, Norman and Gerry Hambridge, Gilda Hammond, Roger Hand, David Hand, Alison Harris, Sarah Harris, Pam Hassell, Kathleen Hesketh, Joan Hornett, Jill Howell, Julie Howard (Temple), Henry and Ruth Howitt, Julie Hughes, Robert Hughes, Sophie Ingham, Ruth Ive, Val Jackson, Eleanor Robert-James, Harry Robert-James, Sheila Jamieson, Patricia Jochem, Jac Jones, Ron and Monica Jones, robby Keen, Mike Kendrick, Helen Koffman, Barbara Koffman, Liz Lowsby, Susan Kondryn, Kate Law, Joanna Lea, Maria Longman, John Maitland, Donnette Mars, Emma Marshall, Sarah Marshall, Lynette Marshall, Tanya Martin, Pammy Matheson, Maria Maw, Dennis and Beth McCleod, Brian and Tuula McClusky, Jayne Morgan, Stephen Morris, Maureen Moss, Rachel Mossey, Janet Mott, Janice and Mike Nickson, Linda and Geoff Oliver, Mary Orchard, Sue Owst, Russ and Margaret Pattinson, David and Marjorie Pearson, Ken Payne, Sally Pearson, Hamish and Jemma Pearson, Christine Phillips, Alys Powell, Sue Pratt, Linda Price, Stephen and Joan Proctor, Julie Pugh, Olivia Pumphrey, Katie Puttick, Alia Rashid, Sandra Ratcliffe Mark Rimmington, Rebecca Probets, Paul Sabine, Judith Scriven, Lizzie Scriven, Nigel Shaw, Liz Skirrow, Mike Spry, Carol Stanton, Michelle Stennet, Nicola Stevens, Jean Sutton, Clare Sweasey, Lizzy Timpson, Julie Tonks, Margaret Tonks, Jim Tryon, Frances Turner, Walter Turner, Lesley Twigg, Ann West, Liz Westaway, Lynne Westhead, Siobhan Wilson, Brian and Kath Wood, Richard and Shifa Wood, Bethan Wootton, Kath Young.

Thank you David Young from 'Children for Christ' in Sydney Australia. For the privilege of allowing me to facilitating your first trip to Uganda and subsequently Alan Martin, Ron Howarth, Ivan and Jane Mills, Patrick

Kennedy, Pat Pearce, Sue Leckenby, John Eattell, Graeme Young and Eric Wieckmann from CHIPS (Christian's in Primary Schools) Adelaide followed by Sharon O'Brian and others from Australia, such wonderful brothers and sisters in Christ. You all heard the call, had a choice to make and now you are doing some fantastic God given work of your own in Uganda.

I am still facilitating groups of volunteers who want to come on a 'Ugandan experience.' Each trip is unique and this gives me immense joy. I remember on one occasion a lady who had been with us for nearly three weeks saying to Barbara:

"I know you two are good, but not that good." She had witnessed so many God incidences in such a short time that she knew it was impossible for the two of us to have organised this ourselves. Within five minutes of her saying that she sat on her bed and committed her life to the Lord. It was wonderful seeing God move in such an extraordinary way. Barbara and I had the pleasure of being at her baptism and later in the year we were asked to take the service at her church in Sheffield.

It transpired there were issues in my friend's life that needed addressing and this was the time to give them to God. Please don't leave it too long to give your life to God. If you feel God is calling you then respond to his call. Jesus bore the cost on the cross at Calvary and you have a choice. If you choose to become a Christian you will have eternal life with him; if you don't that is your choice and you will have eternal life without him. We have been given free will; you choose. 1 John 5:11-12 says: "...*and this is the testimony: God has given us eternal life, and this life is in his Son. He who has the Son has life; he who does not have the Son of God does not have life.*"

This is a prayer you can pray from the heart:

Dear Lord Jesus, I am sorry for the things I have done wrong in thought, word and deed, please forgive my sins. I ask you to come into my life and make me the person you want me to be. Please be my Lord and Saviour, fill me with your Holy Spirit and give me the gift of eternal life. In Jesus' precious name. Amen.

Over many years I have been involved with the Maranatha Community in England, an ecumenical movement; God led me to set groups up in Uganda and I have taken people from the UK to visit Maranatha groups there. This is another opportunity the Lord has given me to share his love wherever we go. I am now the Maranatha International Coordinator.

I started this book by saying: 'How does an insecure young girl from a non Christian family in Liverpool find herself years later in Uganda doing extraordinary things for God?' It is God who qualifies: giving thanks to the Father who has qualified you to share in the inheritance of the saints in the kingdom of light. For he has rescued us from the dominion of darkness and brought us into the kingdom of the Son he loves, in whom we have redemption, the forgiveness of sins. Colossians 1:12-14.

It is also due to people who believed in me, spent time encouraging me and empowering me; people who told me to look at the good qualities within, who cut me spiritually free from all the negative words and actions dumped on me.

Having time in Uganda has taught me to use the words 'I can' instead of 'I can't'. Above all I have been taught to listen to God, to obey him and to surrender all to him; to stand on his living word the Bible, which is truth and follow him. God is a God of order not chaos, he will never leave us or forsake us. God has said: *"Never will I leave you; never will I forsake you."* Hebrews 13:5.

I hope and pray you will hear the Lord speak to you, encourage you and empower you. May the Lord bless you as you go minute by minute, hour by hour, day by day in his strength and the knowledge that you are following him.

My Thanks..........

Thank you Sarah and Emma my two lovely daughters, for your encouragement and support, especially as I dash off time and time again to Uganda, and a double thank you to Sarah for designing the book cover; it is stunning.

Thank you to all the people who chose to join me on the trips to Uganda and experienced many amazing God incidents with me; your lives have been changed by God as you used your gifts and talents in extraordinary ways. It has given me great pleasure to be part of your journey and I have learnt so much from you.

Thank you Larry and Gill for allowing me to share your home in Weston Super Mare. It was wonderful to be able to hide away and write without any disturbances. Also for the opportunities given me to go to the local primary schools and present Ugandan experiences during the assemblies. Thanks too to Harry and Ellie for the trips I made to your home in Spain, often feeling as though I was climbing Mount Everest trying to write this book. You were great encouragers and spurred me on to the top of the mountain! The wonderful meals and refreshing dips in your pool added to my delightful time with you. Thanks to my brother Graeme and his wife Christina, for letting me have time, space and comfort in your cosy home to finish the book; for sharing the wildlife in your garden and for laying on the birth of my great nephew Malachi Jack to proud parents Sam and Jenna.

Thank you to Betty and the late George Norbury who initially prompted me to write my diary in the first place; from those diaries a book was born.

Thank you to all who have provided the finance and sponsorship over many years for myself and the projects in Uganda.

Thank you to local friends who have written books that have inspired and encouraged me; Myra and the late Douglas Kjeldson, Chris Whiteley, Andy Hawthorn and Debra Green, Daisy Kapasa, Dennis Wrigley, Anne Coombs, the late George Norbury and Christine Cartwright, who also encouraged me and said she always knew I would finish this book.

Thank you to people on the early CRU committee who didn't come to Uganda but were in the background making things run smoothly in the UK: Ian & Myra Fallows, David Humphreys, Pam Jagger, Ken and Sue Johnson, Wendy Mosley, Sue Russell, the late Angela Knopp, and the late Gerald and Hilda Moss who also thought up the name of the charity. Thank you Richard Charnley for designing the first web site. Thank you to all of the CRU committee members who chose to be faithful and obedient to God, using your gifts and talents to serve him both in England and Uganda. Thank you for your help, encouragement, prayers, finance and support.

Thank you to my trusty friend and companion Barbara Koffman, who in the early days with faltering foots steps visited Uganda with me; I praise God we both chose to follow his calling on our lives and marvel how he and only he could have directed our path. I praise God for the fantastic dental ministry that has now blossomed through Barbara's obedience, and the help that has been given by professional people she has encouraged, which has made such a difference too many Ugandan people.

The Call, the Cost, the Choice

Thank you Maria Maw for choosing to follow the call God gave you to go to Uganda. Thank you for inviting me to be part of your life; without you I would not have made the choice to go to Uganda and had the experiences to record in this book.

Weebale to all the Ugandan people who have crossed my path; without you this book would never have been written.

Thanks also to my encouraging friends and prayer partners: Val Sillavan, Pammy Matheson, Pam Jagger, Jim Tryon, George Fraser, Granny Densham and everyone at Tytherington Family Worship Church in Macclesfield, friends in other church fellowships; all of your encouragement has been invaluable. I am the only one who knows what a difference you have made in my life and it has been phenomenal.

Thanks to Alan Batchelor for encouraging me; you were my first contact point with all the manuscripts. You told me: "You have a story to tell, just get it written down," and Andy Hollis who gave me that last push when he said: "You can do it Rho; it's just one word after another!" He was right.

And last but certainly not least my trusty friend and wonderful editor Annie Roebuck; you have worked tirelessly through hundreds of manuscripts with a red pen editing thousands of words and made huge decisions as to what we kept in the book and what we took out. We have laughed and nearly cried as we edited the pages together; we drank endless cups of tea and coffee and worked through all seasons to get this book ready for publishing. Then eventually Alan and Annie worked together to produce the final script ready for print. Thank you. I never thought I would see the day this book was published!

Above all I thank God; without him I could not have accomplished any of the things written in this book. Before the beginning of time he knew what I and each one of you would be doing, he has the blueprint for all of our lives. When we are in tune with him it is amazing what he can do in and through us! I heard the call and had a choice to make; I chose life in abundance, I chose to listen and follow his still small voice, I chose to follow the Lord Jesus Christ and the plan he has for my life. "*Therefore, my dear brothers and sisters stand firm. Let nothing move you. Always give yourself fully to the work of the Lord because you know that your labour in the Lord is not in vain.*" 1 Corinthians 15:58.

Thank you for reading this book; an account of the remarkable work

Your labour in the Lord is not in vain

God has used us to do for people in Uganda, a place deep in his and my heart. *"Let us fix our eyes on Jesus, the author and perfecter of our faith, who for the joy set before him endured the cross, scorning its shame, and sat down at the right hand of the throne of God."* Hebrews 12:2.

I encourage you to contact me if you have been touched by this book in any way. I would feel it a real privilege to be informed of happenings going on in your life. I may be able to help, pray or pass you on to other contacts.

I would be delighted to hear from you if you would like to go to Uganda, or support the work there, or invite me to speak at your local group or school. Please contact me.

Rhona Marshall MBE
email: rhonaccc@gmail.com
The Call, The Cost, The Choice
Web site: thecallthecostthechoice.co.uk

Christian Reliof Uganda
Web site: www.christianreliefuganda.org
Email: info@christianreliefuganda.com

Barbara Koffman: Dentaid's Ugandan Volunteering Coordinator
Web site: www.dentaid.org

Dennis Wrigley: Leader and Co-Founder of the Maranatha Community
Web site: www.maranathacommunity.org.uk

Andy Hawthorn OBE: CEO The Message Trust
Web site: www.message.org.uk

Debra Green OBE: National Director, Redeeming our Communities
Web Site: www.roc.uk.com

David Young: Children for Christ.
Web site: www.childrenforchrist.org.au

Other books that you might find inspiring:

Christine Cartwright:
Glory Unveiled
Web site: www.gloryunveiled.co.uk

Daisy Kapasa:
Every Child is Special.
An amazing true story of how God's love restores the fatherless
Email: restorationhouse@hotmail.co.uk

Philippa Skinner:
'See you soon'
A mother's story of drugs, grief and hope
Web site: www.seeyousoon.me.uk